Learn How to Program
Using Any Web Browser

Learn How to Program
Using Any Web Browser

Harold Davis

Apress®

Technical Reviewer: Beth Christmas

Editorial Board: Dan Appleman, Craig Berry, Gary Cornell, Tony Davis, Steven Rycroft, Julian Skinner, Martin Streicher, Jim Sumser, Karen Watterson, Gavin Wray, John Zukowski

Assistant Publisher: Grace Wong

Copy Editor: Kim Wimpsett

Production Manager: Kari Brooks

Proofreader: Carol Burbo

Compositor and Artist: Diana Van Winkle, Van Winkle Design

Indexer: Michael Brinkman

Interior and Cover Designer: Kurt Krames

Manufacturing Manager: Tom Debolski

Distributed to the book trade in the United States by Springer-Verlag New York, Inc., 175 Fifth Avenue, New York, NY 10010 and outside the United States by Springer-Verlag GmbH & Co. KG, Tiergartenstr. 17, 69112 Heidelberg, Germany.

In the United States: phone 1-800-SPRINGER, email orders@springer-ny.com, or visit http://www.springer-ny.com. Outside the United States: fax +49 6221 345229, email orders@springer.de, or visit http://www.springer.de.

For information on translations, please contact Apress directly at 2560 Ninth Street, Suite 219, Berkeley, CA 94710. Phone 510-549-5930, fax 510-549-5939, email info@apress.com, or visit http://www.apress.com.

The source code for this book is available to readers at http://www.apress.com in the Downloads section. You will need to answer questions pertaining to this book in order to successfully download the code.

For the next generation of
potential programmers in my family:
Peter, Emma, David, Steven, Julian, and Nicholas

Contents at a Glance

Contents

Foreword

Programs drive the world. Literally. Heck, there's more software in the average car than was used to run an airline when I grew up in the '60s. But it sure is a different world than when I grew up. And that's nowhere more so than in the programming world. When I learned programming in the '70s, it was all punch cards and big machines—no PCs and no Internet.

But, too many books that try to teach you programming haven't gotten the message that it's a different world: It's the world of the Internet! Why, they still use an archaic language called BASIC that's 40 years old and was designed for Teletype machines to teach you programming. The book you have in your hand is unusual because it accepts that the programming world has changed. The browser is all-important: Controlling your browser isn't only an exciting way to learn to program, it's darn useful if you ever want to make your own home page interactive.

But that isn't the only way this book is different from all the other beginning programming books out there that use BASIC. Feeding you BASIC as your first programming language is a terrible idea. Why? Because the BASIC programming language is old and tired and doesn't use *object-oriented programming* (OOP) as its fundamental paradigm. OOP was developed in the '80s and '90s, and every programmer must be familiar with it. OOP is how programmers can hope to piece together the very large programs they need to build in the 21st century.

(If you're wondering what OOP is, well, you'll just have to read this book—I won't try to explain it here because then I'd have to do a better job than Harold Davis does in this book, and that's not likely to happen.)

So sit back in front of any computer (heck, even some personal digital assistants) and learn to program by taking full control of your browser (fun!) and learning OOP (useful!) with one of the best writers I know.

Gary Cornell
Apress, Publisher/Author/Cofounder

About the Author

Harold Davis is a strategic technology consultant, hands-on programmer, and the author of many well-known books.

His books on programming and technology topics include *Red Hat Linux 9: Visual QuickPro Guide* (Peachpit Press, 2003), *Visual Basic .NET for Windows: Visual QuickStart Guide* (Peachpit Press, 2003), *Visual C# .NET Programming* (Sybex, 2002), *Visual Basic .NET Programming* (Sybex, 2002), *The Wi-Fi Experience: Everyone's Guide to 802.11b Wireless Networking* (Que, 2001), *Visual Basic 6: Visual QuickStart Guide* (Peachpit Press, 1999), *Red Hat Linux 6: Visual QuickPro Guide* (Peachpit Press, 1999), *Visual Basic 6 Secrets* (IDG Books, 1998), *Visual Basic 5 Secrets* (IDG Books, 1997), *Visual Basic 4 Secrets* (IDG Books, 1996), *Web Developer's Secrets* (IDG Books, 1997), and *Delphi Power Toolkit: Cutting-Edge Tools & Techniques for Programmers* (Ventana, 1995).

In addition to technical books, Harold has written about a wide range of topics, from art and photography to business and the stock market. His *Publishing Your Art As Cards, Posters & Calendars* (Second Edition: Consultant Press, 1996) is the definitive work on the topic and has been in print for more than 20 years.

Harold has served as a technology consultant for many important businesses, including investment funds, technology companies, and Fortune 500 corporations. In recent years, he was vice president of Strategic Development at YellowGiant Corporation, chief technology officer at an expert systems company, a technical director at Vignette Corporation, and a principal in the e-commerce practice at Informix Software.

Harold started programming when he was a child. He has worked in many languages and environments and has been lead programmer and/or architect in projects for many corporations, including Chase Manhattan Bank, Nike, and Viacom.

Harold was a professional photographer for 15 years, and he maintained a studio in New York City. His photographs have been widely exhibited and published. While a professional photographer, he founded Wilderness Studio, a national distributor of posters and greeting cards.

He has earned a bachelor's degree in Computer Science and Mathematics from New York University and a doctor's of jurisprudence degree from Rutgers Law School, where he was a member of the law review.

Harold lives with his wife, Phyllis Davis, who is also an author, and their two sons, Julian and Nicholas, in the hills of Berkeley, California. In his spare time he enjoys hiking, gardening, and collecting antique machines including typewriters and calculation devices.

Acknowledgments

First and foremost, thanks go to my friend Gary Cornell, whose idea this book was. Thanks, Gary, for believing in me! Second, great thanks go to Grace Wong, without whom this book wouldn't exist in its current form (dare I say this is true of most Apress books?).

I also owe a debt of gratitude to Beth Christmas, Martin Davis, and Phyllis Davis, each of whom read this book carefully in manuscript and made many helpful suggestions.

1

Getting Started

If you've picked up this book, it's a pretty good guess that you'd like to learn how to program. Well, you've come to the right place!

This book will teach you the basics of programming. Because this book emphasizes good programming practices, you won't learn any bad habits that you might have to "unlearn" later. Programming is—among other things—a craft. *Learn How to Program* will teach you the right way to start learning that craft.

You'll learn how to program with a minimum of fuss and aggravation.

If you have a computer, you won't have to buy fancy new equipment or software. Best of all, the entire process will be great fun.

So, what are you waiting for? Let's get started!

What Is Programming?

There are many ways to "talk" to a computer. You're probably already familiar with some of them. For example, most likely you've "surfed" the Web or created a document using Microsoft Word. You may also have used a voicemail system to leave someone at a big corporation a message or even to check your bank account balance. Indeed, it's hard to do anything in the modern world without communicating with computers.

> *It's hard to do anything at all in the modern world without communicating with computers.*

> *Most computer programs provide a user interface that allows users to interact with the computer nonprogrammatically.*

Programming is a particular way of "talking" with a computer that tells the computer to do something. For example, when you tell your VCR to record a show, you are, of course, programming the VCR.

To take this one step further, each of the examples mentioned earlier—surfing the Web, using a word processor, and navigating an automated phone system—involve using a program created by someone else. The programmer designs the program—the Web browser, word processor, or whatever—so that you can achieve results without having to program anything yourself. The mechanism that you—as opposed to the programmer—use to communicate with the computer is often called a *user interface*. Many, if not most, computer programs provide a user interface that allows users to interact with the computer nonprogrammatically, often using a visual metaphor such as clicking buttons with a mouse.

This has several interesting implications. First, someone who programs a computer has to think about how a computer interacts with the instructions that make up a computer program. Second, the programmer has to manage how people interact with the program.

The point is that programmers interact with computers in a different—some would say deeper and more significant—way than those who only use programs created by someone else.

To drive this home, think of a game that involves racing cars around a speedway. The programmer has created code that lets the game interact with a computer on which it's running. The programmer has to also deliver appropriate effects when a user chooses a car, steers and accelerates with a game stick or other device, and so on. Figure 1-1 shows this relationship.

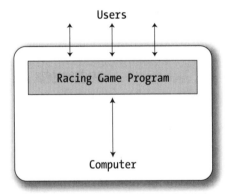

FIGURE 1-1

A program, such as a racing game, interacts with both a computer and users and makes sure that the computer takes the steps requested by the users.

Programmers Can Be Users

In some cases, programmers may be the only people interacting with a particular program. But when they do so, they're interacting as mere users, not as the programmer who is telling the computer what to do.

Understanding Machine Language, Assembly Language, Operating Systems, and All That

From the viewpoint of this book, you don't really need to know much about machine language, assembly language, operating systems, and all that stuff. But, in case you're curious, *machine language* is the underlying two-position native language of computers. You can think of these two positions as a switch with an on and off (or as a zero and a one). The two positions are also called *binary*. Machine language manipulates groups of these switches.

Assembly language, also sometimes called *assembler*, is a somewhat more human-friendly mechanism that can directly communicate with the hardware switches that natively "think" in machine language. Assembly language is specific to a particular processor because its statements correspond to specific machine instructions.

Assembly and machine language are considered *low-level* languages—they allow direct access to all of the capabilities of the underlying system, but they're time consuming and tedious to use. In contrast, the programming languages described in the next section are considered *high level* because they hide the actual low-level details of how something is implemented and combine many low-level commands into single statements.

Operating systems are computer programs—such as Microsoft Windows or Linux—whose principal purposes are to launch other programs, give them resources to run, and keep them out of each other's way. Operating systems vary greatly in functionality and sophistication. Most also provide a high-level mechanism for programmers to utilize underlying system capabilities to perform tasks such accessing files on a disk.

Exploring Programming Languages

Programming languages are the way programmers communicate with computers. As you'll see in this book, in some sense computers aren't inherently very bright. The programmer generally supplies the smarts—which can range from nonexistent to vast.

In the words of Tolstoy, "Happy families are all alike." Similarly, all modern high-level programming languages are really pretty much alike.

To say that all programming languages are pretty much alike might evoke gasps of horror from adherents of one language or another—and, truthfully, it's an exaggeration because some important differences exist between languages. However, it's not a bad generalization.

Like human languages, computer programming languages use specific words, often called *keywords*, to mean specific things. Keywords are typically human-language-like so that their meanings can be intuitive. For example, the keyword if generally tells the computer to do one thing or another thing depending on how a condition is evaluated. This is comparable to the English sentence "If it's after 3 P.M., pick up the baby."

In other words, the *If* in the sentence tells someone to check the time and, if it meets the condition (it's after 3 P.M.), to do something (pick up the baby).

In human languages, rules of grammar and syntax are used to put words together into phrases and sentences, such as the example sentence "If it's after 3 P.M., pick up the baby." Then sentences are combined to tell a story, give directions, or provide a million other purposes.

Computer languages work the same way. In other words, you put keywords and other elements together using rules of syntax to create *statements*. (You can think of a statement as a sentence in a computer program.)

These statements combine to create computer programs.

The syntax of a programming language is the basic scaffolding you use to create programs and applications with that language. Understanding the syntax means understanding how a language works—and knowing what the language can (and can't) do.

If you learn a foreign language, then you can communicate with natives who speak that language. Similarly, if you learn the language of computers, you can "speak" with a computer. Just as it helps to learn a foreign language by thinking the way native speakers do, it helps to learn to think like a computer if you want to learn a computer's language. (So, really, this book is about computer psychology.)

However, before a computer can run a computer program that's written in a human-like language, the program needs to be translated into code that the machine understands. Programmers accomplish this using special programs called *compilers* and *interpreters*.

> ### Understanding Compilers, Interpreters, and Why Not to Worry
>
> A compiler translates a high-level program into machine code and creates an *executable* program that can be processed by the machine. In contrast, an interpreter translates program statements in code that can be processed by the computer on the fly, a kind of "pay-as-you-go" scenario.
>
> Although professional programmers may have to worry quite a bit about the nature of the compiler or interpreter they're working with, often these programs are built into the development environment used to create the program.
>
> In the case of the programs you'll write using this book, you don't have to worry about these things at all because JavaScript—the language used in this book—has an interpreter built into every modern Web browser.

Why Learn to Program?

Let's stand back for a second and ask and answer the question "Why learn how to program?" If you've picked up *Learn How to Program*, it's likely you already have some reasons of your own and don't need to be convinced that learning how to program is a good idea.

But it's important to describe some of the reasons that a person might want to learn how to program. Posing the question "Why learn to program?" and providing some answers now—before you get started with this book—can help you to approach the material presented in this book with the right (positive) attitude.

The following are some good reasons to learn how to program:

- Computer programming is tremendously fun!

- It's challenging and a great intellectual puzzle (much better than crossword puzzles—unless you really like crossword puzzles!).

- Computer programming stimulates creativity.

- If you learn how to program, you can create universes and systems that you alone control.

- You can produce small, but useful, programs. These programs bear the relationship that a bespoke suit bears to ready made—they're customized for your particular needs.

- Programming is tremendously useful. The sound practices and principles you'll learn in this book will give you a leg up if you need to do any kind of programming—from creating Word macros and meeting course requirements to learning to program professionally.

- You have full control of the software you write. If you need to change some of its behavior, you can.

Programming a computer is more fun than doing a crossword puzzle any day of the week!

- Learning to program is educational. You'll gain a great deal of understanding of how computers work, their strengths and weaknesses, what they can do well, and what they have difficulty doing.

- If you learn to program, you'll learn to think like a computer when you need to do so. This will help you be a better computer user, play games better, and much, much more.

What Approach This Book Takes

Ah, the places you'll go! The things you'll see! This book is about a journey, an exciting one at that.

The approach this book takes can be boiled down to four general principles:

- Have fun while learning how to program!

- Learn by doing. Immersion is the best way to learn programming.

- Do it right the first time. If you learn the concepts behind modern programming and good programming practices, then the things you learn in this book will be applicable wherever you go and whatever you do.

Don't let the technology get in the way of learning how to program.

- Don't let the technology get in the way of learning how to program.

My premise in writing this book is that understanding is key. In keeping with that premise, I've decided to use JavaScript as the teaching language throughout *Learn How to Program.* Despite its rather awkward name—it sounds like it has something to do with Java when it doesn't, and it sounds like it's a scripting language or a "lite" programming language—JavaScript is a full-fledged modern programming language, providing the ability (indeed, necessity) of working with objects, understanding event-driven programming, and much more. Best of all, everyone has access to it without needing to buy or install anything new.

Emphatically, *Learn How to Program* isn't a book about the JavaScript language. Also, it's not about adding bells and whistles to Web sites although this can be fun and a good motivation for learning to program (so you'll see a few bells and whistles along the way and specifically in Chapter 11, "Programming with JavaScript").

Learn How to Program is about the how and why of programming languages, about understanding good programming practices, and about helping you learn to think in a new way (that is, like a computer).

Understanding the Conventions and Icons

This book is about programming. You can't learn to program without a way to see what a particular program does when a computer processes it. Setting up a mechanism for observing what a program does is sometimes called creating a *test bed*.

In this case, the test bed consists of Hypertext Markup Language (HTML), or Web pages, that contain JavaScript code. You then open the Web pages in a browser. There also has to be a mechanism for starting the program, but you'll see that later in this chapter.

To conceptually separate the HTML (which isn't programming code) from the JavaScript (which is), this book will use all upper-case letters for HTML most of the time. For example (not worrying for the moment what these things mean), the following code contains HTML:

```
<BODY>
var month_income = new Array(12);
```

In this example, `<BODY>` is HTML and `var month_income = new Array(12);` is a JavaScript statement. Because JavaScript, unlike HTML, is case sensitive, some JavaScript keywords—such as `Array`—must be written using both upper-case and lower-case letters.

I've taken a number of steps to allow you to focus on JavaScript rather than HTML. Later in this chapter, you'll find step-by-step instructions for creating the HTML test bed for your JavaScript programs. Further on, you'll find detailed instructions for creating JavaScript programs, along with JavaScript code listings. Mostly, I'll omit the HTML unless it's necessary for clarity.

In addition, I've added some special graphical features to *Learn How to Program* to make it easier for you to find the information you need:

- **Margin notes** highlight key concepts.

- **Sidebars** explain concepts that you may be curious about but aren't really on the critical path of learning to program.

- **Step-by-step** sections provide detailed directions (so that the technology doesn't get in the way).

You'll also find the following special icons highlighting important points in the text:

WAY COOL

Way Cool means, as you'd expect, that this is something real neat and groovy!

DO IT RIGHT

Do It Right! explains the right way to do something as opposed to a way that merely "works."

TRY THIS
AT HOME

Try This at Home highlights fun projects that I encourage you to work out—and extend—on your own.

ADVANCED

Advanced Topic means, as you'd suspect, that the text marked with this icon is relatively advanced. I've included the advanced material because it's important and for completeness. However, don't worry if you find it difficult—you can simply move on to the next topic. You can always come back later and reread the Advanced Topic sections when they'll likely make more sense to you.

By the way, you'll find the code for all the programs explained in the book on the Apress Web site (`http://www.apress.com/`) in the Downloads section. But I encourage you not to download the code. You'll learn much more if you enter it yourself at the keyboard.

Let's Talk Some More About JavaScript

Now that you know why this book will use JavaScript to teach programming and why—everyone has it, it's free, you can do neat things with it, it's a modern programming language—let's talk a little more about JavaScript.

Scripts vs. Programs

Because the name of the JavaScript language contains the word *Script*, it leads to the natural question "What is the difference between a script and a program?" Actually, there's no difference. Officially speaking, a script is a program. However, the term *script* tends to connote a lightweight program, one that's run in an interpreted rather than a compiled environment. (A *macro* is a term for an even lighter weight program than a script.)

It really doesn't matter whether you call code intended for execution a *macro*, a *script*, or a *program*. I prefer to use the term *program* because it emphasizes the programmatic nature of the challenge involved. If you think of it as a program, rather than a script, your attitude may embrace the Zen necessary for proper planning and best coding practices. This attitude will help you be successful with JavaScript (or any other programming language). Besides, *object-oriented scripting* sounds like a bit of an oxymoron.

> *Good coding takes a Zen attitude.*

Understanding the History of JavaScript

Although JavaScript is a little bit Java-like, JavaScript isn't Java and isn't even Java's cousin.

Netscape originally developed JavaScript in the mid-1990s under the name *LiveScript*. LiveScript was intended as an easy language for Web developers—including hobbyists—to add interactivity and movement to static HTML pages. The companion product LiveWire was intended for use on the server side to script connections between Web servers and back-end programs such as databases.

Netscape changed the name of LiveScript to JavaScript for marketing reasons. (You may recall that a few years ago any software name that bore any relationship to coffee was very cool.) This may have been a valid marketing decision, but it created considerable confusion in the marketplace. Netscape is still the official owner of the name *JavaScript*, which is why Microsoft's version is called *JScript*.

Deciphering JavaScript, ECMAScript, and JScript

In the beginning, there was LiveScript, which became JavaScript. As such, *JavaScript* is a proprietary name for a language running in the Netscape browser. As noted previously, Microsoft developed its own version of the language under the name *JScript* that runs in Internet Explorer browsers.

The official, standardized cross-platform language is defined by the European Computer Manufacturers Association (ECMA) standard 262. (If you're curious, you can find the full text of the standard online at `http://www.ecma-international.org/`.)

So, officially speaking, the name of the language in this book is *ECMAScript 262*. But everyone just calls it *JavaScript*—no matter what browser is interpreting it.

What Tools Do You Need?

As mentioned, one of the main reasons this book will use JavaScript is that you don't need to buy or install any special software. But what do you need?

You can create the computer programs in this book using a simple text-editing program. I've used Notepad throughout this book, but if you prefer, you can use some other program with comparable functionality. (Mac users should refer to "If You Have a Mac" later in this chapter for information regarding working with their computers.)

Once you enter the program into Notepad, you save it. Next, you open it in a Web browser such as Internet Explorer. That's all there is to it!

Using JavaScript Editors

Although it's perfectly reasonable to write JavaScript programs in a simple text editor such as Notepad (indeed, some professional programmers prefer to do this), specialized editors can make the process of entering and debugging code easier. You can find a number of editors specially designed for working with JavaScript on the Web. The best of these are probably Antechinus JavaScript Editor (`http://www.c-point.com/pjedit.htm`) and JPad Pro (`http://www.modelworks.com/`).

Writing and Running Your First Program

It's traditional to start programming books with an exercise that creates a program that displays the text *Hello, World!* when the program runs. This is, in some respects, an inside joke: The computer is coming to life and speaks its first words, "Hello, World!"

From a practical viewpoint, starting with a computer program that displays a phrase of text (it really doesn't matter if it's *Hello, World!* or something else) makes some sense. First, it should be a pretty easy thing to do. You'll probably need to know how to do this before you can write a program to do anything more significant. So, you can think of displaying text as a good warm-up exercise.

Second, it provides instant feedback that your program is working—if the computer does indeed display the designated text. The only way to be sure you've got something right is to try it. The ability to display text allows the display of programmatic values, which allows you to easily try many of the examples in this book and be certain they're right.

Your first program will display the text *I think therefore I am* in the Web browser.

 TIP Of course, you could achieve the same result using just plain HTML—but that's not the point of this exercise, which is to make an easy transition into programming.

Getting the browser to programmatically display text when it loads is a three-phase operation:

1. You create the HTML scaffolding for the program.

2. You add the program that actually writes the text.

3. You save the completed file containing the HTML and the program and then open it in a browser.

So, let's take these phases from the top!

To Create the HTML Scaffolding:

1. Open a text editor such as Notepad (if you're running a Mac, see "If You Have a Mac" later in this chapter). You can find Notepad in the Accessories group; you can open it by selecting Programs ➤ Accessories ➤ Notepad on the Start menu.

2. Create a simple HTML document with a place in the body of the document to put the program (within the <SCRIPT></SCRIPT> tags). To do this, type the following tags into your document:

```
<HTML>
<BODY>
<SCRIPT>

</SCRIPT>
</BODY>
</HTML>
```

3. Save the file using a name and an HTML file suffix. To do this, when you're in Notepad's Save dialog, you must select All as the file type and then manually enter a filename ending in *.html*. For example, save the file as *myfile.html* or *0101.html*.

 TIP It's a good idea to create a special folder for the files you'll be creating in this book. That way, you'll easily be able to find them when you want to see what they do in a browser.

If you opened this file now in a browser, you wouldn't see anything much (see Figure 1-2).

The next step is to add the program. This is the most fun part and the start of seeing what you'll learn in this book.

This program consists of one line, which displays the text *I think therefore I am* when you load it into the browser. This is the program code:

```
document.write("I think therefore I am");
```

Understanding Methods and Objects

The point of this exercise is mastering the mechanics of writing and saving a short program that displays text—not, at this point, understanding the concepts involved in the program. Later chapters will explain these concepts.

However, I don't like to use terms without explaining them. So here goes:

- An *object* is a collection of data and procedures—or short programs— that can be used in code.

- A *method* is a procedure belonging to an object that does something.

- The *document object* is a JavaScript object that can be used to manipulate a document that's loaded in a Web browser.

You'll find more information about methods and objects in many places in *Learn How to Program*—and particularly in Chapter 7, "Working with Objects." In addition, Chapter 11, "Programming with JavaScript," explains some of the ins and outs of the JavaScript document object.

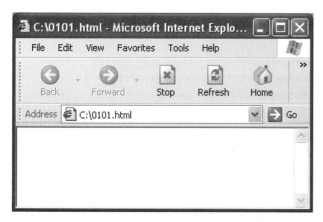

FIGURE 1-2

The HTML scaffolding appears as an empty document in a Web browser.

This line of program code goes between the `<SCRIPT></SCRIPT>` tags in your HTML scaffolding. It uses the write method of the document object to display the designated text in the current document.

Listing 1-1 shows the HTML scaffolding with the line of program code.

LISTING 1-1

HTML and Program Code

```
<HTML>
<BODY>
<SCRIPT>
 document.write("I think therefore I am");
</SCRIPT>
</BODY>
</HTML>
```

You're ready for the final phase—which is to save the HTML file and open it in a browser.

TRY THIS
AT HOME

To Open the HTML File (Including the Program) in a Web Browser:

1. If you haven't already saved the file, in Notepad, save the file with an HTML file extension. For example, save it as *0101.html*.

2. Double-click the saved file in Windows Explorer to open it in your default Web browser, likely Internet Explorer. The file will open, the program code will run, and the text will display (see Figure 1-3).

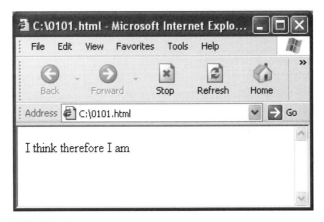

FIGURE 1-3

You know that the one–line program has run because you can see the text displayed in the browser.

> ## JavaScript Code in HTML: Best Practices
>
> This book isn't really about HTML and browsers. But if you were intending to add JavaScript code to Web pages on a production basis, it would be a good idea to use a more extensive script tag than I've shown you. For example:
>
> ```
> <SCRIPT LANGUAGE=JAVASCRIPT TYPE="TEXT/JAVASCRIPT">
>
> </SCRIPT>
> ```
>
> Also, it's a good idea to use *code hiding*, which makes sure older browsers that can't process JavaScript don't end up displaying the program code literally as text. You do this using HTML comments to hide the JavaScript from browsers that aren't capable of interpreting JavaScript:
>
> ```
> <SCRIPT LANGUAGE=JAVASCRIPT TYPE="TEXT/JAVASCRIPT">
>    <!--Hide that code from very old browsers
>
>    // End code hiding from ancient browsers -->
> </SCRIPT>
> ```

If You Have a Mac

Although the example files in this book were all written in Notepad, there are simple text-editing programs that come free with your Mac and can be used to perform the same job. In other words, things work in pretty much the same way whether you're running a Windows or a Mac computer.

This section explains how to save an HTML file if you're using a Mac. The two main programs are:

- TextEdit (in the Applications folder in Mac OS X), capable of creating both rich-text and plain-text documents

- SimpleText (in the Applications folder of Mac OS 9), limited to file sizes of 32 kilobytes

To build the simple HTML file, follow these steps:

1. Open your preferred text editor. If you're working in TextEdit, make sure you're in Plain Text edit mode by selecting Format ➤ Make Plain Text (if you're already in Plain Text edit mode, the option will appear as Make Rich Text). This ensures that no formatting, font styles, and so on are included in the file. You just want to create the pure HTML code.

   If you're using SimpleText, check that you're in Plain Text edit mode by selecting Style ➤ Plain Text.

2. Create a simple HTML document with a place in the body of the document to put the program (within the <SCRIPT></SCRIPT> tags). To do this, type the following tags into your document:

```
<HTML>
<BODY>
<SCRIPT>

</SCRIPT>
</BODY>
</HTML>
```

3. Enter a single line of program code between the <SCRIPT></SCRIPT> tags in your HTML scaffolding so that the file looks like this:

```
<HTML>
<BODY>
<SCRIPT>
 document.write("I think therefore I am");
</SCRIPT>
</BODY>
</HTML>
```

4. Now you need to save your file with an HTML suffix. To do this in TextEdit, go to File ➤ Save As and manually enter a filename finishing in *.html*. For example, save it as *myfile.html* or *0101.html*. When you click Save, a pop-up informs you that the "Document name myfile.html already seems to have an extension. Append '.txt' anyway?" Click Don't Append to save your HTML file (see Figure 1-4).

FIGURE 1-4

Click the Don't Append button to save your HTML file.

If you're using SimpleText, go to File ➤ Save As and type your filename including the .html suffix into the Save Your Document As field. Click the Save button and you're done.

You can test the file (and run the programs contained in the file) by double-clicking them to open in your Web browser.

Contacting the Author

If you have any questions or comments about the material in this book, please feel free to send me an email. I'll do my best to answer any questions about programming topics.

The best email address to use is `learntoprogram@bearhome.com`.

What's It All About?

Perhaps you remember the old Burt Bacharach song, "What's It All About, Alfie?" You may know this song as "What's It All About, Austin?" updated for the *Austin Powers* movie series.

This chapter has covered a great deal of ground, most of it about giving you a feel for things. What things, and what's it all about, Alfie (or Austin)?

In this chapter, you've learned about the nature of computer programming and about computer languages. I've asked, and answered, the question "Why learn to program?" I've also explained the approach taken by this book.

Finally, and perhaps most important, you've written and run your first computer program. Congratulations!

2

Understanding Types, Variables, and Statements

In Chapter 1, "Getting Started," I told you that a computer program is made up of statements in much the way that an essay written in English is comprised of sentences. These statements, which follow specific rules of syntax and grammar, tell the computer what to do. This chapter explains what goes into a statement and how you put statements together.

A computer statement includes keywords, which, as I explained in Chapter 1, are words that are reserved for a special meaning and usage within the computer language and that are usually English-like. You'll learn the important JavaScript keywords as you go on in *Learn How to Program*—there aren't many of them.

In addition, a statement can contain values, which are of a type recognized by the computer, and variables, which are used to hold values.

Variables and values play the role of nouns in a computer statement. They're acted upon. But to make a complete statement, you also need to describe the action—what's being done to the object and subject. The role of the verb is played by keywords and operators, such as the assignment operator. The assignment operator is indicated using an equals sign (=) and serves to copy the value on the right side of an equals sign to the variable on the left side.

This may all sound rather abstract, but it's pretty down to earth! By the end of this chapter, you'll understand the basic nature of types, values, statements, and operators—which are the building blocks that are used to create programs.

Understanding Types

Programming languages can only deal with a limited number of types of things. By way of illustration, suppose you're at the beach building a sand castle. There are three buckets you can use. One bucket can hold only sand, another bucket can only hold water, and the final bucket can only hold pebbles. So the types you have available for building your castle in the sand are sand, water, and pebbles—and each type must go in the appropriate bucket for its type. In other words, you're not allowed to put water in the sand bucket and so on.

In the context of a programming language such as JavaScript, the values that programs manipulate are of various kinds called *types*.

JavaScript has three basic types (or kinds of value):

> *The values that programs manipulate are of kinds called* types.

Boolean: A Boolean type stores logical information. It has a value of either `true` or `false`. (Note that the constant values `true` and `false` are case sensitive, meaning that they have to be written exactly as either *true* or *false* in all lower-case letters.)

Number: A Number type is an integer or floating-point value. For example, as I'm sure you know, 42 is a number, as is 3.1415.

String: A String type is some text, for example, `"I think, therefore I am"`. Strings start and end with either matching single quotes or matching double quotes. If you don't have the quotation marks, you don't have a string. You should also know that you can have a string with no characters (the empty string). Here's how it looks: `""`. Strings are so important in programming that I've written a whole chapter (Chapter 9, "Manipulating Strings") just about them.

ADVANCED

Fancy Ways to Write Numbers

You can write numbers in standard decimal notation or in exponential, hexadecimal, or octal notation. For example, the four numbers shown in Table 2-1 all are 255, each notated as indicated. If this makes sense to you, fine; if not, please don't worry about it—we'll only use simple integers in this book, anyway!

TABLE 2-1

Fancy Numerical Notation

Notation	Representation
Decimal	255
Exponential	2.55e+2
Hexadecimal	0xFF
Octal	0377

Understanding Variables

Just a moment ago, I explained types by asking you to imagine you had three buckets—one for sand, one for water, and one for pebbles—to build a sand castle. The types were sand, water, and pebbles. The buckets are the variables. In other words, a *variable* is used to hold values (with the kinds of values limited by the kinds of types). So you can think of a variable as a placeholder for data. As such, variables are an important underlying part of any computer program. If you just have a value—for example, the number 42—you can perform operations on that particular number. But if you have a variable that holds numerical values, you can invent an operation once—and then apply it to a whole mess of values.

Using variables, you can invent an operation once and apply it to a whole mess of values.

For example, a store might want to give a five-percent discount on the price of all items on a particular day. The computer program that generates the total at the checkout register doesn't have to provide instructions for each item if the item price is stored in a variable. It just applies the discount to the price stored in the variable for the item being purchased. Figure 2-1 shows this simplification.

FIGURE 2-1

By storing values in variables, each operation doesn't have to be written in code.

Naming Variables

It's easy to name a JavaScript variable because variables can be named pretty much anything you'd like provided the name begins with a letter. Variable names can also begin with an underscore (_) or a dollar sign ($).

Any characters after the first character can be a letter, digit, underscore, or dollar sign. (Digits aren't allowed as the first character so that JavaScript can easily distinguish identifiers from numerical values in your code.)

 NOTE Variable names are *identifiers*—in other words, they're made up by the programmer to identify something, in this case a variable. Other kinds of identifiers include labels (used with looping and explained in Chapter 4, "Working with Loops") and function names (discussed in Chapter 5, "Understanding Functions"). All identifiers follow the same official rules as identifiers used to denote variables.

There are only a couple of "don'ts" and "gotchas" when dealing with variable names:

A variable name can't be the same as any JavaScript keyword. For example, you can't name a variable if.

In JavaScript, variable names are case sensitive. This means that myVariable identifies a different variable than Myvariable, both of which are different animals than myvariable. Watch out for this one; this kind of thing can introduce errors into programs and be tricky to spot!

Here are some examples of legal JavaScript variable names:

```
Whale
salmon
pelham123
SSN
total_cost
L_Name
```

Don't get too excited just because you can name a variable pretty much anything you'd like! These are only the *official* variable-naming requirements.

Following the official rules of the Uniform Building Code is probably necessary for building sound houses that can be resold, but it's not sufficient for creating well-designed, intuitively functional homes. In the same way, as a matter of good programming practice, you should be careful with variable names. For example, in the list of variable names I just gave you, some identify their likely contents (SSN, total_cost, L_Name) and others don't (Whale, salmon, pelham123).

A good variable name tells someone reading your code what the variable is supposed to contain. The name should be simple, clear, and—to avoid potential confusion—not too close to any other variable name. (This is also handy for you if you need to change the code at a later date—in case you've forgotten, a good variable name will tell you what the variable does!)

> *A good variable name makes clear what the variable is supposed to contain.*

Creating Variables

You can create variables in your code in two ways:

> *You should always declare your variables using the var keyword.*

- Using the var keyword. For example, var trekVerb; uses the var keyword to create a variable named trekVerb.

- Just by using an identifier as a variable.

Creating a variable just by using it—in other words, without declaring it using var—works okay but is not good practice. If the JavaScript interpreter sees the identifier trekVerb without a declaration, and it makes sense to use the identifier as a variable, that's what will happen. But it's bad programming practice because it's not necessarily clear at a casual glance what the identifier is.

You should always declare your variables so that it's clear what they are.

DO IT RIGHT

Assigning Values to Variables

Once you've created a variable, you can easily assign a value to it using the assignment operator (which is represented by the equals sign). The assignment operator works in the way you'd think it should—namely, it assigns a value. The later "Understanding Operators" section explains operators, including the assignment operator, in greater detail.

It's high time to work through a few examples of creating variables and assigning them values.

To Create a Variable Containing a Value:

Use the var statement to assign a value to a variable. For example:

```
var trekVerb = "Make ";
```

Or you can do the following:

1. Create a variable using the var statement. For example:

```
var trekObject;
```

2. Assign a value to the variable. For example:

```
trekObject = "it so!";
```

> **NOTE** If you prefer, you could combine step 1 and step 2: `var trekObject = "it so!";`.

Now you have two variables, the first containing "Make" and the second containing "it so!" Let's combine them to create the phrase (from *Star Trek: The Next Generation*) *Make it so!* The new, combined phrase will be stored in a new variable. The contents of the new variable will then be displayed in a Web page using the document.write method I showed you in Chapter 1.

Let's take this from the top, one step at a time.

You already know how to create the first two variables and assign text to them:

```
var trekVerb = "Make ";
var trekObject;
trekObject = "it so!";
```

Next, create a third variable, trekQuote, and assign the values of the first two variables to it, using the *string concatenation operator* (+) to connect them:

```
var trekQuote = trekVerb + trekObject;
```

Using the String Concatenation Operator

In everyday usage, the plus sign (+) is used to add two numbers together. For example, $1 + 1 = 2$. The plus sign is used this way in JavaScript, as well—and is called the *addition* or *additive* operator.

However, when strings are involved rather than numbers, the plus sign tells JavaScript to *concatenate* the string values. This means to append the string on the right of the operator to the string to the left of the operator. In the following example:

```
var trekVerb = "Make ";
var trekObject;
trekObject = "it so!";
var trekQuote = trekVerb + trekObject;
```

the concatenation operator is used to assign the concatenated string "Make it so!" to the variable trekQuote.

The following is another example of string concatenation, which makes a variable named tharn and stores the value "cat" in it. Next, tharn is assigned the value of itself concatenated with the string literal "atonic", and the result is displayed:

```
var tharn = "cat";
tharn = tharn + "atonic";
document.write(tharn);
```

As you can see in Figure 2-2, "cat" concatenated with "atonic" makes *catatonic*.

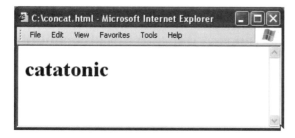

FIGURE 2-2

Concatenation appends the string on the right of the string concatenation operator to the end of the string on the left of the operator.

The final step in the *Star Trek* quotation example is to display the value stored in the variable trekQuote, using the document.write method I explained to you in Chapter 1:

```
document.write(trekQuote);
```

Note a subtle, but important, difference between this line of code and the line of code in Chapter 1. In Chapter 1, we displayed a line of text after the French mathematician and philosopher Descartes:

```
document.write("I think therefore I am");
```

In that case, the text displayed was a *string literal*—in other words, the literal text contained between the quotation marks. In this example, we're doing something a bit more abstract and powerful: We're telling the computer to display the contents of the variable trekQuote, whatever that may happen to be.

Listing 2-1 shows making the variables, assigning them values, and concatenating them into the trekQuote variable. As you can see in Figure 2-3, the full phrase is correctly displayed.

 NOTE I've added HTML <H1></H1> tags to the listing simply to make the display text larger.

LISTING 2-1

Concatenating Variables and Displaying the Value Contained

```
<HTML>
<BODY>
<H1>
    <SCRIPT>
    var trekVerb = "Make ";
    var trekObject;
    trekObject = "it so!";
    var trekQuote = trekVerb + trekObject;
    document.write(trekQuote);
    </SCRIPT>
</H1>
</BODY>
</HTML>
```

FIGURE 2-3

The contents of the trekQuote variable is displayed.

Using Some Fancy Characters

ADVANCED

You may not need to know about the special fancy characters known as *escape sequences* (or *escape characters*), but they sure are useful—and fun! Strictly speaking, it's not necessary to learn about escape sequences to learn how to program. But most languages use them, and they make some tasks much easier.

All the JavaScript escape sequences begin with a backslash (\). Table 2-2 shows some of the JavaScript escape sequences you can use.

TABLE 2-2

JavaScript Escape Sequences

Escape Sequence	Meaning
\b	Backspace
\t	Tab
\n	New line
\f	Form feed
\h	Hexadecimal sequence
\r	Carriage return
\u	Unicode sequence (see http://www.unicode.org for more information about Unicode)
\"	Double quote
\'	Single quote
\\	Backslash (\)

Here's how this works: Suppose you have a sentence full of single and double quotes that you'd like to display. For example, this if from *Harry Potter and the Sorcerer's Stone*:

```
"I want to read it," said Harry furiously, "as it's mine!"
```

To change the double quotes and single quote (that is, the apostrophe) in this sentence so that they can be displayed as a JavaScript string, they must be escaped. Here's how this looks:

```
\"I want to read it,\" said Harry furiously, \"as it\'s mine!\"
```

Next, the whole thing must be surrounded by single or double quotes before you can assign it to a variable or display it as a string literal:

```
"\"I want to read it,\" said Harry furiously, \"as it\'s mine!\""
```

Listing 2-2 shows assigning the escaped string to a variable and then displaying the value stored in the variable. You can see in Figure 2-4 that the quotes are properly displayed.

LISTING 2-2

Displaying a String Containing Escaped Quotations

```
<HTML>
<BODY>
<H1>
    <SCRIPT>
var potterSays = "\"I want to read it,\" said Harry furiously, \"as it\'s
mine!\"";
    document.write(potterSays);
    </SCRIPT>
</H1>
</BODY>
</HTML>
```

WAY COOL

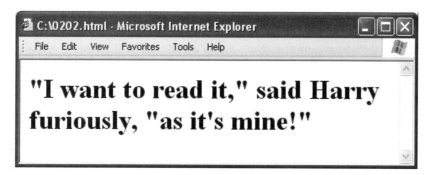

"I want to read it," said Harry furiously, "as it's mine!"

FIGURE 2-4

It's easy to display quotations using escape sequences.

Let's Have HTML for Dinner!

TRY THIS
AT HOME

If you play with the example I just showed you with escaped quotations, you'll see that the place where the line of text breaks and forms a new line depends on the size of the browser window and is out of the programmer's control. (If you look closely at Figure 2-4, you'll see that with the browser sized as shown, the line break occurs between the words *Harry* and *furiously*.)

You may have wondered if you can embed HTML within JavaScript strings. The answer is that you can—HTML is just plain text like any other text string. Let's use the HTML line break tag—
—to create line breaks where we'd like them in a JavaScript string displayed with the document.write method. This will also give us a chance to practice assigning and concatenating variables.

First, create a variable named newLine and store the HTML <BR> tag in it:

```
var newLine = "<BR>";
```

WAY COOL

Next, create variables for each word in the text you want to display:

```
var One = "One";
var line = "line";
var at = "at";
var a = "a";
var time = "time!";
```

Note that I've named the variables to match their contents, but the variable name isn't the same thing as its contents.

> *Even though the variables have been named to match their contents, the variable name is a different thing from its contents.*

Next, concatenate the variables with display text and the newLine variable containing the HTML line break tag and then assign the results to a variable named splitLine:

```
var splitLine = One + newLine + line  + newLine + at  +
   newLine + a  + newLine + time;
```

Finally, display the text including HTML:

```
document.write(splitLine);
```

As you can see in Figure 2-5, the HTML works: The line of text is displayed with breaks where the <BR> character was placed.

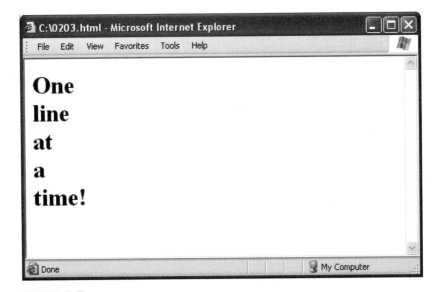

FIGURE 2-5
You can include HTML tags in JavaScript strings.

Listing 2-3 shows the complete code for concatenating the words and HTML line breaks.

LISTING 2-3

Embedding HTML in a JavaScript String

```
<HTML>
<BODY>
<H1>
    <SCRIPT>
    var newLine = "<BR>";
    var One = "One";
    var line = "line";
    var at = "at";
    var a = "a";
    var time = "time!";
     var splitLine = One + newLine + line + newLine + at
         + newLine + a  + newLine + time;
    document.write(splitLine);
    </SCRIPT>
</H1>
</BODY>
</HTML>
```

Examining Some Special Types

ADVANCED

In addition to the three standard types—Boolean, Number, and String—that I've told you about earlier in this chapter, there are two other special types in JavaScript: Null and Undefined.

The Null type has only one value, null. The null value means that there's no data in a variable.

The Undefined type also has only one value, undefined. This is the value of a variable whose contents are unclear because nothing has ever been stored in it. (Interestingly, a variable that has never been mentioned in a particular program also has the value of undefined.)

You should also know about NaN. NaN is an important property of the JavaScript Number object. It's short for *Not a Number* and is the result of a mathematical operation such as dividing a number by zero that has no numerical answer. NaN is unequal to any number and doesn't even equal itself.

You'll find out more about Null, Undefined, and NaN as you go on in *Learn How to Program*.

Implementing Type Conversion

JavaScript is a *loosely typed* language. This means you don't specify the type of a variable when you create it. Variables are automatically converted to reflect the type of values stored in them during program execution depending on the JavaScript interpreter's analysis of the context in which a variable is being used. This makes things seem easy because you don't have to manually specify type conversions, but it also means that there's a greater possibility of error because of unexpected consequences of automatic type conversion.

In contrast, in a *strongly typed* language you must specify the type of every variable. Unless there's absolutely no possibility of data being lost, in a strongly typed language automatic type conversion (also called *implicit* conversion) doesn't take place.

It's often the case in programs that you'll need to convert a type. As a simple example, suppose you've performed a calculation and come up with a number. You now want to display the number as part of a string ("Including interest, you owe $42.42. Please pay it at once."). The process involves converting the number (the result of the calculation) to a string for string concatenation and display.

As a matter of good coding practice, you should attempt to perform conversions yourself rather than letting JavaScript do it for you automatically. A number of JavaScript functions are available for performing type conversions, including those shown in Table 2-3. (When you perform a type conversion using one of these functions rather than allowing JavaScript to automatically perform a conversion for you, it is called an *explicit* type conversion.)

> *"Including interest, you owe $42.42. Please pay it at once."*

DO IT RIGHT

ADVANCED

TABLE 2-3

JavaScript Type Conversion Functions

Function Name	What It Does
eval	Evaluates an expression and returns its value. If the expression consists of JavaScript statements, these are executed and a value provided by the last executed statement is returned.
parseInt	Converts a string to an integer (NaN returned if this isn't possible).
parseFloat	Converts a string to a floating-point number (NaN is returned if this isn't possible).

As a general rule of thumb, JavaScript automatically converts numbers to strings rather than the other way around. Thus, in these statements:

```
var test = "The answer is " + 42;
var test2 = " and ";
var test3 = 42 + " is the answer.";
```

both occurrences of 42 are converted to strings, no matter whether the number is the first value encountered by the variable. If you concatenate the test variables with an HTML line break:

```
var newLine = "<BR>";
document.write(test + newLine + test2 + newLine + test3 + newLine );
```

you'll get the results shown in Figure 2-6.

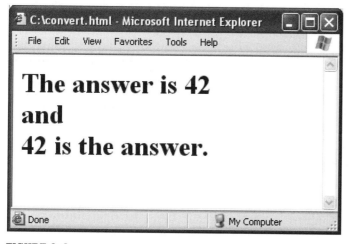

FIGURE 2-6

JavaScript implicitly converts numbers to strings rather than the other way around.

Bear in mind that most conversion bugs happen during comparisons. If you only compare same types—not mixing numbers and strings—you won't run into problems.

Conversions to a Boolean type, which contains logical information as explained at the beginning of this chapter, are generally safe if you know the rules. Chapter 3, "Using Conditional Statements," explains these conversions.

Understanding Statements

Statements are the building blocks used to make a program.

JavaScript statements are the fundamental sentence-like building blocks used to create a program.

You probably have a fairly good, intuitive idea of what's meant by *statement*, and you've already seen quite a few JavaScript statements in this chapter so far. Here are two examples of statements from earlier in this chapter:

```
document.write(potterSays);
var trekQuote = trekVerb + trekObject;
```

JavaScript statements consist of *tokens*, namely keywords, variables, literals, operators, function calls, object references, and so on. (Don't be scared by all these terms; by the time you've finished *Learn How to Program,* you'll be familiar with them all and eating them for breakfast!)

DO IT RIGHT

All JavaScript statements you'll see in this book are ended, also called *terminated,* with a semicolon. But JavaScript is a forgiving language. It's not a good practice, but most of the time if you leave the semicolon off, JavaScript will still know what you mean and act accordingly.

Every JavaScript program consists of a sequence of statements that's nominally processed from top to bottom. (The exception to this processing order is if you put flow control statements in your code that change the order of execution, as explained in Chapters 3–5.)

JavaScript ignores spaces, tabs, and most line breaks that occur between tokens, except those that are part of string literals. This means you can—and should—use spacing and line breaks to format code to be consistent and readable.

As I mentioned a moment ago, it's normal practice to end each JavaScript statement with a semicolon. It's a good idea to follow this practice because you're less likely to inadvertently introduce errors. However, the semicolon isn't required because JavaScript is the kind of language that always tries to fix laziness on the part of the programmer by guessing what the programmer means.

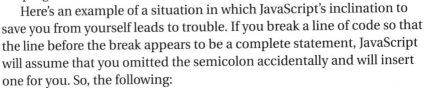

ADVANCED

Here's an example of a situation in which JavaScript's inclination to save you from yourself leads to trouble. If you break a line of code so that the line before the break appears to be a complete statement, JavaScript will assume that you omitted the semicolon accidentally and will insert one for you. So, the following:

```
return
false;
```

is evaluated as this:

```
return;
false;
```

which has a different meaning from the statement you probably intended:

```
return false;
```

Using Comments

Comments are a special and important kind of statement. Comments are intended to explain your code to human readers and aren't processed as part of a computer program.

It's sometimes said that the best comments consist of clearly written code with proper naming of variables and other identifiers. This may be true, but it's still an extremely good practice to add comments to your code.

DO IT RIGHT

Comments can also be used to identify who wrote a program. Because I'm proud of my code, I always sign it in a comment.

There are two styles of JavaScript comments. The first is to use // characters. Any text after the // and before the end of the line is treated as a comment and ignored by the JavaScript processor.

In the second kind of comment, any text between /* and */ is ignored by the processor.

Listing 2-4 shows five comments. To make sure you understand how comments are marked, see if you can count all five comments.

> *I'm proud of my code, so I sign it in a comment!*

LISTING 2-4

Styles of JavaScript Comments

```
// I'm a single-line comment
// This is another comment
/* Real multiple-line comment to follow */ //Yet another comment

/***********************************************************
 * JavaScript module written by Harold Davis
 * Purpose: Rock, Scissors, and Paper game
 * Date:
 * Inputs:
 * Outputs:
 * Of special note: Demonstrates conditional statements
 ***********************************************************/
```

Understanding Operators

Operators are the glue that combines identifiers, variables, and keywords together to create statements. In this chapter, you've already used the concatenation operator—and probably are pretty familiar with some other operators, such as those used in everyday arithmetic.

The following sections explain the operators you're most likely to encounter. (You'll find information about the operators specifically relating to JavaScript objects, such as typeof and new, in Chapter 7, "Working with Objects.")

Using Assignment Operators

One JavaScript operator, the simple assignment operator, represented by an equals sign, has already been frequently used to create statements in this chapter. For example, this statement:

```
var test = "The answer is " + 42;
```

uses the assignment operator to store the value "The answer is 42" in the variable test. Put more generally, the assignment operator assigns the value on the right of the equals sign to the variable on the left.

JavaScript has other assignment operators you can use, all of which assign a value to a left operand based on the value of the right operand. In other words, these operators combine two operations into one step. Here are the "combination" operators:

- x += y assigns the value x + y to the variable x.
  This works for string concatenation as well as numerical addition.

- x -= y assigns the value x - y to the variable x.

- x *= y assigns the value x * y to the variable x.

- x /= y assigns the value x / y to the variable x.

- x %= y assigns the value x modulo y
  (the remainder following division of x by y) to the variable x.

These assignment operators combine two operations into one step.

For example, the modulo assignment operator (%=) combines assignment with modulo (or remainder) arithmetic. If you run this:

ADVANCED

```
var myAssign = 13;
myAssign %= 3; // modulo assignment
document.write("13 modulo 3 is " + myAssign);
```

the modulus—or integer remainder when you divide 13 by 3—will be displayed, as shown in Figure 2-7.

FIGURE 2-7

The modulo operator combines remainder arithmetic with assignment.

Using Arithmetic Operators

In addition to the standard arithmetic operators—plus (+), minus (–), multiplication (*), division (/)—JavaScript supports the arithmetic operators shown in Table 2-4.

TABLE 2-4

JavaScript Arithmetic Operators (in Addition to Standard Arithmetic Operators)

Operator	Functionality
% (Modulus operator)	x % y returns x modulo y (the integer remainder of x divided by y).
++ (Increment operator)	Adds one to the operand. If the increment operator is used as a *prefix* (++x), the operator returns the value after incrementing. If it is used as a *postfix* (x++), the value is returned before incrementing.
–– (Decrement operator)	Works the same way as the increment operator, except subtracts one rather than adds one.

ADVANCED

Listing 2-5 illustrates how the increment operator works (the decrement operator works the same way except that it subtracts rather than adds).

LISTING 2-5
Working with the Increment Operator

```
var Inc = 42;
document.write("Starting value of " + Inc + "<BR>");
var IncPreFix = ++Inc;
var IncPostFix = Inc++;
document.write(" IncPreFix " + IncPreFix + "<BR>");
document.write(" IncPostFix " + IncPostFix+ "<BR>");
document.write("Ending value of " + Inc);
```

In Listing 2-5, the variable Inc starts with a value of 42. This statement:

```
var IncPreFix = ++Inc;
```

increases the value of Inc by one, so it's now 43, and then assigns the value 43 to the variable IncPreFix.

Next, this statement:

```
var IncPostFix = Inc++;
```

first assigns the current value of Inc (43) to IncPostFix and only then increments Inc so that it finally stores 44. Figure 2-8 shows the results of these increment operations.

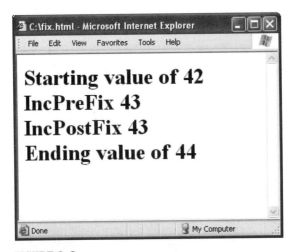

FIGURE 2-8
Results of the increment operations

Using Boolean Operators

ADVANCED

Boolean, or logical, operators let you combine the results of logical evaluation, as shown in Table 2-5, to create logical expressions. In JavaScript, a logical expression consists of values of the Boolean type and Boolean operators. Every logical expression evaluates to true or false.

TABLE 2-5

Boolean Operators

Operator	Meaning
&& (And)	A && B is true if A is true and B is true.
|| (Or)	A || B is true if A is true or B is true.
! (Not)	!A is true if A is false, and false if A is true.

JavaScript Boolean expressions are evaluated from left to right. They're processed using "incomplete" evaluation as follows:

- False && anything always evaluates to false without looking at the anything.

- True || anything always evaluates to true without looking at the anything.

Programmers write code that uses incomplete evaluation as a shortcut to save computer processing time. Of course, it always leads to the correct Boolean result. However, any code to the right of the Boolean operator will not be evaluated (or triggered). In some situations, this might cause unexpected errors or side effects, so you shouldn't write code that depends on the execution of expressions to the right of a Boolean operator unless you are very careful!

Using Comparison Operators

A comparison operator compares its operands and returns a logical value of true or false depending on the results of the comparison. Comparison of strings is case sensitive and is based on a dictionary ordering of the strings. So, this string:

```
"Harry Potter" == "harry potter";
```

> "Harry Potter" *doesn't evaluate as equal to* "harry potter".

returns a value of false because upper-case letters aren't the same as lower-case letters.

However, the following:

```
"Dumbledore" < "Voldemort";
```

evaluates to true because D comes before V in the dictionary.

Table 2-6 shows JavaScript comparison operators.

> "Dumbledore" *is less than* "Voldemort".

TABLE 2-6

JavaScript Comparison Operators

Operator	Meaning
==	Equality. This returns true if its two operands are equal.
!=	Inequality, the exact opposite of equality; if its two operands are equal, it returns false.
===	Identity. Evaluates to true if its two operands are equal without any type conversion.
!==	Nonidentity, the exact opposite of identity; it evaluates to true if its operands have different types or values.
>	Greater than.
>=	Greater than or equal.
<	Less than.
<=	Less than or equal.

Using Operator Precedence

Operator precedence means the order in which operators are applied when evaluating an expression. Order does matter: The order in which operators are applied can change the value of an expression.

You can direct JavaScript to evaluate part of an expression first by enclosing it in parentheses. In the absence of this kind of direction, evaluation is probably more or less what you might expect. The following operators appear in the order of JavaScript evaluation precedence (the highest precedence is first):

- Negation, increment, decrement
- Multiply, divide, modulo
- Addition, subtraction
- Comparison
- Logical And
- Logical Or
- Assignment

Understanding Blocks

Blocks, also called *statement blocks* or *compound statements*, are sequences of statements that are treated as a single JavaScript statement. Blocks can be used any place that JavaScript expects a single statement.

To Create a Statement Block:

Enclose any number of JavaScript statements within curly braces. For example:

```
{
    var test = "The answer is " + 42;
    var test2 = " and ";
    var test3 = 42 + " is the answer.";
}
```

NOTE Although the individual statements within a statement block should end with a semicolon, the statement block itself—even though it's treated as a single statement—doesn't terminate with its own semicolon. The curly brace ends the statement block.

What's It All About?

It's all about building blocks. This chapter was about the basic building blocks that are used to construct computer programs. In addition to keywords, you use variables and operators to build statements. In turn, a computer program consists of a sequence of statements.

If you know how to build statements, then you know how to construct the basic building blocks of any computer program.

In Chapter 3, "Using Conditional Statements," you'll start to look at statements that are a bit more complicated than those presented in this chapter because they involve conditional evaluation, or a choice, often depending on the user's input.

3

Using Conditional Statements

In this chapter, things get kicked up a notch and become really fun!

Conditional statements tell the computer to make a choice depending on the evaluation of a condition. Often, evaluating the condition means checking to see what the user selected—so conditional statements allow you to create programs that are interactive. What the computer does, in other words, depends on what the human interacting with the computer does.

Without conditional statements, it's hard to use a computer as anything much more than a really good calculation engine—so conditionals are crucial to understanding the true potential of computer programs.

In this chapter, I explain how JavaScript conditional expressions work. Next, I show you the three forms of if statements that you can use in JavaScript. To have some fun with if statements, I show you how to write a program that plays a game—Rock, Scissors, and Paper—with the computer against the human race.

The last topic in this chapter is using the switch statement. Switch statements can be a powerful way to code multiple if statements as a single evaluative statement—thus greatly simplifying code, which is always a good thing.

I also show you how to recode the Rock, Scissors, and Paper game more simply, using two switch statements rather than the many if statements in the original version.

ADVANCED

To accomplish the goals of this chapter, particularly creating the Rock, Scissors, and Paper game, we'll have to get a little ahead of ourselves. Some of the code in this chapter uses conceptual material not explained in full detail until later in this book. Don't be scared; I explain things as we go, and nothing in this chapter should give you great difficulty.

Understanding Conditional Expressions

A *conditional expression* has one of two values based on a condition. The general syntax is as follows:

```
(condition) ? val1 : val2
```

If the condition is true, then the expression is the value of val1; if it's false, then the expression evaluates to val2. For example, the following expression:

```
status = (age >= 21) ? "an adult" : "a minor";
```

assigns the value "an adult" to the variable status if the variable age is greater than or equal to 21; otherwise, it assigns the value "a minor".

Let's use this conditional expression in a program in which the user enters a name and age and then clicks a button. The program evaluates the age using the conditional expression I just showed you, and it returns a message depending on whether the user is an adult or a minor.

Before I can show you how to do this, I need to explain some preliminaries.

First, the JavaScript alert statement is used to display a pop-up message window (this kind of window is sometimes called a *message box*). The way it works is that the keyword alert is followed by parentheses. A string value within the parentheses is displayed in the message box when the alert statement is executed.

For example, when the computer processes the following:

```
alert ("Happy Birthday!");
```

it displays a message box like that in Figure 3-1.

FIGURE 3-1
The JavaScript alert statement displays a message box when executed.

Next, you need to know that HTML form elements can be used to interact with JavaScript programs. The HTML form elements can be recognized because they're created using <INPUT> tags. The TYPE attribute of the tag determines the kind of input element it is (text box, button, and so on).

The NAME property of the element is used to reference it from within a JavaScript program. Other properties of an HTML form element—such as its VALUE—can also be manipulated programmatically.

Listing 3-1 shows the HTML form that will be used to set up this program. It contains a text box for the user's name (with the initial value of "Harry Potter"), a text box for the user's age (with an initial value of "12"), and a button to click to run the program.

LISTING 3-1
HTML with Form Elements

```
<HTML>
<BODY>
<FORM>
Enter Your Name:
<INPUT TYPE=text NAME=userName  VALUE="Harry Potter">
Enter Your Age:
<INPUT TYPE=text NAME=userAge  VALUE="12">
<INPUT TYPE=button VALUE="Check Age">
</FORM>
</BODY>
</HTML>
```

TIP In the interests of readability and clarity, I've omitted HTML table, row, and cell tags—<TABLE>, <TR>, <TD>—used to format this HTML form (you can find them in the online version of this program). This means that the figures shown may not quite match the appearance of what you get when you build the programs in this chapter (although the functionality will be the same).

Finally, if you want something to happen, you can add event code to an HTML form element, such as a button. (Chapter 8, "Understanding Events and Event-Driven Programming," explains events and event code in greater detail.)

JavaScript code placed between single or double quotes and assigned to an onClick event of a button is processed when the user clicks the button. The general form of this is as follows:

```
onClick = 'JavaScript code goes here!;'
```

 CAUTION Be careful that you type onClick with a lowercase o and an uppercase C; the event keyword is case sensitive.

 NOTE As you'll see a little later in this chapter, there's an easier way to add click event code than assigning numerous JavaScript statements as one quoted string to an event.

Listing 3-2 shows adding onClick code to the input button that uses the conditional expression we discussed a little while ago to check if the user is a minor or an adult. The results are then displayed in a message box using an alert statement.

LISTING 3-2

Using a Conditional Expression in an onClick Event

```
...
<INPUT TYPE=button VALUE="Check Age"
onClick='var status = (userAge.value >= 21) ? "an adult" : "a minor";
alert(userName.value + " is " + status + ".");'>
...
```

 TIP I've placed the JavaScript code assigned to the onClick event between single quotes. That way, the double-quoted strings within the code still work.

Listing 3-3 shows the onClick code in the context of the HTML form.

LISTING 3-3

HTML Form with onClick Code

```
<HTML>
<BODY>
<FORM>
Enter Your Name:
<INPUT TYPE=text NAME=userName  VALUE="Harry Potter">
Enter Your Age:
<INPUT TYPE=text NAME=userAge  VALUE="12">
<INPUT TYPE=button VALUE="Check Age"
onClick='var status = (userAge.value >= 21) ? "an adult" : "a minor";
alert(userName.value + " is " + status + ".");'>
</FORM>
</BODY>
</HTML>
```

If you open this in your browser and click the Check Age button without entering any fresh data, you'll see the message box shown in Figure 3-2.

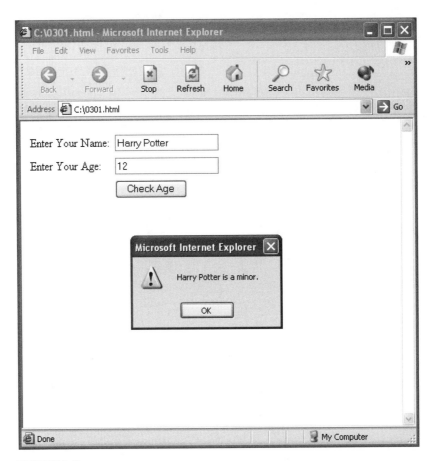

FIGURE 3-2

The alert message box displays the results based on the default values of the HTML form elements.

On the other hand, if you enter your own data into the form—for example, someone very old such as Perenelle Flamel, a character mentioned in *Harry Potter and the Sorcerer's Stone*—the conditional expression will correctly identify an adult (see Figure 3-3).

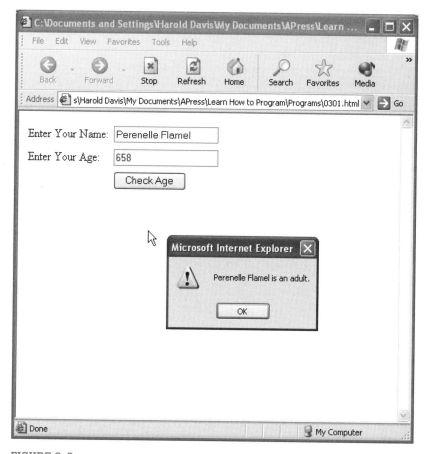

FIGURE 3-3

When you enter new values in the HTML form, they're evaluated using the conditional expression.

CAUTION What happens if the user enters something that's not a number in the age text box? You can try this and find out. (The answer is that a text string converts to NaN, which stands for *Not a Number*, explained in Chapter 2, "Understanding Types, Variables, and Statements.") The point is that this program does nothing to ensure that the user input is of the right type. Doing this is called *input validation*, discussed further in Chapter 10, "Error Handling and Debugging."

Using conditional expressions is a great deal of fun, but it's time to move on to something even more important: if statements.

Using *If* Statements

If statements are used to conditionally execute, or process, code. The conditional code is only executed if the condition evaluates to the Boolean value true.

JavaScript has three forms of the if statement. The first is simply as follows:

```
if (condition)
    statement;
```

In this form of the if statement, the statement executes if the condition is true.

The second form adds an else statement. The else statement executes if the condition is false (implying that the first statement hasn't been executed):

```
if (condition)
    statement 1;
else
    statement 2;
```

It's important to understand that any statement within an if statement can be replaced by multiple statements using curly braces to create statement blocks as explained toward the end of Chapter 2, "Understanding Types, Variables, and Statements."

In general, it's good programming practice to use curly braces with your if statements to make them easier to read and unambiguous. Using curly braces, the second form of the if statement would look like this:

```
if (condition)
    {
      statement 1;
      ...
      statement n;
    }
else
    {
      statement n+1;
      ...
      statement n+m;
    }
```

> ### So, Who Is George Boole, Anyway?
>
> Who is George Boole, and why name the Boolean value type after him? Boole, a nineteenth-century British mathematician, formulated an "algebra of logic" that can be used to mathematically calculate logical values using equations such as X = 1 to mean that the proposition X is true and X = 0 to mean that X is false. The 1 and 0 used in these logical equations is analogous to the true and false values used in modern programming languages.

The third form of the if statement adds else if clauses. You can use this when you have multiple conditions you need to cover. The general form is as follows:

```
if (condition)
   {
      statement 1;
      ...
      statement n;
   }
else if (condition2)
   {
     statement n+1;
      ...
     statement n+m;
   }
else if (condition3)
   {
     statement n+m;
      ...
     statement n+m+q;
   }
else
  {
     // all the other conditions have failed
     statements;
  }
```

The equivalent processing could have been achieved without the else if statement using nested if else statements. (As an exercise, try and see how this is so!) However, else if makes the statement clearer and less likely to contain bugs.

To Create an *If* Statement:

1. Create the scaffolding for the if statement. Experienced programmers have found that you're far less likely to introduce hard-to-find bugs if you first get the structure of conditional statements right. Make sure to use indentation to clarify which statement blocks go with which conditions. For example:

```
if ()
    {

    }
else if ()
    {

    }
else
    {

    }
```

2. Add a comment before the beginning of the if statement that says what the if statement does:

```
/* Tests to see whether a lowercase string is
   greater than, equal to, or less than
   the same string in uppercase characters.
   "HOGWARTS" and "hogwarts" are the test strings. */
```

In this case, we're testing to see how JavaScript ranks, or orders, lowercase and uppercase strings. (You may be surprised at the results!)

3. Add conditional expressions into the parentheses:

```
...
if ("hogwarts" > "HOGWARTS")
    {


    }
else if ("hogwarts" == "HOGWARTS")
    ...
```

4. Add the statements that are to be conditionally executed within the curly braces. Listing 3-4 shows the complete code.

5. Open the HTML page containing the program in a browser, as shown in Figure 3-4.

 TIP It might seem easier to cobble `if` statements together on an ad-hoc basis without first creating the scaffolding. But as these statements get complex, you'll find you save a great deal of time by creating the structure of the statement first.

LISTING 3-4

Determining Whether Lowercase or Uppercase Strings Are "More Equal" Using an `If` Statement

```
<HTML>
<BODY>
<H1>
    <SCRIPT>
    /* Tests to see whether a lowercase string is
    greater than, equal to, or less than
    the same string in uppercase characters.
    "HOGWARTS" and "hogwarts" are the test strings. */
    if ("hogwarts" > "HOGWARTS")
        {
        // lower case wins
        document.write("Lower case is greater than upper case!");
        }
    else if ("hogwarts" == "HOGWARTS")
        {
        // cases the same
        document.write("They are the same!");
        }
    else
        {
        // upper case wins
        document.write("Upper case is greater than lower case!");
        }
    </SCRIPT>
</H1>
</BODY>
</HTML>
```

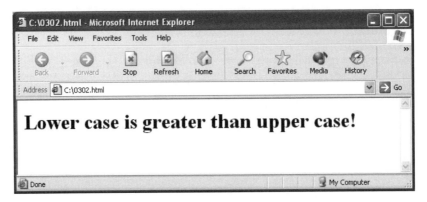

FIGURE 3-4

Using an if statement to test how JavaScript orders lowercase and uppercase strings

Converting to Boolean

As you've seen, an if statement works by performing an evaluation of a condition. The program "branches" to one place or another depending on whether the condition evaluates to the Boolean value of true or false.

However, the types placed in the condition that's evaluated aren't restricted to the Boolean type. This means that it's safe to use any type for a Boolean evaluation in a conditional statement as long as you realize that the implicit conversion forced by the evaluation will follow the rules shown in Table 3-1.

TABLE 3-1

Conversion to Boolean

Type	Converts to Boolean Value As Follows
Null	Converts to false
Number	Converts to false if 0, −0, +0, or NaN; otherwise, true
String	Converts to false if the string length = 0; otherwise, converts to true
Undefined	Converts to false

As a puzzle, try constructing if statements that rely on the conversions shown in Table 3-1—and verify that the conversions work in the way that I've said they do.

Building the Rock, Scissors, and Paper Game

Okay, boys and girls, it's time for something really fun! Now that you know how to work with if statements, we can create an interactive computer game.

WAY COOL

Do you remember the Rock, Scissors, and Paper game from when you were little? Here's how it works: There are two players. Each player selects rock, scissors, or paper. Then the two players simultaneously "show" the other their selection.

If both players have selected the same thing, it's a tie. Otherwise, the winner is determined as follows:

- Rock wins over scissors (because a rock "smashes" scissors).

- Paper wins over rock (because paper "covers" a rock).

- Scissors win over paper (because scissors "cut" paper).

In our case, one of the players is the computer, and the other is the user of the computer program. The user will make a choice between rock, scissors, and paper. The computer's choice will be made at random.

Here are the steps we'll need to build into this program to make the game work:

- A method of *capturing*—another word for *determining*—the user's choice of rock, scissors, or paper

- A way to generate a random choice for the computer

- A way to compare choices and determine the winner (or if it's a tie)

- Finally, a way to display text that indicates the choices and the result

Figure 3-5 shows these steps in a simple *flow chart*—a diagram intended to show the "flow" of execution of statements in a computer program. The flow chart shown in Figure 3-5 is high level, meaning that it doesn't "drill

The rules of Rock, Scissors, and Paper are simple: Rock smashes scissors and so on.

The steps for creating a program that plays Rock, Scissors, and Paper are straightforward.

down" to the level of individual conditional statements. In many circumstances, it may be a helpful part of planning a program to create a flow chart that's more detailed than this one.

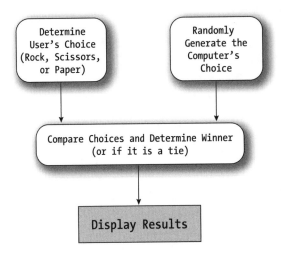

> *A flow chart is a diagram intended to show the order of execution in a program.*

FIGURE 3-5

A high-level flow chart of the Rock, Scissors, and Paper game

I'll show you each of these steps in detail, but before we get there, we need to discuss a few preliminary programming concepts that I haven't explained yet.

ADVANCED

Understanding Some Necessary Preliminaries

To follow the Rock, Scissors, and Paper program, you need to know about some things that are only fully explained later in *Learn How to Program*.

Interacting with HTML Form Elements

You'll need to know how to interact in a simple fashion with HTML form elements and the events fired by an element (Chapter 8, "Understanding Events and Event-Driven Programming," discusses these things). You've already seen in the age check example (Listing 3-3) that you can add code to the onClick event of a form button. The Rock, Scissors, and Paper example uses a similar mechanism to start a play of the game.

In addition, HTML form elements can be referred to by name in JavaScript code. We'll need to know what the user selected—rock, scissors, or paper—which the user sets using option buttons (also referred to as *radio buttons*).

These are HTML <INPUT> elements of `type=radio`.

In JavaScript code, the value stored in a radio button—a Boolean `true` if it has been selected and a Boolean `false` if it hasn't—can be evaluated using the following construction:

```
document.formName.inputElementName.checked
```

In the example, the form is named `gameForm`, and the radio button input elements are an array (I discuss arrays in a second) named `game`. The first radio button on the form is named `game[0]`. So, if it's checked (selected), this expression:

```
document.gameForm.game[0].checked
```

will evaluate to `true`, and if the radio button hasn't been selected, the expression is `false`.

Introducing Arrays

Chapter 6, "Programming with Arrays," fully explains arrays. In the mean-time, you need to know that an array stores values that are of the same type, and they can be accessed using an index.

The index is notated using square brackets. In JavaScript it starts at zero (not as you might expect at one).

So whether (or not) the three radio buttons on the HTML form— one representing the user choice of rock, the next scissors, and the final one paper—are checked can be determined by Boolean evaluation of the expressions:

> Values in an array can be accessed using an index.

```
document.gameForm.game[0].checked
document.gameForm.game[1].checked
document.gameForm.game[2].checked
```

You may be curious to know why I used an array to name these but-tons. If they're named this way, the browser knows the radio buttons are related—and only one can be selected (checked) at a time.

Introducing Functions

A *function* is a piece of JavaScript code—in other words, a series of statements—that's defined once in a program but can be executed many times. Functions (which are explained in detail in Chapter 5, "Understanding Functions") can be passed values, also called *parameters*, to operate on, and they can return a value.

In the Rock, Scissors, and Paper application, functions are used to clarify the organization of the program—and to provide a mechanism so that the program code need not be assigned as a single string to the onClick event.

Listing 3-3 in contrast shows an example of assigning the entire program code as a quoted string to an onClick event. You can readily see why this would get out of hand (and be hard to read) if there were more than one or two lines of code.

Introducing the Random Method

The JavaScript Math object makes available a number of mathematical constants and functions. The Rock, Scissors, and Paper application uses the Random function of the Math object—which returns a pseudorandom number between zero and one.

I say "pseudorandom" because this number isn't really random if you're going to be picky—but it's certainly random enough for playing a game of Rock, Scissors, and Paper.

There's nothing wrong with flipping ahead if you'd like to learn more about these things and then coming back!

But it's not necessary to flip ahead. Now that you have been introduced to the preliminaries, we're ready to forge full speed ahead with Rock, Scissors, and Paper.

Building the User Interface

The first thing we're going to do is build the user interface—or computer screen such as the Web page in which the user enters a choice and starts a play of the game—for Rock, Scissors, and Paper.

The user interface, as you can see in Listing 3-5, is almost entirely HTML (as opposed to JavaScript).

NOTE I'm not going to take much time in this book explaining HTML tags because creating HTML isn't really programming, and it would distract from the subject matter of this book. If you need to better understand the HTML tags used to create user interfaces in the examples, you should pick up one of the many books available that describe HTML in detail, such as *HTML & XHTML: The Definitive Guide*, Fifth Edition, by Chuck Musciano and Bill Kennedy (O'Reilly, 2002).

LISTING 3-5

The Rock, Scissors, and Paper User Interface

```
<BODY>
<H2>
Play "Rock, Scissors, and Paper" the JavaScript way!
</H2>
<UL>
    <LI>Rock smashes scissors!
    <LI>Scissors cut paper!
    <LI>Paper covers rock!
</UL>
<FORM name="gameForm">
<P>Make a choice:
<BR>
<INPUT type="radio" name="game" value="Rock" checked> Rock<BR>
<INPUT type="radio" name="game" value="Paper">Paper<BR>
<INPUT type="radio" name="game" value="Scissors">Scissors<BR>
<INPUT type="button" name="play" value="Play" onClick="shakeIt();">
</FORM>
</BODY>
```

The HTML shown in Listing 3-5 creates the Web page shown in Figure 3-6.

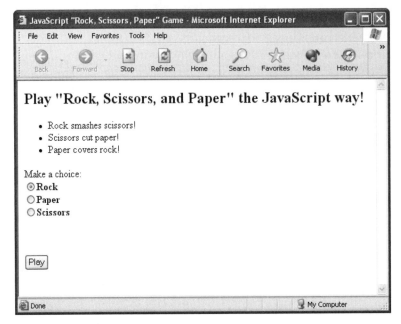

FIGURE 3-6

The Web page (user interface) for Rock, Scissors, and Paper

If you look at the HTML that makes up the Web page, you'll see that there only a few things you need to know from the viewpoint of the JavaScript program. First, the HTML form has a name—gameForm—that we'll need in order to refer to input elements on the form.

Second, the three radio button input elements are all named game and can be referred to using array notation, as I explained a little while ago.

Finally, the user starts a round of the game by clicking the Play button. Clicking this button causes the button's onClick event to fire. The code assigned to the button's onClick event is a single JavaScript function, shakeIt:

```
<INPUT type="button" name="play" value="Play" onClick="shakeIt();">
```

You can tell from this that program execution passes immediately to the shakeIt function when the user starts a round of the game.

Understanding the Organization of the Code

DO IT RIGHT

In contrast to the previous examples in *Learn How to Program*, you can find the program code for the Rock, Scissors, and Paper game in two JavaScript functions, shakeIt and whoWon. This is done for clarity—code organized into conceptual modules is easier to read and, in the long run, easier to maintain.

The function shakeIt is named to suggest the shaking of dice. It performs the following tasks:

- Randomly generates a choice for the computer

- Determines the choice made by the user

- Displays a message box showing both choices and calls the function whoWon with the choices as values

The function whoWon determines the winner and passes back an appropriate message to complete the message box display initiated by shakeIt.

Both functions are placed in the <HEAD> section of the HTML document. One reason for doing this is that everything in the <HEAD> section of an HTML document is loaded—or read by the computer—first. If you put a JavaScript function in the <HEAD> section of an HTML document, then you know it will be available—and the computer will know what you're talking about—when you call it from the body of the document.

Listing 3-6 shows the general structure used for code placement in the Rock, Scissors, and Paper application.

LISTING 3-6

Placement of Code in Rock, Scissors, and Paper

```
<HTML>
   <HEAD>
      <TITLE>
      JavaScript "Rock, Scissors, Paper" Game
      </TITLE>
   <SCRIPT>
   function whoWon (iplay, uplay) {
   ...
   }
   function shakeIt(){
   ...
   }
```

```
    </SCRIPT>
</HEAD>
    <BODY>
    ...
    </BODY>
</HTML>
```

Generating a Choice for the Computer

The first thing that the shakeIt function does is to obtain a random number between zero and one using the Math object's random number generator that I talked about a little while ago:

```
var randGen = Math.random();
```

Next, a choice of rock, scissors, or paper is assigned to the computer using if statements and the random number:

```
if (randGen <= .33)

    var computerPlay = "rock";
if ((randGen >.33) && (randGen <= .66))
    var computerPlay = "scissors";

if (randGen > .66)
    var computerPlay = "paper";
```

Determining the User's Choice

To determine the user's choice, the program uses another series of if statements—combined with the array notation I explained earlier:

```
if (document.gameForm.game[0].checked)
    var personPlay = "rock";
if (document.gameForm.game[1].checked)
    var personPlay = "paper";
if (document.gameForm.game[2].checked)
    var personPlay = "scissors";
```

The value selected by the user is now stored in the variable personPlay, and the value chosen for the computer is stored in the variable computerPlay.

Finding the Winner

The last line in the shakeIt function does a couple of things at the same time:

```
alert ("The computer played: " + computerPlay +
    ". You played: " + personPlay + ".   " + whoWon(computerPlay,
personPlay));
```

The alert keyword tells the computer to display a message box. The string that will be displayed in the message box starts with the value of the choice randomly selected for the computer, computerPlay, followed by the user's selection, personPlay. Next, the whoWon function is called with both values.

The whoWon function, shown in Listing 3-7, compares two variables, iplay and uplay, that are passed to the function. The variable iplay corresponds to the variable computerPlay, and uplay corresponds to personPlay.

The function whoWon first checks to see if the two plays are the same, in which case the game is a tie. Next, it uses if statements to check each possible computer play (for example, rock). If the computer played rock, then the human user loses if the user selected scissors—and wins otherwise.

Each possible combination is checked using conditional statements, and the results are passed back to the shakeIt function as a string using the return keyword.

 NOTE As a reminder, the comparison operator (==) is used to compare two values for equality. On the other hand, the assignment operator (=) is used to assign a value to a variable.

LISTING 3-7

The whoWon Function

```
function whoWon (iplay, uplay) {
    // "I" am the computer
    if (iplay == uplay)
        return "IT'S A TIE! TRY AGAIN, FRAIL HUMAN ENTITY?";
    if (iplay == "rock") {
        if (uplay == "scissors")
            return "I WIN! ROCK SMASHES SCISSORS! COMPUTERS FOREVER!"
        else
            return "YOU WIN. Paper covers rock. Paltry human, how did you ↵
        beat me?";
    }
    if (iplay == "scissors") {
        if (uplay == "paper")
            return "I WIN! SCISSORS CUT PAPER! CHIPS BEAT BRAINS!"
```

```
            else
         return "YOU WIN. Rock smashes scissors. ↵
            Frail human, would you like to try again?";
      }
   if (iplay == "paper") {
         if (uplay == "rock")
                return "I WIN! PAPER COVERS ROCK! ROCK AND ROLL, BABY!"
         else
      return "YOU WIN. Scissors cut paper. Oh, vain flesh and bone entity, ↵
         I'll get you next time!";
      }
}
```

Playing the Game

It's time to have some fun and play Rock, Scissors, and Paper against the computer. The computer, of course, is on the honor system.

WAY COOL

You'll find the complete program code for Rock, Scissors, and Paper in Listing 3-8. But before you go ahead and read it, let's play against the computer a few times (see Figures 3-7, 3-8, and 3-9).

TRY THIS AT HOME

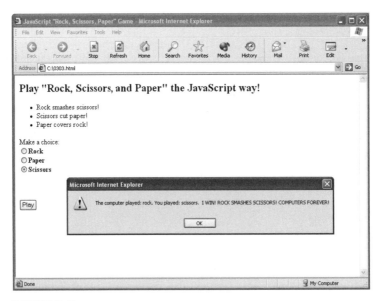

FIGURE 3-7

The computer played rock and the human played scissors—a win for the computer!

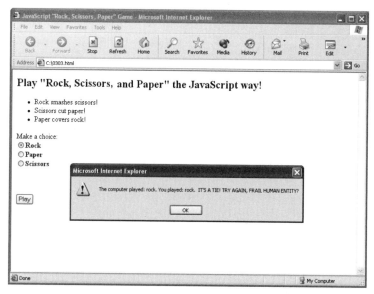

FIGURE 3-8

Both players chose rock; it's a tie.

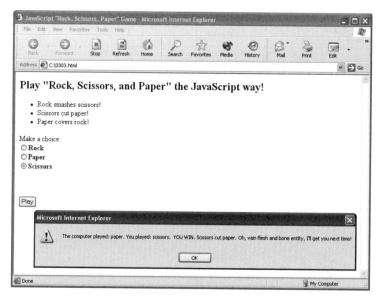

FIGURE 3-9

The computer played paper, and the human chose scissors and wins!

LISTING 3-8

Rock, Scissors, and Paper—the JavaScript Way

```
<HTML>
<HEAD>
<TITLE>
 JavaScript "Rock, Scissors, Paper" Game
</TITLE>
<SCRIPT>
function whoWon (iplay, uplay) {
    // "I" am the computer
    if (iplay == uplay)
        return "IT'S A TIE! TRY AGAIN, FRAIL HUMAN ENTITY?";
    if (iplay == "rock") {
        if (uplay == "scissors")
   return "I WIN! ROCK SMASHES SCISSORS! COMPUTERS FOREVER!"
        else
   return "YOU WIN. Paper covers rock. Paltry human, how did you beat ⟳
      me?";
    }
    if (iplay == "scissors") {
        if (uplay == "paper")
   return "I WIN! SCISSORS CUT PAPER! CHIPS BEAT BRAINS!"
        else
   return "YOU WIN. Rock smashes scissors. ⟳
      Frail human, would you like to try again?";
    }
    if (iplay == "paper") {
        if (uplay == "rock")
   return "I WIN! PAPER COVERS ROCK! ROCK AND ROLL, BABY!"
        else
   return "YOU WIN. Scissors cut paper. Oh, vain flesh and bone entity, ⟳
      I'll get you next time!";
    }
}
function shakeIt(){
    var randGen = Math.random();
    if (randGen <= .33)
        var computerPlay = "rock";
    if ((randGen >.33) && (randGen <= .66))
        var computerPlay = "scissors";
    if (randGen > .66)
```

```
                    var computerPlay = "paper";
            if (document.gameForm.game[0].checked)
                var personPlay = "rock";
            if (document.gameForm.game[1].checked)
                var personPlay = "paper";
            if (document.gameForm.game[2].checked)
                var personPlay = "scissors";
            alert ("The computer played: " + computerPlay +
                    ". You played: " + personPlay + ".  " +
                    whoWon(computerPlay,personPlay));
        }
    </SCRIPT>
    </HEAD>
    <BODY>
    <H2>
    Play "Rock, Scissors and Paper" the JavaScript way!
    </H2>
    <UL>
     <Li>Rock smashes scissors!
     <Li>Scissors cut paper!
     <Li>Paper covers rock!
    </UL>
    <FORM name="gameForm">
    <P>Make a choice:
    <BR>
    <input type="radio" name="game" value="Rock"
checked><STRONG>Rock</STRONG><BR>
    <input type="radio" name="game"
value="Paper"><STRONG>Paper</STRONG><BR>
    <input type="radio" name="game"
value="Scissors"><STRONG>Scissors</STRONG>
    <P>
    <BR>
    <BR>
    <INPUT type="button" name="play" value="Play" onClick="shakeIt();">
 </FORM>
</BODY>
</HTML>
```

Using *Switch Case* Statements

ADVANCED

DO IT RIGHT

Switch case statements are used to control multiple execution branching using the value of a single variable. Multiple if statements could achieve the same results as a switch statement, but the syntax would be complex and confusing. Put another way, a single switch statement can replace a whole bunch of if statements—and make for greater clarity of code.

Switch statements work by telling the computer to conditionally execute blocks of code depending on the value, or *case*, of a variable.

It's probably easiest to understand switch statements when you see them in action, so let's start with a simple switch statement and then follow it up by rewriting part of the Rock, Scissors, and Paper game using switch rather than if statements—because the game is so much fun!

Seeing a Simple *Switch* Example in Action

Listing 3-9 shows an example of a simple switch statement that branches depending upon the value of the variable n. Figure 3-10 shows the results of the program.

Note the use of break statements at the end of each execution block. These cause JavaScript to exit the switch statement. If they were omitted, execution would proceed to the next branch of the switch statement rather than terminating the switch after one block was executed.

LISTING 3-9

A Simple Switch Statement Demonstration

```javascript
var n = 1;
switch (n) {
case 1:
   {
     document.write("n equals 1");
     break;
   }
case 2:
   {
     document.write("n equals 2");
     break;
           }
   case 3:
   {
```

```
      document.write("n equals 3");
      break;
   }
default:
   {
      document.write("No match!");
      break;
   }
}
```

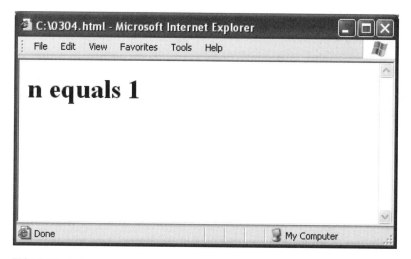

FIGURE 3-10

This simple demonstration shows how switch statements work.

Rewriting Rock, Scissors, and Paper

Listing 3-7 shows the original whoWon function in the Rock, Scissors, and Paper program. If you look at the code, you can see that it's organized around four top-level if statements that test for the value of the variable iplay—the play randomly selected by and for the computer. These if statements, in the order shown, use conditionals to check for the following values of iplay (see Table 3-2).

TABLE 3-2

iplay Values and Conditionals

Value	Conditional Expression
uplay	if (iplay == uplay) Note: If this is true, the game is tied.
"rock"	if (iplay == "rock")
"scissors"	if (iplay == "scissors")
"paper"	if (iplay == "paper")

The top-level conditional expressions shown in Table 3-2 create the structure of the whoWon function. If control passes via any but the first conditional, other if statements are still required to determine the winner.

In fact, the whoWon function could be diagrammed as shown in Figure 3-11.

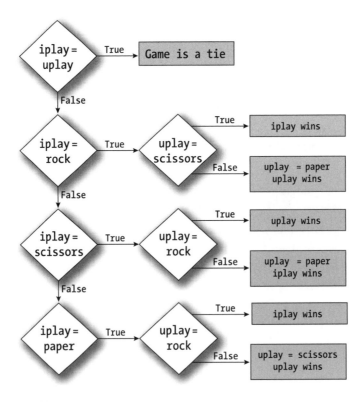

FIGURE 3-11

Flow chart of the whoWon function

NOTE By convention, a diamond shape is used in flow charts to represent conditionals.

The cool thing we can now do is replace the four conditionals shown in Listing 3-7 and Table 3-2 with a single switch case statement. Listing 3-10 shows how to do this.

ADVANCED

LISTING 3-10

The whoWon Function with Top-Level If Statements Replaced by a Single Switch Case Statement

WAY COOL

```
function whoWon (iplay, uplay) {
   // "I" am the computer
   switch (iplay) {
      case uplay:
          return "IT'S A TIE! TRY AGAIN, FRAIL HUMAN ENTITY?";
      case "rock": {
          if (uplay == "scissors")
             return "I WIN! ROCK SMASHES SCISSORS! COMPUTERS FOREVER!"
          else
return "YOU WIN. Paper covers rock. Paltry human, how did you beat me?";
      }
      case "scissors": {
          if (uplay == "paper")
             return "I WIN! SCISSORS CUT PAPER! CHIPS BEAT BRAINS!"
          else
return "YOU WIN. Rock smashes scissors. Frail human, would you like to ⤶
   try again?";
      }
      case "paper": {
          if (uplay == "rock")
               return "I WIN! PAPER COVERS ROCK! ROCK AND ROLL, BABY!"
          else
return "YOU WIN. Scissors cut paper. Oh, vain flesh and bone entity, ⤶
   I'll get you   next time!";
      }
   }
}
```

So this is pretty neat, and it makes for much more readable code, always a good thing. Because it's a good idea to try new code after you've written it and because Rock, Scissors, and Paper is so much fun, let's play a round! Naturally, the computer wins (see Figure 3-12). I think maybe it's cheating with that random number generator....

ADVANCED

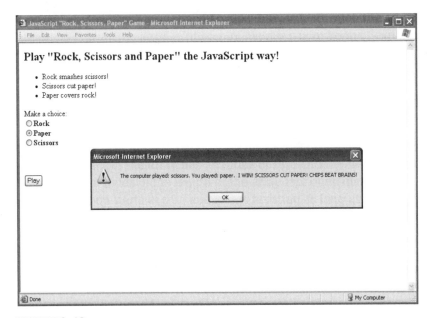

FIGURE 3-12

The computer wins again.

Using Break *Statements and* Return *Statements*

You may have noticed that when I showed you the general form of the switch case statement (see Listing 3-9), I said that a break statement had to be used with each case. Otherwise, program control simply continues to the next case, which is not generally what you want to happen. Why didn't I use break statements in the switch case statement shown in Listing 3-10?

The answer is that each of the cases within the statement ends with a return statement. When JavaScript hits a return statement within a function, processing returns to the place that called the function originally. So, these return statements serve the same purpose as a break statement (while also returning a value, namely the string to be displayed).

You'll learn much more about functions in Chapter 5, "Understanding Functions."

What's It All About?

You've come a long way in this chapter, Alfie (or Austin) baby! We're way beyond the preliminaries now, doing cool and fun things. In this chapter, you learned how to program a real, live computer game that evaluates user input, relies on random number generation, and does much more. You also learned how to use a number of different kinds of conditional statements.

I think you'll agree that this is great stuff—lots of fun and useful. Keep it up and you might get hooked on programming!

In Chapter 4, "Working with Loops," we'll move on to another important topic: looping and iteration.

4

Working with Loops

As you may have gathered by now, computers are not very bright. Let's shout that out loud and say it from the rooftops: "COMPUTERS ARE NOT VERY BRIGHT!"

What do I mean by the statement that computers are not very bright considering that they do all kinds of difficult things? (There, I get to say "Computers are not very bright" again!)

The fact of the matter is that if you tell a computer what to do within the parameters of the kinds of things it can do, and if your instructions are given in the right language and are sufficiently precise, it'll probably be able to do it. Put this way, it's clear that computers by themselves, and innately, don't have the ability to take initiative, behave creatively, exercise intuition—and do the myriad things that make up human intelligence. However, and it's a big "however," computer software can be written that allows computers to at least mimic these kinds of characteristics (and perhaps do more than merely mimic them) and to do many things better than people do. Perhaps, after reading this book, you'll start on your journey toward writing this kind of intelligent software.

So, if computers are so bloody stupid, how come they can do so many wonderful things? An important part of the answer is that computers will perform repetitive tasks without complaint. Computers will and can do this repetition a great many times.

Thomas Alva Edison famously called genius 1 percent inspiration and 99 percent perspiration. Computers are very good at the perspiration part.

They will keep doing one simple thing—this is called *iterating*—until they're told to stop or they run out of computing resources.

The key to a great many computer programs is *iteration* (the process of iterating). The actual step performed can be quite simple. For example, a loop might compare two variables to see when they're of equal value (this is the iteration). When they're equal, code within the loop might do something. Then the loop might continue with an increment of one of the two variables after each comparison. But the net effect of the iterated simple action can be to achieve a quite sophisticated result.

From within a computer program, iteration usually looks like a *loop* (this is where I got the title for the chapter, "Working with Loops.") Loops are used to control execution flow by repeatedly executing a statement or a number of statements. You go back to the beginning—or loop—and do it again until a condition is met, usually with a small change to one of the variables controlling the condition with each increment.

Once again, this will be easier to understand when you see it in practice than in the abstract. This chapter starts by explaining the mechanics of the statements used to loop. In JavaScript, these statements are for, while, and do/while. (Although the specifics may vary in other computer languages, the concepts are essentially the same.)

With the mechanics down, I move on to show you how to use nested looping—placing one loop within another. (The example will use for loops inside other for loops, but you could achieve the same results with while loops.)

We won't do too much with nested looping (I show you how to draw a Christmas tree on screen). But this introduction should stand you in good stead when you have to program with complex looping logic.

If this sounds like great fun, it is! So let's get started with some preliminaries so we can move on to the fun stuff.

Creating a Prompt

In a moment, I'll show you how to do something really fun with a for loop—namely, reverse the text entered by the user. But before we get there, I need to show you a preliminary example.

In Chapter 3, "Using Conditional Statements," I showed you how to display an alert box, which provides a message to the user.

A prompt box provides a similar sort of facility except that it also lets the user enter input.

NOTE By the way, you should expect the appearance and user prompt to vary in different browsers. I show Internet Explorer in these figures, but things won't quite look the same in Mozilla or Netscape.

Just as the alert function displays an alert box, there's a JavaScript function, prompt, that displays a prompt box and requests input from the user. The general form is as follows:

```
ReturnValue = prompt (message, default text);
```

For example, this assignment:

```
retVal = prompt("Enter your text, please!", ↵
    "How doth the little crocodile?");
```

produces the prompt box shown in Figure 4-1.

FIGURE 4-1

The prompt function displays a box that accepts user input.

As you can see, by *default text* in the general form provided previously, I mean the text initially seen by the user in the prompt box. If the user doesn't change the default text and clicks OK, the default text is the value sent back to the JavaScript variable (retVal in the example). However, if the user enters their own value in the prompt box—for example, *I'll do it my way, thank you very much!*—then that's the value passed back to the JavaScript variable.

Now that you know how prompt boxes work, let's go ahead and put them to use in conjunction with a loop.

> ### I'm Blocked, How About You?
>
> A prompt box is *modal,* meaning that no further program statements will be executed until the user chooses OK or Cancel. Another way of putting this is that all other code statements in the program are *blocked* until the user takes action.

Working with *For* Statements

For statements are an exciting kind of looping statement that many people find it easy to wrap their brains around when they're first learning to program.

ADVANCED

For statements are particularly easy to write in conjunction with arrays, as I show you in Chapter 6, "Programming with Arrays."

A while statement can be written that does exactly what a for statement does. But for statements are easy to understand because the "business end" of the statement—the initial value of the counter, the terminating condition, and the increment—are all in one place.

> *Everything that makes up the "business end" of a for statement is all in one place.*

So that you can see exactly how for statements work, in a moment we're going to reverse an input string. Later in this chapter, I show you how to do the same things using a do/while statement rather than a for statement. This will show you how the two compare.

The generalized form of the JavaScript for statement is as follows:

```
for ( initial counter value ; condition ; increment)
    statement
```

This statement is itself usually a statement block of multiple statements enclosed in curly braces as I explained in Chapter 2, "Understanding Types, Variables, and Statements" (see the "Understanding Blocks" section):

```
for ( initial counter value ; condition ; increment)
    {
        statement1;
        statement2;
        ...
        statementn;
    }
```

As with any looping statement, it's a good idea to create the statement framework before filling it in with other program statements. You're less likely to make errors that way!

Reversing the String

It's time to move along and write a program using a for loop that reverses the text string input by the user.

To Create a *For* Statement That Reverses a String:

1. Create the framework for a script within the body of an HTML document:

```
<HTML>
   <BODY>
   <H1>
   <SCRIPT>

   </SCRIPT>
   </H1>
   </BODY>
</HTML>
```

2. Create the scaffolding, or structure, for the for statement:

```
for (   ;   ;   )
   {


   }
```

3. Initialize a variable before the for statement to hold the value of the reversed text string:

```
var newString = "";
```

4. Use the prompt function to obtain a string from the user:

```
var newString = "";
var theString = prompt("Enter a string for reversal","");
```

When the prompt function runs, the user will be prompted for input as shown in Figure 4-2. The value entered by the user will be assigned to the variable theString. (Because the default value is the empty string (""), if the user doesn't enter text, that will be the value assigned.)

FIGURE 4-2

The string that will be reversed is entered in a prompt box.

5. In JavaScript, each string variable has an associated attribute, known as a *property*, called its length. As you might expect, a string's length property contains the number of characters, including spaces, in a text string. (If the same letter occurs twice, it's counted twice so that the value of the length property of the string "iiiuuu" is 6.) Use the length property to store the length of the string in a counter variable:

```
var theString = prompt("Enter a string for reversal","");
var counter = theString.length;
```

(For more information on working with properties, see Chapter 7, "Working with Objects.")

6. Create the iteration expressions for the for statement:

```
var newString = "";
var theString = prompt("Enter a string for reversal","");
var counter = theString.length;
for (counter  ;counter > 0 ;counter -- )
{

}
```

This for condition means that the loop uses the variable counter to track iterations; it continues while counter > 0; and decrements the counter each time the loop is passed through.

 NOTE As a reminder, the decrement operator (--) subtracts one from its operand. So writing counter -- is equivalent to the statement counter = counter -1.

7. Enter the statement (or statements) to be executed within the for loop:

```
for (counter  ;counter > 0 ;counter -- )
{
    newString += theString.substring(counter-1, counter);
}
```

This statement uses the substring method of the string object (this is all explained further in Chapter 7, "Working with Objects") to extract a letter from the old string and add it to the new string. The extracted letter is assigned using concatenation to the right of the existing contents of the new string.

In other words, the statement could be rewritten in a longer way as follows:

```
newString = newString + theString.substring(counter-1, counter);
```

The first time the statement is executed, the new string is empty and the last letter of the old string is assigned to its leftmost place. The next time the statement is executed, the counter has already been decremented, meaning that the second-to-last letter of the old string is concatenated with the new string.

8. Add a statement after the for loop to print the results:

```
document.write(theString + " reversed is " + newString + "!");
```

9. Run the program to verify that it works. As before, after the user enters a text string as shown in Figure 4-2 and clicks OK, the reversed string is displayed (see Figure 4-3). Listing 4-1 shows the complete code used.

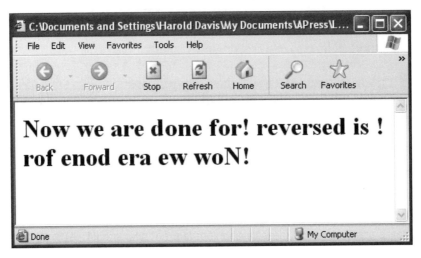

FIGURE 4-3

The reverse text is displayed in the browser.

LISTING 4-1

Using a for Loop to Reverse a String

```
<HTML>
  <BODY>
  <H1>
  <SCRIPT>
    var newString = "";
    var theString = prompt("Enter a string for reversal","");
    var counter = theString.length;
    for (counter  ;counter > 0 ;counter -- )
    {
      newString += theString.substring(counter-1, counter);
    }
    document.write(theString + " reversed is " + newString + "!");
  </SCRIPT>
  </H1>
  </BODY>
</HTML>
```

If the code in this example seems difficult to you, don't worry about it too much! It has introduced a number of new concepts in addition to the for loop, including the prompt function, the length property of a text string, and the substring method of a string.

These aren't easy things to wrap one's brain around. The best thing you can do is play with the code in the example. What happens if you change things around a little?

 TIP A variation of the `for` statement, the `for/in` statement, is used with JavaScript objects. For more information about `for/in`, see Chapter 7, "Working with Objects."

Play with the code.

What happens if you change things around a little?

Understanding *While* Statements

The `while` statement is probably the simplest JavaScript statement that allows a program to perform repetitive tasks. A `while` statement (or statement block) executes as long as an expression evaluates to `true`.

The syntax of the `while` statement is as follows:

```
while (expression)
    statement
```

When the JavaScript processor hits a `while` statement, the first thing it does is evaluate the expression. If the expression evaluates to `false`, the processor skips the rest of the `while` statement and moves to the next statement. If, and only if, the expression is `true`, the statement part of the `while` statement is processed. Once again, you should understand that a JavaScript statement means a single statement *or* a statement block made up of multiple statements.

After the statement block has been processed, the expression is evaluated again. If it's still `true`, the statement block is executed again. This process is repeated until the expression evaluates to `false`.

When you're creating `while` statements, you must be sure to add code within the executed statement block that will eventually turn the expression that's controlling the `while` statement false. If you don't do this, you'll probably create an *infinite loop*. Once the execution of an infinite loop starts, it'll never terminate and go round and round forever until the application or computer is shut down, usually because it has run out of resources. This is one of the easiest kinds of programming mistakes to make and can be frustrating, so watch out for it.

DO IT RIGHT

TRY THIS
AT HOME

To Create a *While* Statement That Counts Down from 10 to 1:

1. Create the framework for a script within the body of an HTML document:

```
<HTML>
    <BODY>
        <H1>
        <SCRIPT>

        </SCRIPT>
        </H1>
    </BODY>
</HTML>
```

2. Within the <SCRIPT> tag, create the framework for the while statement:

```
while ()
    {

    }
```

3. Declare and give an initial value to a counter variable before the start of the while loop:

```
var counter = 10;
while ()
    {

    }
```

4. Create the expression that the statement will evaluate:

```
while (counter > 0)
```

5. Add code within the statement block that performs a repetitious task:

```
while (counter > 0)
    {
        document.write (counter + "<br>");
    }
```

6. Add code within the statement block that decrements the counter variable used within the evaluation expression:

```
{
  document.write (counter + "<br>");
  counter--;
}
```

7. Open the JavaScript code within a browser (Listing 4-2 shows the complete loop). The countdown will display as shown in Figure 4-4.

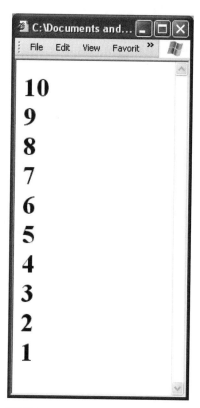

FIGURE 4-4

The while loop decrements from 10 to 1.

 TIP As with conditional statements, it's always a good practice to build the scaffolding of a loop before you start populating it with actual statements and expressions.

LISTING 4-2

A While Loop That Decrements from 10 to 1

```html
<HTML>
    <BODY>
    <H1>
    <SCRIPT>
        var counter = 10;
        while (counter > 0)
        {
            document.write (counter + "<br>");
            counter--;
        }
    </SCRIPT>
    </H1>
    </BODY>
</HTML>
```

DO IT RIGHT

So-called "one-off" errors—in which a loop counter is off by one—are one of the most common and pesky programming bugs. Make sure you haven't introduced one-off bugs into your loops by testing "boundary" values of your counter variables—typically those one greater than and one less than the value at which the expression is supposed to fail. For example, in the program shown in Listing 4-2, if you changed the condition to (counter >= 0), you'd get a countdown to zero instead of one. That's fine if it's what you want, but not otherwise. The point is, the difference can be confusing, and you should be sure to "dial up" the precise condition that's necessary to make your program work right.

How Many Ways Can You Write a While?

Generally, the expression that's being evaluated can be written in many ways that are logically equivalent. For example, asking if the counter is greater than zero (counter > 0) is equivalent to asking if the counter is not less than one (!(counter < 1)).

That said, it's best if you create the expression that's used by a while statement as simple and unconvoluted as possible. The easier it is to understand, the less likely you are to make a mistake.

Doing the *Do/While* Thing

A do/while statement is like a while statement except that the expression is evaluated after the statement has been executed rather than before. You can think of this as testing at the bottom of the loop rather than the top. The impact is to ensure that the statement in a do/while statement is executed at least once, even if the condition evaluates to false.

The general form of the do/while statement is as follows:

```
do
    statement
while (condition);
```

As with while loops, you can replace the single statement in this syntax with a statement block, provided you put the statements in the block with curly braces:

```
do
{
    statement1;
    statement2;
    ...
    statementn;
}
while (condition);
```

To see how easy it is to use while statements, let's go ahead and rewrite the program that reverses a string using a do/while loop instead of a for statement.

TRY THIS
AT HOME

To Create a *Do/While* Loop That Reverses Text Entered by the User:

1. Create the framework for a script within the body of an HTML document:

DO IT RIGHT

```
<HTML>
  <BODY>
  <H1>
  <SCRIPT>

  </SCRIPT>
  </H1>
  </BODY>
</HTML>
```

2. Create the scaffolding for the do/while statement:

```
do
  {

  }
while ();
```

3. Initialize a variable before the do/while statement to hold the value of the reversed text string:

```
var newString = "";
```

4. Use the prompt function to obtain a string from the user:

```
var newString = "";
var theString = prompt("Enter a string for reversal","");
```

When the prompt function runs, the user will be prompted for input as shown in Figure 4-5.

FIGURE 4-5

The user is prompted for a text string to reverse.

5. Use the length property of theString to store the length of the string in a counter variable:

```
var theString = prompt("Enter a string for reversal","");
var counter = theString.length;
```

6. Create the expression for the do/while statement:

```
var newString = "";
var theString = prompt("Enter a string for reversal","");
var counter = theString.length;
do
  {

  }
while (counter > 0 );
```

In this case, the conditional statement means that the statement will stop being processed when the counter variable, which is the length of the string the user entered, is zero.

7. Enter the statement to be executed:

```
do
  {
      newString += theString.substring(counter-1, counter);

  }
```

8. Decrement the counter:

```
do
  {
      newString += theString.substring(counter-1, counter);
      counter--;
  }
```

Decrementing the counter ensures that the loop will terminate and enables the reversal process to work.

9. Add a statement after the do/while loop to print the results:

```
document.write(theString + " reversed is " + newString + "!");
```

10. Run the program. After the user enters a text string as shown in Figure 4-5 and clicks OK, the reversed string is displayed (see Figure 4-6). Listing 4-3 shows the complete code used.

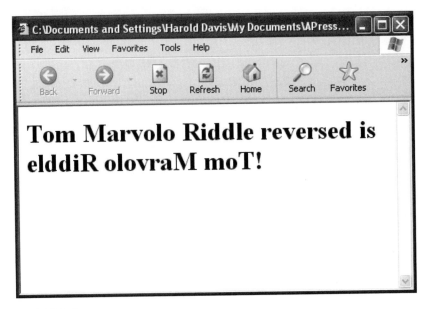

FIGURE 4-6

The reversed text string is displayed.

LISTING 4-3

Using a Do/While Loop to Reverse a Text String

```
<HTML>
   <BODY>
   <H1>
   <SCRIPT>
      var newString = "";
      var theString = prompt("Enter a string for reversal","");
      var counter = theString.length;
      do
      {
         newString += theString.substring(counter-1, counter);
         counter--;
      }
      while (counter > 0 );
      document.write(theString + " reversed is " + newString + "!");
   </SCRIPT>
   </H1>
   </BODY>
</HTML>
```

Of course, the two programs (one shown in Listing 4-1 using a for loop and the other shown in Listing 4-3 using a do/while loop) aren't different except at the heart—the loops.

So, it's a good idea to look closely at the essential difference between the two programs. Behind door number one, we have the do/while loop:

```
do
{
    ...
    counter --;
}
while (counter > 0 );
```

Here's the door number two entrant, the for loop:

```
for (counter  ;counter > 0 ;counter -- )
{
...
}
```

Can you see how these two loops amount to the same thing?

Whichever loop you use, neither program is really that polished.

In the real world, you'd probably want to add some niceties to the program. For example, you should check the input string to make sure the user hasn't pressed Cancel in the prompt box. Otherwise, the variable theString will not have a string stored in it, and the following statement:

```
var counter = theString.length;
```

will cause a JavaScript syntax error when the program runs. To see this error, try running the program and clicking Cancel in the prompt box. A blank browser window will open, and if you look on the browser's status bar, you'll see a message like that shown in Figure 4-7 (this figure shows the error message in Internet Explorer; it will look slightly different in other Web browsers).

DO IT RIGHT

> *The two programs aren't different except at their heart, the loops!*

Done, but with errors on page.

FIGURE 4-7

If you try to assign the length property of an empty object, you'll get a syntax error.

To get a more complete explanation of the error, you can double-click the icon in the browser status bar. You'll get an explanatory message describing the error and providing a line number where it occurred, like that shown in Figure 4-8.

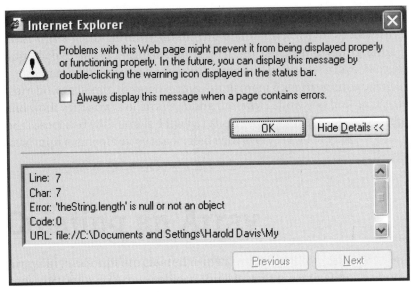

FIGURE 4-8

The Web browser provides an explanation of JavaScript errors and the line number in the program where they occurred.

Another problem you might want to handle is the case of a user who inputs an empty string. As things stand now, you'll get the display shown in Figure 4-9, which isn't incorrect but somewhat sloppy. It'd be better to display a message such as "You didn't enter any text to reverse. Please try again by clicking the Refresh button on your browser."

For more on error handling, debugging, and writing code that's not error-prone, see Chapter 10, "Error Handling and Debugging."

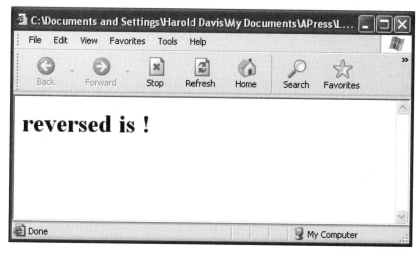

FIGURE 4-9

If the user enters an empty string, the browser display looks kind of weird.

Trimming a Tree with Nested Loops

By now, you've probably pretty much gotten the hang of all kinds of iterations and how to use while statements, do/while statements, and for loops. It's a good thing because we'll be using these techniques a great deal in the rest of *Learn How to Program*. You can do all kinds of things using loops, and there isn't all that much you can do without them. So learning to use iterative statements is a crucial step on your journey to becoming a programmer.

But before moving on, let's look at one final example. It may not be Christmas when you read this book, but quite likely you're familiar with Christmas trees. This example shows you how to draw a Christmas tree, complete with ornaments, on the screen. As you can see in Figure 4-10, the tree is mostly "drawn" using the letter X, and ornaments are made out of capital letter Os. (Will this really be as much fun as Christmas? I think not.)

You can do all kinds of things with loops, and there isn't much you can do without them!

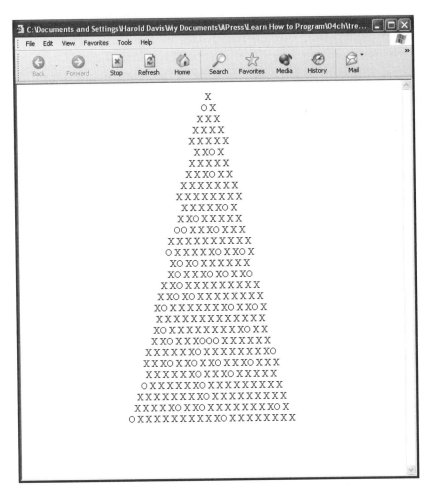

FIGURE 4-10

Nested loops are used to draw a tree using Xs and Os.

The point of this example is that it takes three for loops to accomplish the task. Not unlike wooden dolls that you may have seen—you can open up the largest one to find another one inside, which you can, in turn, open—there's an outermost loop. Within it, there's another loop, and within that loop there is the innermost loop. Loops that are set up this way are called *nested* loops. So you can add another line to the song about partridges and pear trees: On a certain day of Christmas, my true love gave to me, one nested loop....

> *My true love gave to me one nested loop!*

Seriously, folks, before we get to the actual code, let's look at what each loop does. The outer two loops control the height of the tree and where its width is "stepped back." (If you look at Figure 4-10, you can see a "step back" in the width of the tree every five rows, which corresponds to the maximum value in the middle loop.)

Each row in the tree is created by writing an HTML <BR>, or line break, tag.

Within the innermost loop, the "tree" and ornaments are drawn by writing X and O characters. X represents the tree's branches, and O represents ornaments. The positioning of ornaments is determined somewhat at random (so if you refresh your browser, you'll get a somewhat different layout).

To "Draw" a Tree Using Nested Loops:

TRY THIS
AT HOME

1. Create the framework for a script within the body of an HTML document:

```
<HTML>
    <BODY>
    <CENTER>
    <SCRIPT>

    </SCRIPT>
    </CENTER>
    </BODY>
</HTML>
```

By the way, I've added a <CENTER> tag to this so that the tree will appear in the middle of the browser.

2. Declare and initialize the variable width, which controls the number of characters written per line of the tree:

```
var width=1;
```

3. Create the scaffolding, or structure, for the outermost for loop:

```
for (   ;   ;   )
{

    }
```

4. Nest within the outermost loop another loop framework:

```
for (  ;  ; )
{
   for (  ;  ; )
   {

   }
}
```

5. Create the innermost loop framework within the other two loops:

```
for (  ;  ; )
{
   for (  ;  ; )
   {
      for (  ;  ; )
      {

      }
   }
}
```

 NOTE As a reminder, the increment operator (++) adds one to its operand. So writing **i++** is equivalent to the statement **i = i + 1**.

6. Fill in the loop conditions:

```
for (i=0; i <= 5 ; i++)
{
   for (x=0; x<=4; x++)
   {
      for (y=1; y<=width; y++)
      {
      ...
```

What this amounts to is that the outermost loop goes from zero to five, including five (from one to six would have been another way to write the same thing); the middle loop goes from zero to four, including four (this would be the same as from one to five); and the innermost loop goes from one to the value of the width variable. This is relatively complex code. You can get a good feeling for what it's doing by sitting down with pencil and paper and pretending you're the computer, following directions, and seeing what you draw. It's also educational to modify the code and see what happens.

7. Add the logic to the innermost loop that uses the JavaScript random number generator—explained in Chapter 3, "Using Conditional Statements"—to write Os and (mostly) spaces followed by Xs:

```
for (y=1; y<=width; y++)
{
    var Number=Math.random()*10;
    var Ornament=Math.round(Number);
    if (Ornament<=1)
    {
        document.write("O");
    }
    if (Ornament>=2)
    {
        document.write(" X");
    }
}
```

8. Below the end of the innermost loop, so that it's controlled by the middle loop, write a line break and increment the width variable by one:

```
document.write("<BR>");
width=width+1;
```

Incrementing the width variable will cause each subsequent, and lower, row of the tree to be one character wider than the previous row.

9. Below the end of the middle loop, decrement the width variable by two:

```
width = width - 2
```

This has the effect of taking two characters off the width of the next tree row each time the middle loop completes—or every five rows—and program control returns to the outermost loop.

Listing 4-4 shows the complete code for this program. If you run it in your browser, you'll get a Christmas tree that looks pretty much like the one shown in Figure 4-10.

LISTING 4-4

Drawing a Christmas Tree Using Nested For Loops

```
<HTML>
<BODY>
<CENTER>
<SCRIPT>
    var width=1;
    for (i=0; i <= 5 ; i++)
    {
        for (x=0; x<=4; x++)
        {
            for (y=1; y<=width; y++)
            {
                var Number=Math.random()*10;
                var Ornament=Math.round(Number);
                if (Ornament<=1)
                {
                    document.write("O");
                }
                if (Ornament>=2)
                {
                    document.write(" X");
                }
            }
            document.write("<BR>");
            width=width+1;
        }
        width=width-2;
    }
</SCRIPT>
</CENTER>
</BODY>
</HTML>
```

If you look closely at Figure 4-10, and at the code for the program, you can see that the innermost loop writes the lines. The line break and increment to the width variable in the middle loop are controlling line width in five row groups; every sixth row, the subtraction from the width variable gives the tree an indent.

You can count the rows in the tree and verify that it has 30 rows. This is the product obtained by multiplying the upper bounds of the middle and outer loops.

These numerical values and relationships are essentially arbitrary. I encourage you to play with them to create your own tree!

The important point is that in many programs it is common to see loops within loops—you often need to do this to get the functionality a program requires. It can be a little difficult to keep different loops and how they interact straight. As always, I want to get you off on the right foot, so things will not be hard for you later.

The Christmas tree program is a (I hope) gentle introduction to the concepts and techniques that you need to work with multiple nested loops.

Create your own tree today!

What's It All About?

This chapter is all about doing things over and over and over again. (This reminds me of the movie *Groundhog Day*, in which actor Bill Murray's character had to live the same day over and over again.)

Iteration and looping are some of the most important techniques you can use in working with computer programs. You'll need to iterate and loop, you'll want to iterate and loop, and there won't be much you can do without iterating and looping. This chapter has explained the basics of working with JavaScript's looping statements: while, do/while and for. Loops will be used many times in later chapters in this book, so you'll have the opportunity to hone your knowledge and skills.

In the meantime, let's move on to another very important topic in Chapter 5, "Understanding Functions."

5

Understanding Functions

A *function* is a small program that often—but not always—returns a value to the code that invoked the function. You can use functions to organize a program by breaking the program up into small functional units. These small functional units (each one a function!) can be reused to perform the same task over and over again without having to rewrite the code in the function each time. Therefore, the best-written functions tend to be somewhat general in flavor (so that they can be reused).

You've already seen a number of examples in *Learn How to Program* of programs that use functions. For instance, the Rock, Scissors, and Paper program in Chapter 3, "Using Conditional Statements," is implemented using a number of functions to help organize the code. For example, in that program, the whoWon function works as a general mechanism for determining if the human player or the computer player won a particular round. Two variables are passed as input to the whoWon function. The variables represent "plays" of the game: iplay, the computer's move, and uplay, the human's move. The function returns a value, namely a text message stating whether the computer or the human is the winner of the round of Rocks, Scissors, and Paper.

In Chapter 3, in the Rock, Scissors, and Paper program, I used functions to organize the program because it was the right thing to do—and because it seemed intuitive as to how they worked. This chapter looks at functions in greater depth. It's an important topic because most well-written programs are largely made up of functions.

Differentiating Between Functions, Methods, and Subroutines

You may have noticed that I've used the word *method* earlier in this book to refer to something that pretty much seems like a function. So, how are functions and methods different? The truth is that they're more or less the same thing except that a method is related to an object, and this isn't necessarily the case for a function. Moreover, internally a method is implemented (meaning "made to work") using a function. Put another way, the word *method* is object-speak for a function, and if a function is associated with an object ("encapsulated by the object"), then it's called a *method*. I show you how to work with objects in detail in Chapter 7, "Working with Objects."

Now that we've cleared up the difference between a function and a method (or the lack of any difference), let's also have a look at subroutines. Some programming languages (for example, Visual Basic but not JavaScript) let you place code in small internal programs called *subroutines*. Subroutines are just like functions except that they can't return a value.

To start with, I show you how to construct your own functions. This is fun and useful material.

Next, you'll learn how to use the array of arguments associated with a function. Finally, I show you how to use a *recursive* function, which is a function that calls itself. The recursive function will be used to display the Fibonacci series of numbers, a series that comes up in nature, architecture, and many other contexts.

The chapter concludes by showing you how to work with some of the methods associated with the JavaScript window object. You can think of these methods as built-in, or premade, functions. In fact, you've already used a number of them, such as the alert method, which displays a message box (although I'll show you again how the alert method works).

Functions and methods are pretty much the same things. Technically, a *method* is a function associated with an object. For more on the distinction, or lack thereof, between functions and methods, see "Differentiating Between Functions, Methods, and Subroutines."

Creating a Function

Functions are defined in JavaScript using the following syntax:

```
function myFunc (parameter1,...,parametern) {
  statement1;
  ...
  statementn;
  return retval; //specify optional return value
}
```

In plain English, the following are the steps involved in creating a function.

To Create a Function:

1. Start with the keyword `function`.

2. Provide the identifier (or name) that will be used for the function.

3. Within parentheses, provide a list of names for the parameters (also called *arguments*) that will be passed to the function. The parameter names are separated by commas. If there are no parameters, just use empty open and close parentheses, like so: ().

4. Place the code statements that will comprise the function within curly braces. Here are some curly braces: { }.

5. If the function returns a value to the code that called it, use the `return` keyword within the function statements to specify the return value. Note that when the return keyword is used, program execution returns to the code that invoked the function—so any statements in the function following the return statement will not be processed.

You invoke (or *call*) a function by using the function as a statement or assignment. Here are a number of examples:

```
myFunc();
x = myFunc2();
myFunc3 (par1, par2, par3);
result = myFunc4 (par1, par2, par3);
```

Functions and Children First!

You should know that if you're placing JavaScript code in a Web page (as in the examples in this book), you need to define a function before it can be used. Web pages are processed by the browser from the top down, so a function must be located above the code that calls the function in the Web page. This isn't the case in many programming environments. It's far more typical to be able to place your functions anywhere in your program that you'd like.

One way to make sure that a function has been processed before the code that calls the function is encountered is to place your functions in an HTML document head section rather than in the body of the HTML document.

The first of these statements, myFunc();, calls the function named myFunc, which neither takes nor returns any values.

The next statement, x = myFunc2();, calls the function myFunc2, which doesn't accept a passed value but does return a value. The returned value of the function myFunc2 is then assigned to the variable x.

The statement myFunc3 (par1, par2, par3); calls the function myFunc3 with three passed values, but no value is returned. (The values passed to a function are often called *arguments* or *parameters*.)

The final statement, result = myFunc4 (par1, par2, par3);, calls the function myFunc4 with three arguments. The function returns a value, which is assigned to the variable result.

> *I think you get the idea of how functions work!*

I think you probably get the idea of how functions work and how to call them! But, as always, it's easiest to see how functions work in practice. So it's time to create a simple example.

The Only Good Return Is a Hard Return

> *The sample function is simple, but it has some practical use.*

The example I'll show you for creating a function, and then calling it, is pretty simple. But it actually has some practical use.

A lot of times, when you display text, you'd like to split it up on more than one line. Lines of text are broken up for printing or display using a hard return. In the HTML used to create Web pages, a hard return is created using the <br> tag.

For example, the following HTML fragment:

```
<HTML>
   This is one line; <br>
   this is another line; <br>
   and this is the final line
</HTML>
```

uses a hard return generated with the <br> tag to display text on three lines, as shown in Figure 5-1.

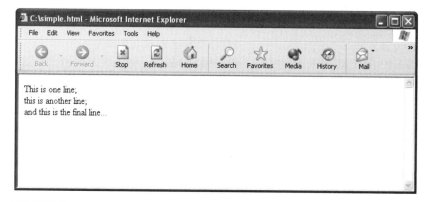

FIGURE 5-1

In an HTML document, the <br> tag is used to create a line break.

If you know you're going to be inserting line breaks in your text, wouldn't it be nice not to have to type all those <br> tags? It's easy enough to write a JavaScript function that extends the text display generated by the JavaScript document.write method, adding a <br> tag to the end of the text to be displayed. This kind of extension of an existing function or method is sometimes called *wrapping*—because the inner function is wrapped in another function.

Wouldn't it be nice not to have to type all those <br> tags?

 NOTE   To *wrap* a function or method means to call it from within another function. The wrapping function generally adds some functionality to the wrapped function.

We'll call the function that adds a line break to the HTML text displayed: writeMyWay.

To Create a Function That Adds a Line Break to Displayed Text:

1. In an HTML document, above the place you want to use the function (possibly in the <HEAD> section of the document), start by entering the keyword `function`.

2. Name the function (writeMyWay).

3. Provide an input parameter (`textIn`) so that the function knows it'll be passed a value.

4. Enter an opening and closing curly brace: {...}. In many languages, including JavaScript, it's conventional (but not required) to skip some lines between the curly braces—that's where the actual work of the function is accomplished.

> *The business end of the function takes place between the curly braces.*

So far what we've entered is called the *declaration* of the function, and it looks like this:

```
function writeMyWay (textIn) {


}
```

5. Next, within the curly braces, add the code that makes the function work. This code calls the JavaScript document.write method, using the text passed into the function with a line break appended to the text. Here's the writeMyWay function including the code that displays the text with an added line break:

```
function writeMyWay (textIn) {
    document.write (textIn + "<br>");
}
```

Note that the writeMyWay function doesn't return a value to the call code—it just displays text.

You'll find the function in an HTML page that also invokes it in Listing 5-1.

The next thing to do is to create an example that calls the function. This is easy enough!

To Call the writeMyWay Function:

1. Within an HTML document, after the function has been defined, call the writeMyWay function with the text you want displayed on its own line:

```
writeMyWay ("I");
writeMyWay ("did");
writeMyWay ("it");
writeMyWay ("my");
writeMyWay ("way!");
```

2. Open the HTML document in a Web browser. Each bit of text will be displayed on its own line, as you can see in Figure 5-2.

> *Calling a function means using the function's name with the right number of arguments.*

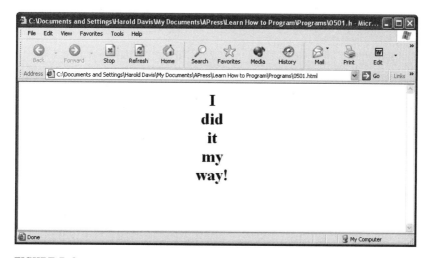

FIGURE 5-2

The function adds a line break to the text passed to it.

Listing 5-1 shows the writeMyWay function and the code for calling it.

LISTING 5-1

The Function That Wraps Document.Write, Adding a Line Break

```
<HTML>
<BODY>
  <CENTER> <H1>
  <SCRIPT>
  function writeMyWay (textIn) {
     document.write (textIn + "<br>");
  }
  <!-- Call the writeMyWay function-->
  writeMyWay ("I");
  writeMyWay ("did");
  writeMyWay ("it");
  writeMyWay ("my");
  writeMyWay ("way!");
  </SCRIPT>
  </CENTER> </H1>
</BODY>
</HTML>
```

This seems (and is) easy enough. Let's have a look at another example in which the function returns a value.

Returns Are Good

Let's have a look at another simple function, one that returns as a value the sum of three numbers. Obviously, there's no great intellectual feat in adding three numbers together. But this example shows you how to return a value from a function (and this works the same way even if the function is a great deal more complicated). In addition, the example allows you to start having a look at two other important topics:

- Types and type conversion

- Creating an HTML form to use JavaScript code to allow interactivity

As I explained earlier in this chapter, to return a value from a function, you simply use the return keyword and specify the value to be returned. (When a function is processed, execution of code statements within the function stops after the value is returned, and execution control returns to the code that called the function.)

So you'd think it would be a simple enough matter to write a function that returns the sum of three numbers. Except for one wrinkle, it is!

Let's start with a function that accepts three inputs as passed values (or arguments):

```
function addThreeNums (inOne, inTwo, inThree) {

}
```

Except for one wrinkle, it's a simple matter to write a function that returns the sum of three numbers.

As in normal, everyday arithmetic, the plus sign (+), called the plus *operator*, is used to sum (add) numbers. So, logically, it's easy to add the three input numbers:

```
inOne + inTwo + inThree
```

If you add the return keyword, for a first attempt, the function that adds three numbers and returns the sum would look like this:

```
function addThreeNums (inOne, inTwo, inThree) {
    return inOne + inTwo + inThree;
}
```

This looks pretty good, but as I mentioned, there's a wrinkle (which is another way of saying that there's a problem with this code).

There's a problem with this code.

If the computer thinks that the inputs to this function are text strings rather than numbers, it'll also think that the plus sign is used for string concatenation rather than numeric addition.

Here's an example of string concatenation: Let's suppose you have three text strings: *I, love,* and *you.* You can then use the string concatenation operator like this:

```
var kissyFace = "I" + "love" + "you";
```

The string value stored in the variable kissyFace is now "I love you".

Returning to our function, let's suppose that the computer thinks that the plus sign means that string concatenation (rather than numeric addition) is taking place. In this case, have a look at the function's `return` statement:

```
return inOne + inTwo + inThree;
```

Suppose the value stored in the variable `inOne` is 1, the value stored in `inTwo` is 2, and the value stored in `inThree` is 3. If these values are concatenated together, the result returned will be 123. This is a pretty far cry from adding the values, which returns a result of 6.

It's important to understand that a value stored in a variable can appear to be numeric and still be a string. In other words, as an example, 2 can be either the number 2 or the string "2". The computer decides that the + operator means to concatenate rather than to add if at least one of the values being operated on is a string.

So how does the computer decide whether a value is numeric or a text string? When a *loosely typed* computer language such as JavaScript is used, basically the computer makes a gut assessment depending on the context of the value. Like many human gut assessments, or best guesses, this can often be wrong!

As I've already said, if the computer thinks that the values passed to the addThreeNums function are strings—such as the string "2" rather than the numeric value 2—the function will produce the wrong result. Specifically, it'll concatenate the inputs rather than adding them.

The worst part of it is that the way this function is likely to be used in the real world is that much of the time the values passed to it will be taken for strings rather than numbers. In the example I'm about to show you, the user inputs three numbers. Then the addThreeNums function is called to sum the user's input and display the results. The problem is that by definition in JavaScript a user input is a string, even when it's a number.

How can we correct this problem?

The answer is that we can explicitly convert each input to the addThreeNums function to a number using the Number function built into JavaScript. Here's what the revised function looks like:

```
function addThreeNums (inOne, inTwo, inThree) {
    var inOne = Number(inOne);
    var inTwo = Number(inTwo);
    var inThree = Number(inThree);
    return Number(inOne + inTwo + inThree);
}
```

> *Concatenation is a pretty far cry from addition!*

> *The number 2 can mean a number or a string.*

> *The problem is that, by definition, a user input in JavaScript is a text string, even when it's a number.*

ADVANCED

Understanding Loosely and Strictly Typed Computer Languages

Computer languages can either be loosely typed, such as JavaScript, or strictly typed (such as Java and C#). (Some other languages, such as Visual Basic .NET, are actually hybrids, and can be used in either a loosely typed mode or a strictly typed mode.)

In a strictly typed language, as opposed to a loosely typed language, the programmer must specify the type of each variable that will be used to store values. In the context of a programming language variable, a type isn't an animal, vegetable, or mineral—but rather refers to the types available in the programming language. In most modern programming languages, *primitive* types such as integer number, floating-point number, and text string are available. (I say *primitive* types because in modern programming languages it's also generally possible to define your own types.)

In addition to specifying the types of all variables, in a strictly typed programming language the programmer is responsible for specifying methods for converting values from one type to another, at least if there's any possibility of losing data in the conversion. In other words, for the most part, type conversions won't take place automatically.

In contrast, in loosely typed languages you don't have to specify the type of a variable. (In fact, in JavaScript you can't specify a variable's type when the variable is declared even if you wanted to specify it.) The computer does the best job it can figuring out the variable type based on the value assigned to the variable. Conversions take place automatically when the computer figures it's appropriate, using the computer's best guess for the conversion method to use.

In favor of loosely typed languages, they're easier to use and require less up-front work. For better (and worse), strictly typed languages require programmers to be more precise. This means that programmers have to think a little harder about the types of values that will be used in their programs. The up-front work of understanding the types of the values that will be used in the program and specifying the conversion methods to be used generally leads to fewer errors in the finished code.

Each of the values passed to the function, as represented by a function parameter such as inOne, are converted to a new variable (with the same name, for example, inOne) using the Number function:

```
var inOne = Number(inOne);
```

Then the three inputs are added, and the resulting value is returned:

```
return Number(inOne + inTwo + inThree);
```

A few comments are worth making. If the inputs to the function are already of numeric type, then calling the Number function has no effect—which is just fine!

But what happens if one of the inputs to the function is something that can't be converted to a number, for example, the text string *Harold*? Good question! In that case, the results of the conversion using the Number function are a JavaScript value of NaN, which is short for *Not a Number*. In fact, if you add a value of NaN to numbers, you still get NaN. So, if our addThreeNums function tries to add the text string *Harold* to 1 and 2, the result will be NaN.

It's a good criticism of the example I'm about to show you that there's no testing to make sure that only values that can be converted to numbers are sent to the addThreeNums function. It's actually pretty easy to make this kind of test—called *validating user input*—by first attempting to convert the value input to a number and then checking to see that result isn't NaN. In fact, if you wanted, you could "bullet proof" the addThreeNums function by adding a test of this sort for each input to the function before attempting to add the inputs.

The Number conversion function is closely related to the JavaScript Number object. You'll learn more about objects in JavaScript in Chapter 7, "Working with Objects."

 NOTE By the way, sometimes you'll need to explicitly force a conversion of a number to a text string—in other words, convert in the opposite direction from the Number function. You do this using the String function built into JavaScript.

Getting back to our function, and our example, it's time to construct an HTML form that will allow the user to enter three numbers. When the user clicks the Add Them button, the AddThreeNums function adds the numbers. Finally, the results are displayed using the document.write method.

To Allow User Input of Three Numbers and Display The Sum:

1. Place the addThreeNums function in the <HEAD> section of an HTML document:

```
<HTML>
<HEAD>
   <SCRIPT>
   function addThreeNums (inOne, inTwo, inThree) {
      var inOne = Number(inOne);
      var inTwo = Number(inTwo);
      var inThree = Number(inThree);
      return Number(inOne + inTwo + inThree);
   }
   </SCRIPT>
</HEAD>
<BODY>
...
</BODY>
</HTML>
```

2. In the <BODY> section of the HTML document, add an HTML form:

```
<BODY>
   <FORM>
   ...
   </FORM>
<BODY>
```

3. So that the elements of the HTML form can be referred to in JavaScript code, use a Name attribute to name the form:

```
<BODY>
   <FORM Name="theForm">
   ...
   </FORM>
<BODY>
```

4. Within the HTML form, add three text input elements, one for each of the numbers to be input, and name each element:

```
<INPUT Type=Text Name="num1">
<INPUT Type=Text Name="num2">
<INPUT Type=Text Name="num3">
```

5. Within the HTML form, add a button element:

```
<INPUT Type=Button>
```

6. Provide a Value attribute for the button (this is the text that will appear on the button in the browser):

```
<INPUT Type=Button Value="Add Them">
```

7. Add an onClick handler to the button:

```
<INPUT Type=Button Value="Add Them" onClick= >
```

8. The JavaScript code placed within quotes and assigned to the onClick handler is executed when the button is clicked by the user. Single quotes are used so that double quotes can be employed within the JavaScript code. (You'll find more about JavaScript events, such as the onClick event in Chapter 8, "Understanding Events and Event-Driven Code"). Here's the code assigned to the onClick event that calls the addThreeNums function with the values entered by the user and uses the document.write method to display the results:

```
<INPUT Type=Button Value="Add Them"
onClick='document.write("The sum of the three numbers is " +
addThreeNums(theForm.num1.value, ⏎
   theForm.num2.value, theForm.num3.value));'>
```

9. Save the HTML file (Listing 5-2 shows the complete code).

10. Open it in a Web browser to test the function.

11. Enter a number in each of the text boxes (see Figure 5-3).

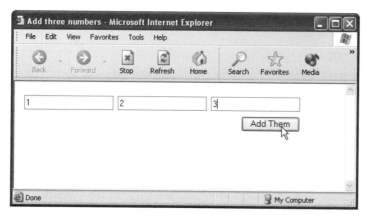

FIGURE 5-3

The user can enter a number in each of the text boxes.

12. Click Add Them. The document.write method is used to display the sum of the three numbers (see Figure 5-4).

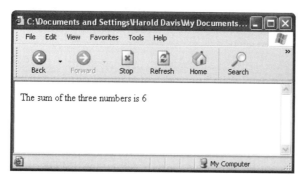

FIGURE 5-4

The sum of the three numbers is displayed.

Learning More About HTML Table Tags

You don't really need to use the HTML shown in Listing 5-3 to get the programming point of the exercise. And I can't really explain HTML (which isn't programming anyhow) within the scope of this book. (There are quite a few good books just about HTML that you can get.) But let me quickly explain some of the table tags shown in Listing 5-3:

- <TR></TR> tags mark a row in a table.

- <TD></TD> tags mark a cell within a row in a table.

- The cellspacing attribute of the <TABLE> tag determines the number of pixels separating each table cell.

There are some "gotchas" with this application. First, as I've already mentioned, no validation of user input is performed to make sure that the user has entered something that can actually be converted to a number (this validation check could be performed when the user enters a value or in the function itself).

Second, it's of course no big shakes to add three numbers. The important point is that this example shows how to return a value from a function.

Finally, I lied to you. What, an author who lies? Never! The HTML shown in Listing 5-2 would never look as clean and orderly as the user interface shown in Figure 5-3. As experienced creators of HTML documents understand, HTML tables are generally used to organize screens in HTML applications. This is a book about learning the craft of programming, not about creating HTML documents. So I thought it was a good idea in Listing 5-2 to show the HTML form and JavaScript code it invokes without complicating matters by showing the HTML table tags used for formatting purposes. But, if you want to see the HTML form, JavaScript code, and HTML table tags used for formatting, look at Listing 5-3.

An author who lies! Never!

LISTING 5-2

A Function That Returns the Sum of Three Numbers (Stripped-Down Version)

```
<HTML>
<HEAD>
   <TITLE>
   Add three numbers
   </TITLE>
   <SCRIPT>
```

```
    function addThreeNums (inOne, inTwo, inThree) {
       var inOne = Number(inOne);
       var inTwo = Number(inTwo);
       var inThree = Number(inThree);
       return Number(inOne + inTwo + inThree);
    }
    </SCRIPT>
</HEAD>
<BODY>
   <FORM Name="theForm">
   <INPUT Type=Text Name="num1">
   <INPUT Type=Text Name="num2">
   <INPUT Type=Text Name="num3">
   <INPUT Type=Button Value="Add Them"
         onClick='document.write("The sum of the three numbers is " +

addThreeNums(theForm.num1.value,theForm.num2.value,theForm.num3.value));'>
   </FORM>
</BODY>
</HTML>
```

LISTING 5-3

The Function That Returns the Sum of Three Numbers Including Table Codes

```
<HTML>
<HEAD>
   <TITLE>
   Add three numbers
   </TITLE>
   <SCRIPT>
   function addThreeNums (inOne, inTwo, inThree) {
      var inOne = Number(inOne);
      var inTwo = Number(inTwo);
      var inThree = Number(inThree);
      return Number(inOne + inTwo + inThree);
   }
   </SCRIPT>
</HEAD>
<BODY>
   <FORM Name="theForm">
   <TABLE cellspacing=5>
```

```
     <TR>
        <TD><INPUT Type=Text Name="num1"></TD><TD><INPUT Type=Text
           Name="num2">
        </TD><TD><INPUT Type=Text Name="num3"></TD>
     </TR>
     <TR>
        <TD></TD><TD></TD><TD align=right><INPUT Type=Button Value="Add
Them"
        onClick='document.write("The sum of the three numbers is " +
        addThreeNums(theForm.num1.value, theForm.num2.value,
theForm.num3.value));'>
        </TD>
     </TR>
  </TABLE>
</FORM>
</BODY>
</HTML>
```

Using a Function's Arguments Array

In the example in the previous section, I showed you how to use a function to add three numbers. Let's suppose you want to use a function that adds some numbers, but you don't really know how many numbers you're going to need to add. It's easy to do this in JavaScript using the properties of the function.

As I'll show to you in Chapter 7, "Working with Objects," everything in JavaScript is an object. This is also true for most modern programming languages. (We'll have to leave for Chapter 7 a discussion of the nature of objects.)

In JavaScript, as in most modern programming languages, everything is an object.

Most objects have properties, which are settings related to the object. In the case of a function, one of the properties associated with the function is an array, or list, of the arguments passed to the function. (Chapter 6, "Programming with Arrays," explains arrays in detail.)

The array that stores the arguments of a function can be used to access the arguments passed to the function by means of an index mechanism. Furthermore, when you write a function without knowing how many arguments will be passed to it, you can use the length property of the arguments array to find out in your code exactly how many arguments were passed to it. In other words, the length property is a property of the arguments property of a function, and it contains the number of arguments passed to the function. If the function were named addNums, the value contained in the following code:

```
addNums.arguments.length
```

would tell you the number of arguments passed to the function.

If this sounds a little complicated to you, don't worry! An example will help. But first, here's what it boils down to: The function's arguments array can be used to access arguments passed to the function, even if you don't know how many arguments to expect. In addition, the function's arguments.length property will tell you how many arguments were, in fact, passed to the function.

Let's go over how you would rewrite the addThreeNums function explained in the previous section so that it'll add however many numbers are passed to it. (The new function is called addNums because it adds any number of numbers!)

First, remove the parameters from the function declaration so that it now appears to not take any arguments:

```
function addNums () {

}
```

Next, at the top of the function, declare a variable, theAnswer, with a starting value of zero:

```
var theAnswer = 0;
```

 TIP Because the variable **theAnswer** has been given a numerical value to start with, the computer knows that it stores a numerical type. If I had used the statement **var theAnswer = "0"** (note the quote marks), the computer would have known that a string value was being stored. In other words, if you store an unquoted number in a variable in JavaScript, the computer assumes you want to store a numerical type.

The variable theAnswer will be used to return the sum of all the numbers passed to the function.

Here's what it boils down to: The function's arguments array can be used to access arguments passed to a function, even if you don't know how many arguments there are!

The function adds the numbers passed to it.

Next, create a `for` loop that will be used to cycle through the addNums function's arguments array (Chapter 4, "Working with Loops," explained for loops):

```
for (var i = 0; i < addNums.arguments.length; i++) {


}
```

NOTE The arguments array is *zero-based*, meaning that the first element in the array has an index of zero and the last element has an index of the length of the array less one. That's why the `for` loop starts at zero and keeps iterating as long as the counter variable, `i`, is less than the number of elements in the arguments array (`addNums.arguments.length`).

Within the `for` loop, explicitly convert each argument passed to the array to a number in case it's actually a text string, as explained in the previous section "Returns Are Good":

```
var theNum = Number(addNums.arguments[i]);
```

Finally, use the incremental assignment operator (+=) to add the argument to the variable theAnswer that's being used to store the sum of all the arguments passed to the addNums function.

TIP The incremental assignment operator (+=) adds the value on the right side of the operator to the variable on the left side and stores the incremented total in the variable on the left side of the operator. In other words, the statement `Answer += theNum;` is the same as (the longer) `Answer = Answer + theNum;`.

Once all the arguments have been saved in the variable theAnswer, outside (and beneath) the `for` loop, return the total stored in the variable:

```
return theAnswer;
```

Listing 5-4 shows the complete addNums function, which will return the sum of the numbers passed to it, without knowing in advance how many numbers there are to sum. (Of course, the HTML user interface only allows the user to enter three numbers, even though the function will accept more.)

LISTING 5-4

Adding Numbers Within a Function Using the Function's Arguments Array

```
function addNums () {
  var theAnswer = 0;
  for (var i = 0; i < addNums.arguments.length; i++) {
    var theNum = Number(addNums.arguments[i]);
    theAnswer += theNum;
  }
  return theAnswer;
}
```

Let's take this function for a test drive!

I've replaced the function used in the HTML page shown in the earlier section "Returns Are Good" in Listing 5-3 with the new addNums function, modified the HTML to accept four (rather than three inputs), and modified the onClick event handler of the HTML button to call the new function (see Listing 5-5).

If you open the HTML page shown in Listing 5-5 in a Web browser and enter four numbers, it'll appear as shown in Figure 5-5.

> *You can easily modify the HTML page used in the "Returns Are Good" section to take the new function for a test spin!*

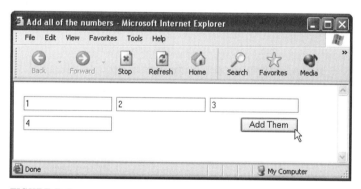

FIGURE 5-5

The function can be used with four boxes (or any number of boxes).

Click Add Them to test the program. The correct sum of the numbers is displayed (see Figure 5-6).

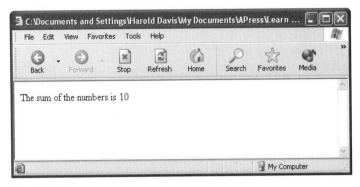

FIGURE 5-6

The sum of the numbers passed to the function is displayed.

LISTING 5-5

Using the addNums Function to Add Four Numbers from an HTML Form
(and Display the Results)

```
<HTML>
<HEAD>
   <TITLE>
   Add all of the numbers
   </TITLE>
   <SCRIPT>
   function addNums () {
      var theAnswer = 0;
      for (var i = 0; i < addNums.arguments.length; i++) {
         var theNum = Number(addNums.arguments[i]);
         theAnswer += theNum;
      }
      return theAnswer;
   }
   </SCRIPT>
</HEAD>
<BODY>
   <FORM Name="theForm">
   <TABLE cellspacing=5>
      <TR>
         <TD><INPUT Type=Text Name="num1"></TD><TD><INPUT Type=Text
            Name="num2">
         </TD><TD><INPUT Type=Text Name="num3"></TD>
      </TR>
```

```
        <TR>
          <TD></TD><TD></TD><TD align=right><INPUT Type=Button Value="Add
Them"
          onClick='document.write("The sum of the numbers is " +

addThreeNums(theForm.num1.value,theForm.num2.value,theForm.num3.value,
              theForm.num4.value));'>
          </TD>
        </TR>
      </TABLE>
    </FORM>
  </BODY>
</HTML>
```

Don't Curse: Be Recursive

Cursing is bad, as your mother may have told you, but being recursive can be good—very, very good! A *recursive* function is one that calls itself.

Our example of a recursive function will be one that calculates numbers in the Fibonacci series.

The Fibonacci series is named after Leonard Pisano, a mathematician who lived in the 1200s and, for some reason, called himself *Fibonacci*. This series of numbers is calculated by starting with zero and one, adding them, and then adding the two previous numbers to obtain the next number. In other words, the Nth number in the Fibonacci series equals the Nth – 1 number plus the Nth – 2 number.

As you'll see, using this formula, the Nth number of the Fibonacci series can easily be calculated using a recursive function—one that calls itself to determine the Nth – 1 and the Nth – 2 Fibonacci numbers.

By the way, the Fibonacci series is famous because it often occurs in natural phenomena such as spiraling plants, chambered nautilus shells, and so on. Fibonacci first discovered these numbers during a calculation of how many rabbits could be eventually expected when starting out with one mating pair.

ADVANCED

Understanding Fibonacci Numbers and the Rabbit Problem

"A certain man put a pair of rabbits in a place surrounded on all sides by a wall. How many pairs of rabbits can be produced from that pair in a year if it is supposed that every month each pair begets a new pair, which from the second month on becomes productive?" asked the mathematician Fibonacci, writing in 1202 in his book *Liber Abaci* ("Book of the Abacus"), describing the rabbit reproduction problem that gave rise to the Fibonacci series.

To answer the rabbit problem, imagine that there are X_N pairs of rabbits after N months. To find out how many pairs of rabbits there will be in the next month, month N + 1, you'd start with X_N and add the new pairs of rabbit born in the month. (This, of course, assumes that rabbits are immortal and never die—a true Malthusian nightmare.)

As the problem is defined, new pairs of rabbits are only born to rabbits at least one month old. So, the number of new pairs is X_{N-1}.

This means that the number of rabbit pairs in the N + 1 month can be calculated as $X_{N+1} = X_N + X_{N-1}$, which is the same thing as the Fibonacci series I just described.

Coming down from planet rabbit to planet earth, let's see how we can use a recursive function (one that calls itself) to generate the Fibonacci series of numbers. To see how to do this, let's have a look at the first few numbers in the series, starting with the first, or zero, Fibonacci number, as shown in Table 5-1.

TABLE 5-1

The First Numbers in the Fibonacci Series

Number in Fibonacci Series	Value
0	0
1	1
2	1
3	2
4	3
5	5
6	8
7	13
8	21

Here's how to declare a function (named fib) that calculates the Nth number in the Fibonacci series:

```
function fib (inNum) {

}
```

The argument inNum in this function declaration represents the number in the series, and the return value of the fib function will be the Fibonacci series value for the number in the series.

The first thing to do within the fib function is to set up an if statement that provides values for the first two Fibonacci numbers (fib(0) and fib(1)). (Chapter 3, "Using Conditional Statements," explained if statements.) Here's the if statement:

```
if (inNum == 0)
    var fibNum = 0;
 else {
     if (inNum == 1)
         fibNum = 1;
     else {

     }
}
```

So far, this if statement uses the comparison operator (= =) to check to see if the Fibonacci number is the zero element in the series, and, if it's the zero element, assigns the value 0 to the variable fibNum. (The variable fibNum will be used to store the value of the Fibonacci number and returned as the value of the fib function.)

NOTE In JavaScript, the comparison operator (==) checks to see if two values are the same. Comparison isn't to be confused with assignment, which assigns a value to a variable. The assignment operator is a single equals sign (=). In some languages, such as Visual Basic, comparison and assignment are both represented by the same symbol, usually a single equals sign.

Next, the if statement uses the comparison operator to check to see if the Fibonacci number is the next element in the series, fib(1):

```
if (inNum == 1)
    fibNum = 1;
else {

}
```

If it's `fib(1)`, then the value 1 is assigned to `fibNum`. If not, it's time to make rabbits! Here's where the recursive function call, which—rabbits or no rabbits—is truly a sexy thing, comes in:

```
if (inNum == 1)
    fibNum = 1;
else  {
    // recursive function call
    fibNum = fib(inNum - 2) + fib(inNum - 1);
}
```

Rabbits or no rabbits, this is truly a sexy thing!

Essentially, this looks just like the definition of the series. Any given Fibonacci number, after the first two, is calculated recursively as the sum of the two numbers that came before it in the series.

✓ **TIP** Recursive algorithms, such as this one, are great for simplicity and clarity, but they may result in programs that are computationally slow. Can you come up with a nonrecursive, faster way to calculate the numbers in the Fibonacci series?

All that remains is the return of the Fibonacci value. Listing 5-6 shows this, along with the complete recursive Fibonacci function.

LISTING 5-6

Calculating a Fibonacci Number Recursively

```
function fib (inNum) {
    if (inNum == 0)
        var fibNum = 0;
    else {
        if (inNum == 1)
            fibNum = 1;
        else {
            // recursive function call
            fibNum = fib(inNum - 2) + fib(inNum - 1);
        }
    }
    return fibNum;
}
```

Now that we know how to calculate a single Fibonacci number (by passing to the fib function shown in Listing 5-6 the number in the series we'd like to calculate), let's add code that shows all the Fibonacci numbers up to a specified maximum in the series.

 TIP You don't want to attempt to calculate a number too far along in the series. Anything greater than the twenty-fifth number in the series is likely to take a long time to calculate recursively and may cause your Web browser to abort the process.

The following is another function, writeFibs, that uses a for loop to obtain each number in the Fibonacci series by calling the original fib function, up to a maximum series number supplied as input to the function:

```
function writeFibs(topFib) {
   for (var i=0;  i <= topFib ; i++)
   {
      document.write ("Fib(" + i + ") = " + fib(i) + " rabbit pairs<br>");
   }
}
```

Each Fibonacci number obtained is displayed on its own line, along with the phrase "rabbit pairs" (just for fun!).

Listing 5-7 shows the two functions (fib and writeFibs) in an HTML page along with an HTML form for the user to enter the number of Fibonacci numbers to calculate. If you open the HTML page shown in Listing 5-7 in a Web browser, it'll look like Figure 5-7.

FIGURE 5-7

The user enters the number of Fibonacci numbers to display.

Enter a number and click Show Fibs. The numbers in the Fibonacci series will be displayed (see Figure 5-8).

 CAUTION The program shown in Listing 5-7 works in Internet Explorer, but not in Navigator or Mozilla.

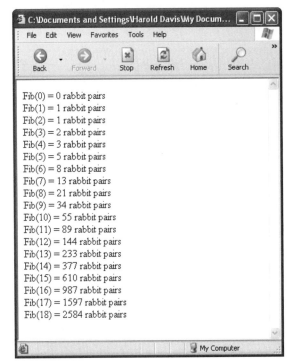

FIGURE 5-8

By the eighteenth generation, there starts to be plenty of rabbits!

LISTING 5-7

Counting Rabbits (Calculating the Fibonacci Series Using a Recursive Function)

```html
<HTML>
<HEAD>
<TITLE>
Counting rabbits...
</TITLE>
<SCRIPT>
    function fib (inNum) {
        if (inNum == 0)
            var fibNum = 0;
        else {
            if (inNum == 1)
                fibNum = 1;
            else {
                // recursive function call
                fibNum = fib(inNum - 2) + fib(inNum - 1);
            }
        }
        return fibNum;
    }

    function writeFibs(topFib) {
      for (var i=0;  i <= topFib ; i++)
     {
      document.write ("Fib(" + i + ") = " + fib(i) + " rabbit pairs<br>");
     }
    }
</SCRIPT>
</HEAD>
<BODY>
<FORM Name="theForm">
   <TABLE cellspacing=5>
      <TR>
         <TD><INPUT Type=Text Name="numFibs">
         <TD>
<INPUT Type=Button Value="Show Fibs" onClick='writeFibs(numFibs.value);'>
      </TR>
   </TABLE>
</FORM>
</BODY>
</HTML>
```

Working with Window Methods

For all practical purposes, the methods associated with the JavaScript window object are used just as if they were functions. So there are a couple of reasons for looking at these methods (functions!) in this chapter. First, if you're writing JavaScript code that will be opened in a browser, they're quite useful.

In addition, because these are essentially built-in functions, using them will give you practice with using functions in general.

 TIP Technically, the methods described in this section are associated with the JavaScript window object (which is discussed more fully in Chapter 7, "Working with Objects"). For example, the alert method actually refers to window.alert. However, you can just refer to these methods without the object qualification—for example, alert—and JavaScript will know what you're talking about.

Let's go ahead and see how to work with some methods for displaying simple dialogs.

 TIP The calls to the methods shown in this section are themselves placed in JavaScript functions (these are shown in Listing 5-8). The reason is that for clarity you want to organize HTML pages using JavaScript so that the code assigned to an event—such as a button onClick event—is kept very short, sweet, and simple. A function call is much shorter than writing out the separate statements contained in the function.

Staying Alert

The alert method displays a simple message box with some text and an OK button.

Here's a function that takes a text value as an input and displays the text value using the alert method:

```
function showAlert(inText) {
    alert (inText);
}
```

Within an HTML form, you could create a text box and a button:

```
<FORM>
...
   <TD><INPUT Type=Text Name="alertText" Size=40>
   <TD><INPUT Type=Button Value="Alert"
onClick='showAlert(alertText.value);'>
...
</FORM>
...
```

The idea is that the user enters the text that will be displayed in a message box when the user clicks the Alert button (as you can see in Figure 5-9).

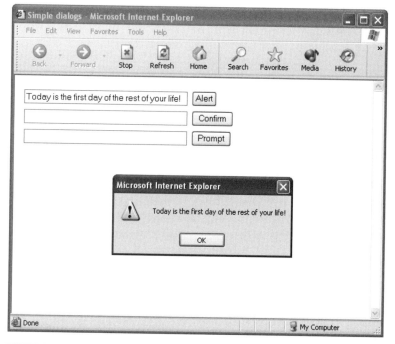

FIGURE 5-9

The text entered by the user is displayed in the message box.

The complete code for an HTML page that includes the showAlert function (as well as functions that display confirm and prompt boxes) is shown a little later in this chapter in Listing 5-8.

Confirming

The confirm method displays a message box with some text and OK and Cancel buttons. The confirm method (read: "function") returns a value of true if the user clicks OK and false otherwise.

Here's a function that shows a confirm box displaying the question "Do you want to dance?" (see Figure 5-10):

```
function showConfirm(){
    if (confirm("Do you want to dance?") == true)
        return "The user wants to dance!"
    else
        return "No dancing tonight!";
}
```

FIGURE 5-10

The confirm method displays a box with text and OK and Cancel buttons.

The showConfirm function returns the text string *The user wants to dance!* if the user clicks OK and the text string *No dancing tonight!* if the user clicks Cancel.

Here's a fragment of HTML form code that calls the showConfirm function when the Confirm button is clicked and displays the return value in a text box, as shown in Figure 5-11.

```
<FORM>
...
    <INPUT Type=Text Name="decisionText" Size=40>
    <INPUT Type=Button Value="Confirm" onClick='decisionText.value =
        showConfirm();'>
...
</FORM>
...
```

By the way, Listing 5-8 shows the complete code for the HTML page that includes the showConfirm method and the form that invokes it.

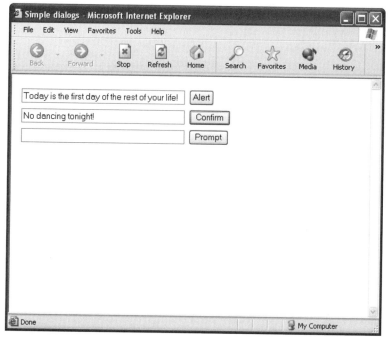

FIGURE 5-11

The return value of the confirm method is either `true` or `false`, and you can branch depending on the value (in the figure, the text message displayed depends on the button clicked).

Being Prompt

As Mel Brooks once said, "It's good to be the king!" And, as the saying goes, "Promptness is the courtesy of kings." Therefore, it's good to be prompt, at least for something nice.

The prompt method displays a prompt box, which consists of some display text, a text box for the user to enter some text, and OK and Cancel buttons. The second parameter passed to the prompt method is the default text that's displayed in the user entry text box (see Figure 5-12). (If you don't want any text displayed in the box, the thing to do is to pass the method an empty string ("") as the second argument.)

FIGURE 5-12

The default text in the prompt box depends on the argument sent to the prompt method.

The following function, showPrompt, displays a prompt box using the text string passed to the function as the message to display (the second argument passed to the prompt method, "John Doe", generates the default value for the text box within the prompt message box):

```
function showPrompt(inText){
    var retVal = ""
    retVal = prompt(inText, "John Doe");
    if (retVal == "" || retVal == null)
        return "nameless one";
    else
        return retVal;
}
```

DO IT RIGHT

Looking at the code for the showPrompt function, I bet you're wondering if it isn't a little overly complicated! Why doesn't the following, simpler function work?

```
function showPrompt(inText){
    return prompt(inText, "John Doe");
}
```

Good question! I'm so glad you asked. There are two problems with the simple version of this function. The first is that if the user clicks Cancel in the prompt box, the value returned from the function is the JavaScript special value null, meaning the return value is nothing at all. The second issue is that an empty string will be returned if the user clears the text box within the prompt and clicks OK.

You could test for both these conditions in the code that calls the showPrompt function, but as I said at the beginning of this section, it's really a bad idea to put JavaScript code in HTML form event handlers. So, it's a much better idea to perform these tests within the function itself. The following code:

```
if (retVal == "" || retVal == null)
    return "nameless one";
else
    return retVal;
```

uses a conditional statement to check whether the return value from the prompt method is the empty string ("") or (|| is the or operator) is null. If either is true, then an appropriate string is passed back ("nameless one"); otherwise, the return value of the prompt method is returned by the function.

The following fragment of HTML form code calls the showPrompt function when the user clicks the prompt button:

```
<FORM>
...
    <INPUT Type=Text Name="nameText" Size=40>
    <INPUT Type=Button Value="Prompt" onClick='nameText.value = "Hello, " +
           showPrompt("What is your name?");'>
...
</FORM>
...
```

The showPrompt method itself shows a prompt message box, as you can see in Figure 5-12 and Figure 5-13.

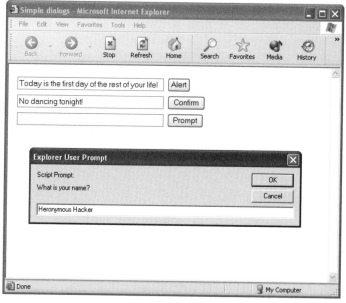

FIGURE 5-13

The user enters text in the prompt box.

If the user enters text in the prompt box and clicks OK, the text is displayed in the HTML page, as shown in Figure 5-14.

By the way, Listing 5-8 shows the complete code for the HTML page that includes the showPrompt method and the form that invokes it.

FIGURE 5-14

The text entered by the user in the prompt box is displayed in the Web page.

LISTING 5-8

Working with the Alert, Confirm, and Prompt Methods

```
<HTML>
<HEAD>
   <TITLE>
   Simple dialogs
   </TITLE>
   <SCRIPT>
   function showAlert(inText) {
      alert (inText);
   }
   function showConfirm(){
      if (confirm("Do you want to dance?") == true)
         return "The user wants to dance!"
      else
         return "No dancing tonight!";
   }
```

```
        function showPrompt(inText){
          var retVal = ""
          retVal = prompt(inText, "John Doe");
          if (retVal == "" || retVal == null)
            return "nameless one";
          else
            return retVal;

          // line below produces ugly result if no user input!
          // return prompt(inText, "John Doe");
        }
      </SCRIPT>
</HEAD>
<BODY>
    <FORM Name="theForm">
    <TABLE cellspacing=5>
      <TR>
        <TD><INPUT Type=Text Name="alertText" Size=40>
        <TD>
<INPUT Type=Button Value="Alert" onClick='showAlert(alertText.value);'>
      </TR>
        <TR>
        <TD><INPUT Type=Text Name="decisionText" Size=40>
        <TD><INPUT Type=Button Value="Confirm"
onClick='decisionText.value =
                showConfirm();'>
      </TR>
      <TR>
        <TD><INPUT Type=Text Name="nameText" Size=40>
        <TD>
<INPUT Type=Button Value="Prompt" onClick='nameText.value = "Hello, " +
                showPrompt("What is your name?");'>
      </TR>
    </TABLE>
</FORM>
</BODY>
</HTML>
```

What's It All About?

From functions to breeding rabbit pairs and back again, this chapter has covered a lot of ground. Using functions in your programs is a good way to organize and simplify your code. If you work with functions, it should help you to understand the way your code is structured. Furthermore, properly written functions allow you to easily reuse code. This saves time and effort.

This chapter has shown you how to write your own functions, how to call functions, and how to use some of the built-in JavaScript functions.

Chapter 6, "Working with Arrays," explains, well, how to work with arrays, which are used to store objects of a similar type and access them using an index.

6

Programming with Arrays

An *array* is a series of variables with the same name. Individual values, also called *elements*, in the series are accessed using an index. You can think of an array as a table with a column. The column contains cells, and in each cell is a value. You can save data to a cell, or retrieve data from the cell, using the row number (or index) in the table.

In JavaScript, arrays are all single-dimensional, meaning that they fit this single table column pattern. By contrast, in many other programming languages you can have multidimensional arrays. Multidimensional arrays use multiple indices to access their values, so (for example) a two-dimensional array can be pictured as a table with rows and columns.

Although all arrays in JavaScript are one-dimensional, you can achieve much the same effect as that of a multidimensional array using arrays of arrays, as I show you later in this chapter.

In the real world, programming usually involves groups of objects. Arrays are specifically designed to store groups of objects (the objects are retrieved using the index). Arrays are important because they make it possible to easily *scale* your code—meaning they deal in an automated fashion with the vast amount of data presented by the real world.

It's common to first write a function (or program) to deal with a single instance of a value. The function can then be generalized, using an array, to deal with many instances of the same type.

Once you have the code working for a single value, it takes little additional work to create code that processes all the values in an array—so in this way it doesn't take much more work to write code that processes many values after you've written the code that processes the first value. (Another way of saying this, in jargon, is that "the program easily scales.")

In the "Using a Function's Arguments Array" section in Chapter 5, "Understanding Functions," I showed you how to use the arguments array associated with any JavaScript function. If you go back and have a look at the example in that section, you'll see that using the function's argument array was a pretty intuitive affair. This chapter takes a bit more formal approach to arrays because they're so important to most programs.

To start with, I show you how to create and populate arrays. Next, you'll learn how to iterate through arrays, implement data structures using arrays, and work with arrays of arrays. Along the way, I show you how to use methods associated with arrays. Finally, I show you how to program with the JavaScript elements array associated with every HTML form.

Creating an Array

Arrays in JavaScript are created using the new operator, which works as the constructor for an Array() object. You'll learn a great deal more about constructors and the new operator in Chapter 7, "Working with Objects." For now, it's enough to know that a constructor is the mechanism for creating an object of some kind (such as an Array() object). Constructors are invoked with the new operator.

The new *operator and the* Array() *object's constructor are used to create arrays for fun and profit!*

With the new operator and the Array() object's constructor, there are a number of variations you can use to create arrays for fun and profit.

The simplest way to create an array is to declare a variable and assign a new Array() object to it. For example, this statement:

```
var theArray = new Array();
```

creates a new array named theArray. One thing that's interesting about this statement is that it doesn't specify how many values, also called *elements*, the array has.

If you know how many elements you'll need to store in your array, it's easy to modify the statement slightly to specify this at the time the array is declared. For example, this statement:

```
var theArray = new Array(42);
```

creates an array with 42 elements.

You should know that JavaScript arrays, like arrays in most modern programming languages, are *zero-indexed*. This means that the first element in the array has an index value of zero (not one, as you might expect). The last element in the array has an index value of the number of elements in the array less one (not the number of elements in the array, as you'd expect if the index started at one rather than zero).

 NOTE The number of elements in an array can be retrieved using the length property of the array, as I explain later in this chapter.

Taking the array created with the statement var theArray = new Array(42);, the elements in the array can be retrieved using a zero-based index as shown in Table 6-1.

TABLE 6-1
Zero-Based Index and Array Elements

Index	Element
0	1st
1	2nd
...	...
40	41st
41	42nd

As you can see in Table 6-1, the index value of N – 1 is used to access the Nth element in an array, which is another way of putting the fact that the index for a 42-element array runs from zero to 41.

I wouldn't be making such a big fuss about the index of an array starting at zero except that it has big practical consequences. It's a true fact (and there are no false facts, at least in this book!) that the vast majority of software errors are caused by being off by one number (so-called "one-off" errors). If you get used to thinking of array indices starting at zero in the first place, you're far less likely to make errors, and your life will be happier.

It's also possible to load an array up with values at the time it's created. To do this, when you create the array using the new constructor, specify the values in order. Here's an example:

The index for a 42-element array runs from zero to 41.

Your life will be happier if you get used to the fact that arrays always start with an index of zero!

```
var trekArray = new Array ("Live", "long", "and", "prosper!");
```

Table 6-2 shows the index and element values for the four-element array created and populated this way.

TABLE 6-2

Index and Element Values for `trekArray`

Index	Element Value
0	Live
1	long
2	and
3	prosper!

ADVANCED

DO IT RIGHT

In case you're wondering, not all the elements in a JavaScript array have to be of the same type. This is different from many other computer languages, in which all the elements in an array have to be of the same type.

As you saw in the "Returns are Good" section in Chapter 5, "Understanding Functions," understanding the type of a variable can be important. So, this can get a bit tricky with JavaScript arrays. JavaScript tries to make the best guess it can for the type of values stored in variables, and this goes as well for values stored as array elements.

Generally, if a number is stored as the first element of an array (with an index of 0), JavaScript will assume that each other element saved to the array is also a number—until it hits something, such as the text string *frodo* that doesn't evaluate to a number. After that, every element stored to the array is taken to be a string.

Conversely, if the first element saved to an array is a text string, then JavaScript goes on the operating assumption that all the elements are string type, even when the element assigned to the array is a number such as 3. (If you put quotes around the 3 so it looked like `"3"`, then JavaScript would know the value is a string.)

It's best not to get too caught up in the details of how JavaScript decides the type of a value. In your programs, check to see if it's important that a value is of a particular type. In the example shown in Chapter 5, JavaScript needed to know that the values passed to a function were numbers, not strings, so that + could be used as the plus operator rather than as the string concatenation operator. As I showed you in Chapter 5, in this kind of situation, you can explicitly convert the values to numerical types using

In JavaScript, as opposed to most languages, elements in an array can be of different types.

the Number function. (Another function I didn't discuss in Chapter 5, String, converts numbers to text strings.)

JavaScript is a great language for learning to program because it's so accessible. (As I said at the beginning of this book, all you need is a Web browser and any operating system.) But it's not the clearest of languages when it comes to understanding the types of values in it. You'll find this issue easier to deal with in other languages when the time comes for you to move on to a language such as Visual Basic, C#, or Java.

Anyhow, I digress. Let's get back to the topic of learning how to work with arrays in JavaScript.

> *It can be tricky to be sure about the type of a value stored in a variable or as an array element in JavaScript.*

> *I digress. But authors never digress!*

Reading and Writing Array Elements

Elements of an array are accessed using square brackets, sometimes termed the [] operator. (In JavaScript, the [] operator can also be used to access object properties, as I show you in Chapter 7, "Working with Objects.")

This means that it's easy to save a value to an array element or to retrieve a value from an array element.

Here are some examples of reading and writing array elements:

```
var theVal = theArray[5];
// retrieves the value of the sixth element of theArray and
// stores the value in the variable theVal

theArray[0] = 256.17;
// stores the floating point numeric value 256.17 in the first
// element of theArray

var i = 1;
theArray[i] = "Good morning";
// stores the text string "Good morning" to theArray[1]

theArray[i +1] = 12
// stores the integral numeric value 12 to theArray[2]
```

Let's look at an example that's a bit more complete. The code shown in Listing 6-1 declares a four-element array, assigns a value to each element of the array, and then retrieves an element and displays it as part of a text string (see Figure 6-1).

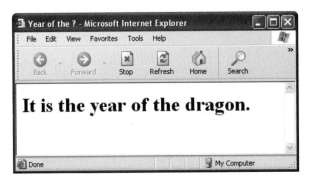

FIGURE 6-1

The text value in the array element is displayed.

In part, the example shown in Listing 6-1 demonstrates that a variable can be used for the index of an array. The ability to do this is part of what gives arrays their power, as you'll see in the examples later in this chapter.

LISTING 6-1

Reading and Writing Array Elements

```
<HTML>
   <HEAD>
   <TITLE>
   Year of the ?
   </TITLE>
   </HEAD>
   <BODY>
   <H1>
   <SCRIPT>
      var myArray = new Array(4);
      myArray[0] = "dog";
      myArray[1] = "cat";
      myArray[2] = "snake";
      myArray[3] = "dragon";
      var i = 3;
      var theYear = myArray[i];
```

```
        document.write("It is the year of the " + theYear + ".");
    </SCRIPT>
    </H1>
    </BODY>
</HTML>
```

As you can see from this example (Listing 6-1), it's really easy to assign values to array elements and to retrieve values from arrays. Because this is so easy to do, you should try it—so you can make sure you're comfortable with arrays!

TRY THIS
AT HOME

Adding and Removing Array Elements

In most modern programming languages, once you declare the number of elements in an array, that number is fixed. Not so in JavaScript. You can change the number of elements in an array at any point.

To add a new element to an array, you just assign a value to the element. For example, let's assume you have an array with two elements:

```
var myArray = new Array(2);
myArray[0] = "dog";
myArray[1] = "cat";
```

The following assignment:

```
myArray[2] = "snake"
```

adds an element with an index of 2 and a value of "snake" to myArray.

> *How do you get to Carnegie Hall? Practice, practice.*
>
> *It's time to practice reading and writing array elements!*

The Undefined Value

If a variable, or array element, doesn't exist, or if the variable (or array element) has been declared but has no value assigned to it, in JavaScript the variable (or array element) evaluates to the special value undefined.

To determine if a variable (or array element) exists and has a value, you can compare the value to undefined. (I provide an example of this in the section "Iterating Through an Array.")

Conversely, if you want to get rid of the value of an array element, you can simply assign the special value undefined to the array element at a specific index. Note that this doesn't actually remove the element, it just makes the value of the element undefined.

To delete the value of an element from an array, assign the special value undefined *to the element using the index of the element.*

For example, let's take the four-element array created with these statements:

```
var myArray = new Array(4);
myArray[0] = "dog";
myArray[1] = "cat";
myArray[2] = "snake";
myArray[3] = "dragon";
```

You can now delete the fourth (and last) element from the array by executing this statement:

```
myArray[3] = undefined;
```

 NOTE You can also delete an element in an array using the delete method. The statement delete myArray[3]; is equivalent to the statement myArray[3] = undefined;.

JavaScript Arrays Are Sparse

There's one other thing you should know about arrays in JavaScript: JavaScript arrays are *sparse*.

JavaScript arrays go around the world with their laptops and wooden begging bowls and nothing else. Not so. No, when an array is sparse, it doesn't mean that the array lives an ascetic, monk-like lifestyle in a small hermit cell with only a few possessions. (I thought I'd state this just in case you decided to ask.)

To say that an array is sparse means that the values of the index for the array doesn't need to be a contiguous range of numbers. Space in the computer's memory is only allocated for the array elements that are actually stored in the array (and not for elements that are undefined).

For example, the following statements create an array with four defined elements:

```
var myArray = new Array();
myArray[500] = "dog";
myArray[1000] = "cat";
myArray[2000] = "snake";
myArray[3000] = "dragon";
```

As you'll see in a moment, the value of the length property of this array is 3001; however, only the four elements referenced in these statements (with an index value of 500, 1000, 2000, and 3000) have been allocated space in memory.

Iterating Through an Array

> *Arrays live to iterate!*

Probably the most important thing you can do to or with an array is *iterate* through it. You could say that "Arrays live to be iterated!"

One could also say "Don't procrastinate, iterate!" But let's move from sayings and slogans toward understanding: What does *iterate* mean?

To iterate through an array means to loop (or cycle) through the array, checking and/or doing something with each and every element.

The easiest and most common way to iterate is to use a variable that represents the index of the array in a for loop. You also need to know how many elements are in an array, and you can determine this using the length property of the array.

> *The length property of an array specifies the index value of the highest element in the array plus one (because arrays have zero-based indices).*

If you know that the range of the index of your array is contiguous and begins at element zero, then iterating through the array is easy. Here's the general pattern:

If you have an array created like this:

```
var theArray = new Array(10);
```

then the index values for theArray range from one to nine. (You don't really need to know the upper bound of the index of the array, but it's good to keep in mind that the array index starts at zero.)

The following statement can be used to iterate through theArray:

```
for (var i = 0; i < theArray.length; i++) {
    // do something with theArray[i]
}
```

This for statement starts with zero, increments by one each time it goes through the for loop (as directed by the i++ clause in the statement), and terminates when the index becomes equal to the value of the array length property. (In the example, the loop terminates after an index value of 9 has been processed.) If you need a refresher on how for loops work, please refer to Chapter 4, "Working with Loops."

As I mentioned earlier, JavaScript arrays aren't necessarily contiguous, another way of saying that they're sparse. This means that if you're iterating through a sparse array, you need to check each element within the loop to make sure it's defined.

For example, suppose you have an array defined as follows:

```
var myArray = new Array(4);
myArray[0] = "dog";
myArray[1] = "cat";
myArray[2] = "snake";
myArray[3] = "dragon";
myArray[6] = "chicken";
myArray[1] = undefined;
```

In this scenario, elements 0, 2, 3, and 6 of the array are defined; elements 1, 4, and 5 are undefined. Let's suppose you'd like to display the index for each defined element of the array along with its value, as shown in Figure 6-2.

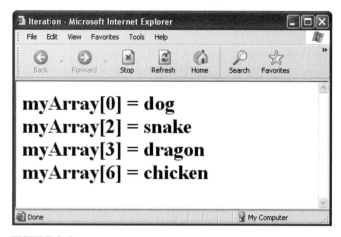

FIGURE 6-2

The defined elements of the sparse array

You can use the normal pattern of statements to loop through the array:

```
for (var i = 0; i < myArray.length; i++){

}
```

Inside the for loop, you'd normally use a statement like this:

```
document.write("myArray[" + i + "] = " + myArray[i] + "<br>");
```

to display the array index and values. Here's the loop code so far:

```
for (var i = 0; i < myArray.length; i++){
    document.write("myArray[" + i + "] = " + myArray[i] + "<br>");
}
```

If the code runs as it stands, you'll see the undefined values (see Figure 6-3).

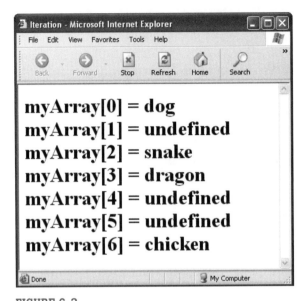

FIGURE 6-3
The undefined values of the array

The way to fix this is to add a conditional statement that checks to make sure that each array element is defined before displaying it. Here's what the loop, modified to check for undefined array values, looks like:

```
for (var i = 0; i < myArray.length; i++){
    if (myArray[i] != undefined)
        document.write("myArray[" + i + "] = " + myArray[i] + "<br>");
}
```

Listing 6-2 shows an HTML page that displays only the defined elements of myArray.

LISTING 6-2

Iterating Through a Sparse Array

```
<HTML>
   <HEAD>
   <TITLE>
   Iteration
   </TITLE>
   </HEAD>
   <BODY>
   <H1>
   <SCRIPT>
      var myArray = new Array(4);
      myArray[0] = "dog";
      myArray[1] = "cat";
      myArray[2] = "snake";
      myArray[3] = "dragon";
      myArray[6] = "chicken";
      myArray[1] = undefined;
     for (var i = 0; i < myArray.length; i++){
       if (myArray[i] != undefined)
         document.write("myArray[" + i + "] = " + myArray[i] + "<br>");
     }
   </SCRIPT>
   </H1>
   </BODY>
</HTML>
```

By the way, you can use Boolean evaluation as another way to determine whether an array element is defined.

 NOTE There's nothing wrong with the test if (myArray[i] != undefined) to determine if an array element is undefined; but there are others way to achieve the same result. (As I explained in Chapter 2, "Understanding Types, Variables, and Statements," != is the comparison operator that means inequality.)

The expression myArray[i] evaluates to true if the array element is defined and false if it's undefined. So, you could replace the iteration code shown in Listing 6-2 with the following loop:

```
for (var i = 0; i < myArray.length; i++){
    if (myArray[i])
       document.write("myArray[" + i + "] = " + myArray[i] + "<br>");
    }
```

This works just fine most of the time except in the situation in which you've stored Boolean values in the array elements. Using if (myArray[i]) as the test, the element myArray[0] = true evaluates to true, but the element myArray[0] = false evaluates to false, which isn't what you'd like from the viewpoint of deciding whether the element is defined (it's defined, but with a Boolean value of false). As long as you're not storing Boolean values in your array, you can use Boolean evaluation as a simple test for whether the array element is defined.

Using the Array Length Property

The length property of an array is an integral number that's one larger than the largest index of a defined element of the array. If you think about this, it means that the length property isn't always equal to the number of elements in an array because JavaScript arrays can be noncontiguous and sparsely populated.

You should also know that an array's length property can be used to write (as well as to read) the length of an array. If you set the value of the length property greater than its current value, new undefined elements are added at the end of the array to extend it to the newly designated size.

If you set the length property to a value that's smaller than its current value, the array is truncated to its new length. Elements with an index value greater than the new length are discarded and their values are gone forever.

Truncating an array by setting its length property to a smaller than current value is the only way to actually remove elements from an array (as opposed to deleting the elements, which makes them undefined and doesn't impact the length of the array).

Seeing Another Array Iteration Example in Action

Let's go ahead and work through another example of iterating through an array. This time, we'll break up the tasks using functions (for more information about functions, see Chapter 5, "Understanding Functions").

There are three tasks to perform:

1. Create a function to create and populate an array.

2. Create another function to generate a text string based on the values stored in the array elements.

3. Display the text string.

Let's take these steps from the top.

To Create and Populate an Array:

1. Create the declaration for the function makeArray that will be used to create and populate the array:

```
function makeArray() {

}
```

Note that there are no arguments passed to this function.

2. Use the new operator to construct a new array with four elements:

```
var myArray = new Array(4);
```

3. Assign values to the elements of the array:

```
myArray[0] = "Live";
myArray[1] = "long";
myArray[2] = "and";
myArray[3] = "prosper!";
```

4. Send the populated array back to the code that called the makeArray function as the return value of the function:

```
return myArray;
```

Here's the complete makeArray function:

```
function makeArray() {
    var myArray = new Array(4);
    myArray[0] = "Live";
    myArray[1] = "long";
    myArray[2] = "and";
    myArray[3] = "prosper!";
    return myArray;
}
```

Next, let's create a function named showArray that iterates through the elements of the passed array to generate a single text string based on the values of the array elements separated by spaces. (Note that the code assumes that the index values of the array elements are contiguous.)

To Generate a Text String by Iterating Through Array Elements:

1. Create a declaration for the showArray function that takes a single argument (the code within the function assumes the argument to be an array):

```
function showArray(theArray){

}
```

2. Declare a variable to hold the text string that will be returned:

```
var quote = "";
```

3. Iterate through the array elements:

```
for (var i = 0; i < theArray.length; i++){

}
```

4. For each iteration, append the value of the array element and a single space to the return string using the concatenation operator:

```
for (var i = 0; i < theArray.length; i++){
    quote += theArray[i] + " ";
}
```

5. Outside, and beneath, the for loop, return the fully generated text string:

```
return quote;
```

Here's the complete code for the showArray function:

```
function showArray(theArray){
    var quote = "";
    for (var i = 0; i < theArray.length; i++){
     quote += theArray[i] + " ";
     }
   return quote;
}
```

The final task is to display the generated text string.

You can easily do this from within the body of an HTML document by calling each of the two functions, makeArray and showArray, in order.

To Display the Generated Text:

1. Within the body of an HTML document, declare a variable x and assign to it the return value of the makeArray function:

```
var x = makeArray();
```

2. Use the document.write method to display the return value of the showArray function when it has been passed the array stored as the value of x:

```
document.write(showArray(x));
```

The actual program in the body of this HTML page consists of only two statements:

```
var x = makeArray();
document.write(showArray(x));
```

These two statements appear to be simple, which is part of the idea. The actual work of making the array goes on in the function makeArray, just as the actual work of showing the array is performed by the function showArray. You don't necessarily need to know exactly how makeArray and showArray do their dastardly deeds to use them. As you'll see in Chapter 7, "Working with Objects," this programmatic separation, and opacity, is at the heart of *encapsulation*, one of the key concepts of object-oriented programming.

Listing 6-3 shows the complete code for creating, populating, and displaying the values in an array in an HTML page. If you open this page in a Web browser, it should look like Figure 6-4.

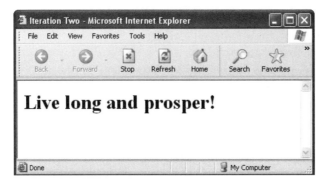

FIGURE 6-4

The value of the elements of an array are displayed as a text string.

The process shown in this example may seem a little convoluted to you, but it's worth following to make sure you understand it. By breaking up the task into three parts, each of the parts has become effectively independent.

The showArray function is completely independent from the function that creates and populates the array. The showArray function is also independent from the code that displays the text string. The three parts of this program even use a different variable name for the array involved (myArray, theArray, and x).

See if you can modify this example for fun and profit!

The only connection between the three parts of the code is that the two statements in the body of the HTML document calls each of the functions in turn.

Can you modify this example to display a saying of your own, perhaps adding line breaks to the text display?

LISTING 6-3

Using Functions to Iterate Through an Array

```
<HTML>
    <HEAD>
    <TITLE>
    Iteration Two
    </TITLE>
    <SCRIPT>
    function makeArray() {
        var myArray = new Array(4);
        myArray[0] = "Live";
        myArray[1] = "long";
        myArray[2] = "and";
        myArray[3] = "prosper!";
        return myArray;
    }
     function showArray(theArray){
       var quote = "";
       for (var i = 0; i < theArray.length; i++){
          quote += theArray[i] + " ";
       }
       return quote;
     }
    </SCRIPT>
    </HEAD>
    <BODY>
    <H1>
    <SCRIPT>
       var x = makeArray();
       document.write(showArray(x));
    </SCRIPT>
    </H1>
    </BODY>
</HTML>
```

Implementing a Stack As an Array

In the beginning of this chapter I defined an *array* as a series of variables with the same name such that individual values in the series are accessed using an index. This means that an array provides a structure for random access to stored values: It's as easy to retrieve a value stored anywhere in the array as it is to retrieve a value stored anywhere else. All you need is the index.

Not every programming problem calls for a data structure that provides random access. For example, suppose you have no idea how many items you'll need to store. But you'd like the data structure you use for this task to have the property that each new item added to it becomes the next item accessed from it. The data structure I've just described is called a *stack*.

By its very nature, a stack isn't a random access structure in the way that an array is. You only have access to the top, or *last in*, item in a stack at any given time. This means that a stack functions in a *first in, last out* (or FILO) fashion. The first item in is the last item out.

NOTE You may have heard of another data structure related to the stack, namely the *queue*. A queue works like a stack except that it's *first in, first out* (or FIFO). Think of people waiting in an orderly line (or queue) and then boarding a bus to get a mental picture of how this data structure works.

In stack lingo, to *push* a stack means to add a new item to the "top" of the stack. To *pop* a stack means to remove the item at the "top" of the stack. When you pop the stack to remove the top item, at the same time you're retrieving the value of the item.

It's easy to make a JavaScript array behave like a stack using the Array object's push and pop methods.

We'll first walk through a simple example of using an array as a stack so that you get the hang of it. Then I'll show you a more general program using a stack for your enjoyment.

The object of the simple stack example is just to give you a feeling for stacks as a data structure and to demonstrate that the push and pop methods work as advertised.

First, within a <SCRIPT> tag in the body of an HTML document, declare a new array named `stack`:

```
var stack = new Array();
```

Next, push two values onto the stack (the text strings *Me* and *Two*):

```
stack.push("Me", "Two");
```

Now, iterate through the `stack` array to display its contents, with a line break placed between each item:

```
for (var i = 0; i < stack.length; i++){
    document.write(stack[i] + "<br>");
}
```

If you open the HTML page as it stands so far in a Web browser, it should display the strings *Me* and *Two* on separate lines, as you can see at the top of Figure 6-5.

> Pushing *a* stack means to put a new item on the top of the stack; popping the stack means to remove, and retrieve, the top item from the stack.

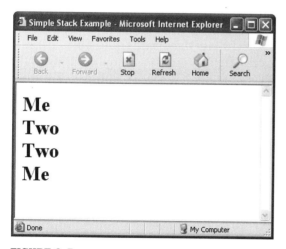

FIGURE 6-5

The contents of the stack (the top two items) are displayed.

Next, pop an item off the stack and display it:

```
document.write (stack.pop() + "<br>");
```

The item popped should be the most recent item added to the stack, also called the "top" item, which is the text string *Two*, as you can see on the third line of Figure 6-5.

The only item left on the stack should be the text string *Me*. But let's prove it by iterating through the stack array again and displaying the contents:

```
for (var i = 0; i < stack.length; i++){
    document.write(stack[i] + "<br>");
}
```

This time only one item, *Me*, is displayed, as you can see in the fourth and final line of Figure 6-5.

Listing 6-4 shows the complete code for the simple stack example.

LISTING 6-4

Simple Stack Example

```
<HTML>
<HEAD>
<TITLE>
Simple Stack Example
</TITLE>
</HEAD>
<BODY>
<H1>
<SCRIPT>
var stack = new Array();
stack.push("Me", "Two");
for (var i = 0; i < stack.length; i++){
    document.write(stack[i] + "<br>");
}
document.write (stack.pop() + "<br>");
for (var i = 0; i < stack.length; i++){
    document.write(stack[i] + "<br>");
}
</SCRIPT>
</H1>
</BODY>
</HTML>
```

Seeing a More General Stack in Action

Now that you have the gist of working with stacks, let's see how a more general stack application stacks up!

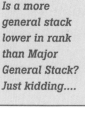

Here's how the general stack application will work: The user will be able to enter a text item and click the Push button to push an item onto the stack. When the user clicks the Pop button, the last-in item is popped off the stack and displayed in a text box. In addition, whenever the Push or Pop button is clicked—which means anytime the stack is changed—the current items on the stack are displayed in an HTML select list.

Figure 6-6 shows the user interface in a Web browser.

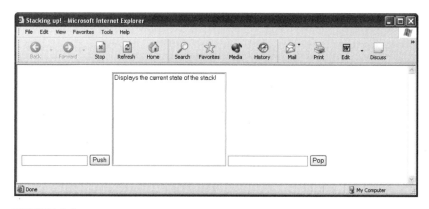

FIGURE 6-6

The HTML page lets you push a text item onto the stack, displays the current state of the stack, and lets you pop the stack.

Using the HTML Form Tags

In case you're wondering, and to get it out of the way, let's look at HTML form tags that create the user interface shown in Figure 6-6. Listing 6-5 shows the HTML for the application.

LISTING 6-5

The HTML for the Stack Application

```
<HTML>
<HEAD>
    <TITLE>Stacking up!</TITLE>
<SCRIPT>
</SCRIPT>
</HEAD>
```

```
<BODY>
<FORM>
<INPUT type=text name=txtPush>
<INPUT type=button value="Push">
<SELECT name="theList" size=12>
<OPTION>Displays the current state of the stack!
</SELECT>
<INPUT type=text name=txtPop size=25>
<INPUT type=button value="Pop">
</FORM>
</BODY>
</HTML>
```

There's no program code in the HTML page shown in Listing 6-5. When code is added to the HTML page, it'll mostly go in the <HEAD> section of the HTML (following the <SCRIPT> tag).

The <FORM> section of the HTML shown in Listing 6-5 creates a text box named txtPush, a Push button, a select list named theList, a text box named txtPop, and a Pop button. You should know that the options array of an HTML select list can be used to populate (and retrieve) the option items associated with the select list. In static HTML, each of these option items can be identified by its <OPTION> tag.

> *The HTML select object is used to display a list of items on the stack.*

With the HTML out of the way, let's move on to pushing an item onto the stack. But first, we need to create the stack.

Pushing the Stack

In the <HEAD> section of the HTML document, create a new Array object named stack:

```
var stack = new Array();
```

 TIP Placing the Array constructor first in the <HEAD> section of the HTML page makes the **stack** array available to any code that comes after it, namely all the code in the HTML page.

Next, write a function, pushStack, that accepts input and pushes it onto the stack using the push method:

```
function pushStack(newVal) {
    stack.push(newVal);
}
```

Finally, in the HTML form, add an onClick event to the Push button that calls the pushStack function, passing the function the value of the txtPush text box:

```
<INPUT type=button value="Push" onClick='pushStack(txtPush.value);'>
```

 TIP This line of HTML and code replaces the original line, `<INPUT type=button value="Push">`.

Now, if you enter a text item in the txtPush text box and click Push, as shown in Figure 6-7, the item will be pushed onto the stack.

It's easy to push items onto the stack!

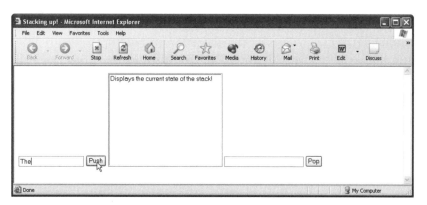

FIGURE 6-7

Enter an item in the leftmost text box and click Push to push it onto the stack.

Displaying the Contents of the Stack

Next, let's write a function, showStack, that displays the contents of the stack in an HTML select list at any given time. Once again, the showStack function should be placed in the <HEAD> section of the document.

Here's the declaration for the showStack function, which assumes that a HTML select object will be passed to it as an argument:

```
function showStack(theSelect){

}
```

Within the function, the first thing to do is to clear the list of options associated with the select list. To do this, set the length property of the select list's options array to zero:

```
theSelect.options.length = 0;
```

Next, create a loop that iterates through the stack array:

```
for (var i = 0; i < stack.length; i++){

}
```

For each item in the stack array, use the new operator to construct a new Option item named theOption that has the value of the stack array item as text:

```
var theOption = new Option(stack[i]);
```

Finally, assign theOption as the value of a new item in the select list's options array. To do this, use as the index value for the options array its length property (theSelect.options.length), which will always be one greater than the highest index value for the array. Here's the statement:

```
theSelect.options[theSelect.options.length] = theOption;
```

I know this seems a little tricky, but it's well worth your while to study it until you get the hang of it. If you understand the showStack function, shown in Listing 6-6, you'll really understand how to work with arrays!

The showStack function is where the rubber meets the road. Can you modify it so that it still works?

LISTING 6-6

Showing the Stack

```
function showStack(theSelect){
    theSelect.options.length = 0;
    for (var i = 0; i < stack.length; i++){
        var theOption = new Option(stack[i]);
        theSelect.options[theSelect.options.length] = theOption;
    }
}
```

Oops! I almost forgot. If we're going to show the contents of the stack every time an item is pushed on it, we need to add code calling the showStack function when a new item is pushed on the stack. This goes in the onClick event of the Push button. Here's the modified Push button onClick event code, which resets the value of the txtPush text box and passes to the showStack function the select list object, using its name theList:

```
<INPUT type=button value="Push" onClick='pushStack(txtPush.value);
    txtPush.value=""; showStack(theList);'>
```

If you open the HTML page as it now stands and push successive items onto the stack, they'll be displayed in the select list, as shown in Figure 6-8.

FIGURE 6-8

The contents of the stack are displayed in the select list.

Popping the Stack

Never pop a stack in haste or anger, only with due deliberation. That said, to pop the stack, we need to add a function, popStack, to the <HEAD> section of the HTML page.

The code for the popStack function assigns to a variable named popVal the return value of the pop method when the function is applied to the stack array.

As you may recall, calling the pop method of an array both pops the stack and returns the popped value.

If popVal is undefined, the text string value *Nothing left on the stack!* is returned. Otherwise, if popVal has been assigned a value, the value is returned.

Listing 6-7 shows the popStack function.

LISTING 6-7
Popping the Stack

```
function popStack() {
    var popVal = stack.pop();
    if (popVal == undefined)
        return "Nothing left on the stack!";
    else
    return popVal;
}
```

To keep the display of the stack synchronized when items are being popped, the onClick event handler for the Pop button needs to both assign the return value from the popStack function to the txtPop text box and also to call the showStack function:

```
<INPUT type=button value="Pop" onClick="txtPop.value = popStack();
    showStack(theList);">
```

 TIP These lines appear in the HTML form and replace the original line `<INPUT type=button value="Pop">`.

The stack program is now complete (and you can find the complete code in Listing 6-8).

If you open the HTML page in a Web browser, push a bunch of items onto the stack, and then click Pop, then the most recently pushed item will be popped off the stack (see Figure 6-9).

FIGURE 6-9

When the user pops an item from the stack by clicking the Pop button, the popped item is displayed in the rightmost text box.

If you keep on popping until the stack is gone, then the txtPop text box will tell you that there's nothing left on the stack (see Figure 6-10).

You can pop, pop, pop until Daddy takes the stack away!

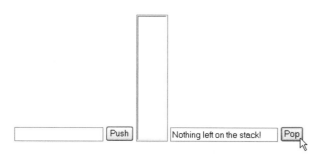

FIGURE 6-10

If you attempt to pop a stack with nothing on it, an appropriate message is displayed.

LISTING 6-8

Pushing, Popping, and Displaying the Contents of a Stack

```
<HTML>
<HEAD>
   <TITLE>Stacking up!</TITLE>
<SCRIPT>
var stack = new Array();
function pushStack(newVal) {
   stack.push(newVal);
}
function popStack() {
   var popVal = stack.pop();
   if (popVal == undefined)
      return "Nothing left on the stack!";
   else
   return popVal;
}
function showStack(theSelect){
   theSelect.options.length = 0;
   for (var i = 0; i < stack.length; i++){
      var theOption = new Option(stack[i]);
      theSelect.options[theSelect.options.length] = theOption;
   }
}
```

```
</SCRIPT>
</HEAD>
<BODY>
<FORM>
<INPUT type=text name=txtPush>
<INPUT type=button value="Push" onClick='pushStack(txtPush.value);
    txtPush.value=""; showStack(theList);'>
<SELECT name="theList" size=12>
<OPTION>Displays the current state of the stack!
</SELECT>
<INPUT type=text name=txtPop size=25>
<INPUT type=button value="Pop" onClick="txtPop.value = popStack();
    showStack(theList);">
</FORM>
</BODY>
</HTML>
```

Understanding Arrays of Arrays

A multidimensional array, sometimes called a *matrix*, lets you process tabular data that has more than one column. For example, suppose you had the table of personal data shown in Table 6-3.

TABLE 6-3

A Two-Dimensional Table of Data (a Matrix)

Name	Height	SSN	Description
Neo	6'	142-1223-689	Doesn't Neo know that life is a dream?
Morpheus	6 '3"		Morpheus? Who is Morpheus?
Trinity	5 '8"		She is a legend.
Mr. Smith	6' 2"		There are many copies of Mr. Smith.

The data in the table shown in Table 6-3 can't easily be stored in a one-dimensional array such as the sort we've used so far in JavaScript. (As you can see, the data in any of the columns in this table could be stored in a one-dimensional JavaScript array.)

Most languages allow you to declare multidimensional arrays. With a two-dimensional array, you would reference the data shown in Table 6-3 with two indices, the first representing the row number and the second representing the column number, as shown in Table 6-4.

TABLE 6-4
. . . .
The Two-Dimensional Table of Data with Index Coordinates

Name	Height	SSN	Description
(0,0) Neo	(0,1) 6'	(0,2) 142-1223-689	(0,3) Doesn't Neo know that life is a dream?
(1,0) Morpheus	(1,1) 6 '3"	(1,2)	(1,3) Morpheus? Who is Morpheus?
(2,0) Trinity	(2,1) 5 '8"	(2,2)	(2,3) She is a legend.
(3,0) Mr. Smith	(3,1) 6' 2"	(3,2)	(3,3) There are many copies of Mr. Smith.

Logically, this table should be represented by a two-dimensional array with four elements in each dimension. Then the data in each cell would be accessible using the index coordinates shown in Table 6-4. For example, if the name of the array were matrix, then the value of matrix[1,3] would be the text string *Morpheus? Who is Morpheus?*

 NOTE The expression matrix[1,3] uses square brackets, the JavaScript array operator, to reference the elements of the array. In many languages, array elements are accessed using normal parentheses, for example, matrix(1,3).

ADVANCED

Unfortunately, we don't have the ability to create two-dimensional arrays in JavaScript. But in many programming situations, we do have the need to easily store and retrieve tabular data that involves two (or more) dimensions (such as the data in the simple table I just showed you). What is the work around?

There's got to be a work around, right? What's the work around, huh?

It's a great thing about programming languages that if you don't have a given facility, there's generally a way to create it or something just about as good.

The answer is to create an array of arrays that's the functional equivalent of a multidimensional array.

Let's see how this works in the context of the two-dimensional array shown in Table 6-4. First, declare a one-dimensional array in the normal JavaScript fashion. For example, if the array is named `matrix`, you could declare a four-element single dimension array as follows:

```
var matrix = new Array(4);
```

Next, declare each of the four elements in the array itself as an array:

```
matrix[0] = new Array(4);
matrix[1] = new Array(4);
matrix[2] = new Array(4);
matrix[3] = new Array(4);
```

We now have the equivalent of a two-dimensional 4×4 array, ready to input the data from Table 6-4.

ADVANCED

NOTE In JavaScript, you don't need to declare the dimensions of the overall array or of the array constituting an element of the overall array. In fact, the arrays making up the elements don't need to be the same length (this is sometimes called a *jagged* array).

As an exercise, can you figure out how to declare and reference the elements of arrays of arrays that are the equivalent of three-dimensional and four-dimensional arrays?

Each of the elements in the array of arrays we've just declared is referenced by using the square bracket array operator twice. For example, to store data in the cell 0,0, we would use a statement like this:

```
matrix[0][0] = "Neo";
```

NOTE This notation differs slightly from what you'd expect as standard notation for a two-dimensional array, which would be `matrix[0,0]`, but it's just as convenient.

Listing 6-9 shows how you would declare the 4×4 two-dimensional array of arrays used to store the data shown in Table 6-4. It also shows how you can use the index values of the element arrays and the overall array to iterate through the arrays, displaying the values of each element:

```
for (var i = 0; i < matrix.length; i++){
    for (var j = 0; j < matrix.length; j++){
        document.write ("Element (" + i + ", " + j + ") is " +
            matrix[i][j] + " -- ");
    }
    document.write("<br>");
}
```

If you open the page shown in Listing 6-9 in a Web browser, you'll see the values contained in each element array displayed on its own line (see Figure 6-11).

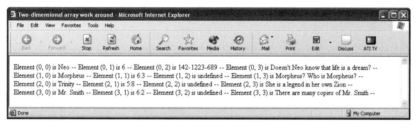

FIGURE 6-11

The values contained in the array of arrays are displayed.

LISTING 6-9

Two-Dimensional Array Work Around

```
<HTML>
<HEAD>
<TITLE>
Two-dimensional array work around
</TITLE>
<HEAD>
    <BODY>
    <SCRIPT>
    var matrix = new Array(4);
    matrix[0] = new Array(4);
    matrix[1] = new Array(4);
```

```
matrix[2] = new Array(4);
matrix[3] = new Array(4);
matrix[0][0] = "Neo";
matrix[0][1] = "6";
matrix[0][2] = "142-1223-689";
matrix[0][3] = "Doesn't Neo know that life is a dream?";
matrix[1][0] = "Morpheus";
matrix[1][1] = "6:3";
matrix[1][3] = "Morpheus? Who is Morpheus?";
matrix[2][0] = "Trinity";
matrix[2][1] = "5:8";
matrix[2][3] = "She is a legend in her own Zion";
matrix[3][0] = "Mr. Smith";
matrix[3][1] = "6:2";
matrix[3][3] = "There are many copies of Mr. Smith";
for (var i = 0; i < matrix.length; i++){
for (var j = 0; j < matrix.length; j++){
    document.write ("Element (" + i + ", " + j + ") is " +
        matrix[i][j] + " -- ");
    }
    document.write("<br>");
  }
</SCRIPT>
</BODY>
</HTML>
```

Using Array Methods

The Array object in JavaScript provides a number of useful built-in methods in addition to the pop and push methods I've already explained in this chapter. These methods make it easy to quickly operate on arrays.

I'm not going to go over all the methods of the Array object here (mostly because they don't necessarily apply to working with arrays in other languages). If you do need to work extensively with arrays in JavaScript, you can get a book specifically intended to help with JavaScript programming and look them up.

But you should have a general sense of how array methods work, so we'll quickly look at the reverse, sort, and concat methods. Rough equivalents to these three Array object methods are available in any modern programming language.

To start with, let's declare and populate a small (four-element) array to use as an example:

```
var theArray = new Array("Neo","Morpheus","Trinity","Mr. Smith");
```

To Reverse the Array:

1. Call the reverse method of the Array object, for example, with this statement:

   ```
   theArray.reverse();
   ```

The array is now reversed as shown in the second line of text in Figure 6-12. Note that the actual elements of the array have been rearranged in reverse order (this is different from returning a copy of the array with its elements reversed).

To Sort the Array:

1. Call the sort method of the Array object, for example, with this statement:

   ```
   theArray.sort();
   ```

The array has now been sorted using a default sort method as shown in the third text line in Figure 6-12. Like the reverse method, the sort method changes the order of the elements in place, this time by sorting them alphabetically (converting numbers to strings as needed).

Note that the default alphabetic sort in JavaScript means—among other things—that all uppercase first letters come before any lowercase first letter. So an array consisting of the elements *Apple, ant, Nancy* would be sorted as *Apple, Nancy, ant*—which may not be what you'd like. I show you how to create custom sorts later in this chapter in the "Making Weird Comparisons" section.

To Concatenate Elements onto an Array:

1. Call the concat method of the Array object with the elements you want to concatenate onto the array. For example, to concatenate two new elements onto theArray, use the following:

```
theArray.concat("Cypher", "Mouse");
```

The fourth line of text in Figure 6-12 shows the Cypher and Mouse elements concatenated to the existing elements of theArray.

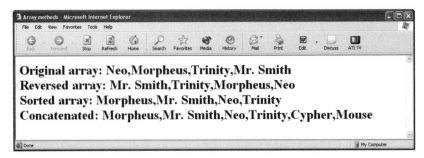

FIGURE 6-12

Reversing, sorting, and concatenating an array

If you open the code shown in Listing 6-10 in your Web browser, you'll see an original array, then the array reversed, sorted, and with the two concatenated elements.

LISTING 6-10

Reversing, Sorting, and Concatenating an Array

```
<HTML>
<HEAD>
<TITLE>
Array methods
</TITLE>
<HEAD>
    <BODY>
    <H1>
    <SCRIPT>
     var theArray = new Array("Neo","Morpheus","Trinity","Mr. Smith");
     document.write ("Original array: " + theArray);
```

```
        document.write ("<br>");
        theArray.reverse();
        document.write ("Reversed array: " + theArray);
        document.write ("<br>");
        theArray.sort();
        document.write ("Sorted array: " + theArray);
        document.write ("<br>");
        document.write("Concatenated: " + theArray.concat("Cypher", "Mouse"));
        </SCRIPT>
        </H1>
        </BODY>
</HTML>
```

Making Weird Comparisons

As I mentioned a little while ago when I described the sort method of the Array object, the default sort is alphabetical, from A to Z and from a to z, meaning that all the uppercase letters come before the lowercase letters. (Numbers come before either uppercase or lowercase letters in the default sort.)

ADVANCED

This default sort may be the wrong sort of sort for you, and it's not at all weird to need a different kind of sort in your array-processing code. Fortunately, this can be achieved by supplying the sort method a custom comparison function. With a custom comparison function, I can sort my way!

The default sort may not be the right sort for you!

Here's how it works: The sort method takes as an optional argument a function that specifies how to do the comparisons for the sort (if one isn't going to accept the default comparison). (For more about how functions work, see Chapter 5, "Understanding Functions.")

By supplying a custom comparison function, I can sort my way!

The function used for the custom comparison must accept two arguments, which represent two elements being compared. If the first argument (element) should appear before the second argument (element) in the sort, then the function needs to return a positive number.

On the other hand, if the first argument should appear after the second in the sorted array, then the function should return a negative number.

 TIP It'll be easiest to wrap your brain around these comparison functions if you think of the process as a kind of game, or puzzle, to figure out!

If the two values are the same in the sort order, then the function should return 0.

Table 6-5 shows these rules for a hypothetical custom sort function that accepts the arguments a and b as representing the elements in an array.

TABLE 6-5

Return Values for a Custom Sort Function That Accepts the Arguments a and b

Sort Evaluation	Function Return
a > b	Positive number, for example, 1
a < b	Negative number, for example, −1
a = b	0

This is really a lot less difficult than it sounds, as you'll see in the context of a couple of practical examples. Coming up with sort functions is a lot of fun if you think of it as a kind of game. That's why I ask you at the end of this section to invent your own sort functions!

Inventing sort functions is useful and fun, too!

Sorting Numerically

The first example I show you will sort the elements of an array in numerical order. This is quite different from alphabetic order in JavaScript. Take the pair of numbers 17, 2 to understand why. Clearly, sorting them numerically would produce 2, 17. But the standard alphabetic sort converts each numeral in 17 to a string, and the first numeral (1) is ahead of 2 in alphabetic order. So the standard sort for the pair stays at 17, 2.

Here's a function that provides the correct returns, as shown in Table 6-5, for a numerical sort:

```
function numSort(a,b){
    return a - b;
}
```

Think about it: If you pass this function the 17, 2 pair, it'll return a positive number (17 – 2 = 15). Returning a positive number means that 17 is greater than 2, so the pair will be correctly ordered 2, 17. You can also easily see that this function would return the correct result (a negative number) if the first argument passed to it were less than the second; for example, the pair 2, 17 would return –15, so the pair would be ordered from smallest number to highest.

Let's use this function in a small program that first populates and displays an array of numbers:

```
var numArray = new Array (59, 4, 63, 12, 17, 3, 2, 1)
document.write ("Original array: " + numArray);
```

Next, let's display the array the way it would be sorted with the default Array.sort method:

```
document.write ("Default Sorted array: " + numArray.sort());
```

The default-sorted array appears as 1,12,17,2,3,4,59,63. Although it's easy to see how this ordering was arrived at (I explained it a little earlier), the ordering could give your program fits and starts if it was expecting a numerically sorted array.

Finally, display the array sorted numerically using our custom function:

```
document.write ("Numerically sorted array: " + numArray.sort(numSort));
```

Sorting numerically is easy and useful, too!

This time the array is correctly sorted from lowest to highest: 1,2,3,4,12,17,59,63.

There, that was easy (and useful, too)! Figure 6-13 shows the display generated by this code, with the complete HTML page that includes the code shown in Listing 6-11.

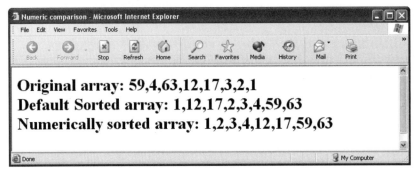

FIGURE 6-13

Default sort comparison and custom numeric comparison

LISTING 6-11

Custom Numeric Comparison for the Array.Sort Method

```
<HTML>
<HEAD>
<TITLE>
Numeric comparisons
</TITLE>
<HEAD>
   <BODY>
   <H1>
   <SCRIPT>
    function numSort(a,b){
       return a - b;
    }
    var numArray = new Array (59, 4, 63, 12, 17, 3, 2, 1)
    document.write ("Original array: " + numArray);
    document.write ("<br>");
    document.write ("Default Sorted array: " + numArray.sort());
    document.write ("<br>");
    document.write ("Numerically sorted array: " +
       numArray.sort(numSort));
   </SCRIPT>
   </H1>
   </BODY>
</HTML>
```

Performing a Case-Insensitive Sort

Suppose you'd like to do a case-insensitive sort. This means that the sort evaluates lowercase and uppercase (capital) letters in the same way. If you compare a big A with little a, they should evaluate as equal. This is very much not the case for the default sort order, in which all the uppercase letters (up to Z) come before the first lowercase letter (a).

Case-insensitive sorting is something that comes up often in the course of programming. It's pretty easy to do using String object methods. However, I don't want to put the cart before the horse.

Working with strings is an important topic for most programmers. It's the subject of entire chapter in this book, Chapter 9, "Working with Strings." There's just enough about it here to show you how to implement the case-insensitive string comparison. If you want to delve more deeply into strings, please turn to Chapter 9.

Let's not put des Carte before the horse!

 NOTE You'll find lots of information about working with strings in Chapter 9, "Working with Strings."

First, let's create, populate, and display a string array:

```
var theArray = new Array("a","Neo","Morpheus","Trinity",
    "Mr. Smith", "N", "n", "A",2);
document.write ("Original array: " + theArray);
```

Next, let's display the array the way it would be sorted with the default Array.sort method:

```
theArray.sort();
document.write ("Default Sorted array: " + theArray);
```

Here's the code that performs the case-insensitive sort using a custom function and displays the results:

```
theArray.sort(function(x,y){
    var a = String(x).toUpperCase();
    var b = String(y).toUpperCase();
    if (a > b)
        return 1
    if (a < b)
        return -1
    return 0;
});
document.write ("Custom sorted array: " + theArray);
```

Figure 6-14 shows the display generated by this code, with the complete HTML page that includes this code shown in Listing 6-12.

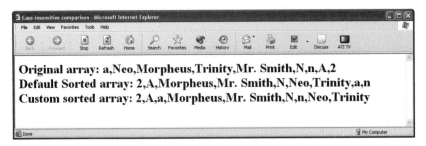

Original array: a,Neo,Morpheus,Trinity,Mr. Smith,N,n,A,2
Default Sorted array: 2,A,Morpheus,Mr. Smith,N,Neo,Trinity,a,n
Custom sorted array: 2,A,a,Morpheus,Mr. Smith,N,n,Neo,Trinity

FIGURE 6-14

Default sort comparison and case-insensitive comparison

A couple of words about the function I just showed you: First, this function is never named and appears in place in code. There's no real need to name it because it's used only once. A function used this way is called a *function literal*, or sometimes a *lambda* function.

Second, if you look at what the function does, it converts each of the two inputs explicitly to the String type using the String function. The String object's toUpperCase method is then used to convert both input strings to all upper case so that a case-insensitive comparison can be performed. Normal string comparison is then used to see which, if either, uppercase string "is greater" than the other, and the appropriate positive, negative, or 0 value is returned.

LISTING 6-12

Case-Insensitive Comparison for the Array.Sort Method

```
<HTML>
<HEAD>
<TITLE>
Case-insensitive comparison
</TITLE>
<HEAD>
   <BODY>
   <H1>
   <SCRIPT>
    var theArray = new Array("a","Neo","Morpheus","Trinity",
      "Mr. Smith", "N", "n", "A",2);
```

```
      document.write ("Original array: " + theArray);
      document.write ("<br>");
      theArray.sort();
      document.write ("Default Sorted array: " + theArray);
      document.write ("<br>");
      theArray.sort(function(x,y){
        var a = String(x).toUpperCase();
        var b = String(y).toUpperCase();
        if (a > b)
          return 1
        if (a < b)
          return -1
        return 0;
      });
      document.write ("Custom sorted array: " + theArray);
    </SCRIPT>
    </H1>
    </BODY>
</HTML>
```

I've shown you two custom sort functions for use with the Array.sort method: sorting numerically and using a case-insensitive string sort. The best way to learn is by doing.

Now that you know how to do weird comparisons, can you create your own interesting custom sort functions?

> *The best way to learn is by doing. If you create your own sort functions, you too can sing "I sorted my way!"*

> *Can you create some other genuinely useful custom array sort functions?*

Using the Form Elements Array

If you're using JavaScript code to enhance the capabilities of HTML pages (or, perhaps to provide the core functionality of the HTML pages), it's good to know that there are a number of useful arrays of HTML objects you can access. This section shows you one of those arrays, the HTML form elements array. Each object in the form elements array is an element of the HTML form with which the array is associated. It's important to understand that arrays are often made up of objects that are more complex than text string or numbers (such as the HTML form elements in this example). In addition, this section serves as a bridge to the next chapter of this book, Chapter 7, "Working with Objects," which begins the discussion of programming with objects in earnest.

*How many
check boxes
can you check
if you could
check check
boxes?*

The point of this example is to see how many check boxes you can check if you could check check boxes. Well, not exactly. Seriously, the point is to show you that you can work with the HTML form elements array in JavaScript, which is an array of objects—and not to do anything terribly important with that array.

As a preparatory step, let's add JavaScript code that adds an HTML form and 100 check boxes to an HTML page, as shown in Listing 6-13.

LISTING 6-13

Adding 100 Check Boxes to an HTML Page

```
document.write("<FORM><CENTER>")
document.write("<font size=6 face='Courier'>");
for (var i = 0; i < 10; ++i) {
    document.write(i);
}
document.write("</font> <br>");
for (var i = 0; i < 10; ++i) {
    document.write("<font size=6 face='Courier'>");
    document.write(i);
    document.write("</font>");
    for (var j = 0; j < 10; ++j) {
        document.write('<INPUT TYPE="checkbox" ');
        document.write('onClick="uClicked(this)">');
    }
    document.write("<BR>");
}
```

WAY COOL

NOTE I'm sneaking in something a little bit new and pretty cool here, namely the HTML for the form is itself written in JavaScript. (All those document.write statements are inserting HTML, not just literal text.) You can use this technique to programmatically vary the HTML written (and used for display).

Each HTML check box element is supplied with an onClick event handler that calls the function uClicked. (Event Chapter 8, "Understanding Events and Event-Driven Programming," explains event-driven programming in detail.) The uClicked function is passed the object that was clicked (the check box) using the this keyword.

The uClicked function itself merely determines if the check box that invoked the function was checked or unchecked and displays an appropriate alert box depending on its state (see Figure 6-15):

```
function uClicked (theBox){
    if (!theBox.checked)
        alert ("You unchecked the box.");
    else
        alert ("You checked the box.");
}
```

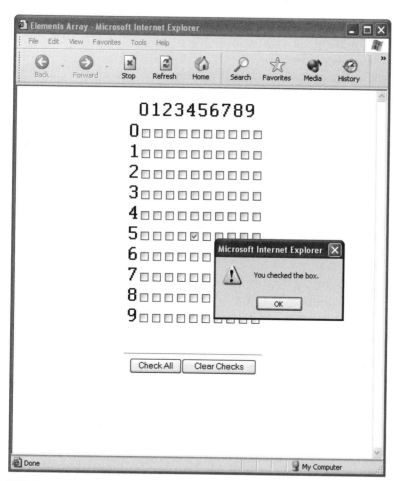

FIGURE 6-15
An alert box shows that the box was checked.

Next, let's add two buttons at the bottom of the form. The Check All button will be used to check all the check boxes that are in the HTML form. The Clear Checks button will clear all the checks. Here are the document.write statements that create the buttons and invoke the checkAll and clearChecks functions, respectively, when clicked:

```
document.write('<INPUT TYPE="button" VALUE="Check All" ');
document.write('onClick="checkAll(this.form)">')
document.write('<INPUT TYPE="button" VALUE="Clear Checks" ');
document.write('onClick="clearChecks(this.form)">')
```

Here's the checkAll function itself, which iterates through the form elements array to check all the check boxes:

```
function checkAll(form){
    for (var i = 0; i < 100; ++i) {
        form.elements[i].checked = true;
    }
}
```

Note that the code in the checkAll function, as well as the code in the clearChecks function, relies on the fact that the 100 elements of the form elements arrays are check boxes (and therefore have a checked property). If you didn't know for sure which kind of element you were dealing with, you'd have to check its type to make sure it had a checked property before trying to set the checked property. I'll show you more about this in Chapter 7, "Working with Objects."

Here's the clearChecks function, which unchecks where checkAll checked but is otherwise the same:

```
function clearChecks(form){
    for (var i = 0; i < 100; ++i) {
        form.elements[i].checked = false;
    }
}
```

Listing 6-14 shows the entire code. If you open it in a Web browser, you can click the Check All button to check all the check boxes (as shown in Figure 6-16).

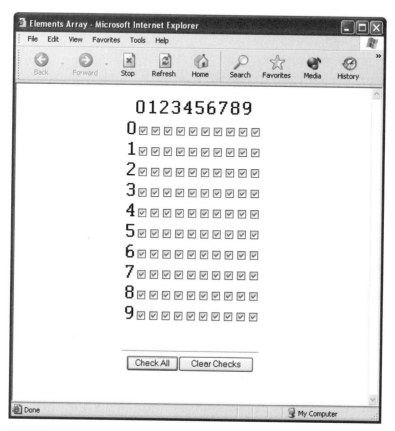

FIGURE 6-16

When the Check All button is clicked, the form elements array is used to check all the check boxes.

Unchecking a check box causes the appropriate message to be displayed (see Figure 6-17).

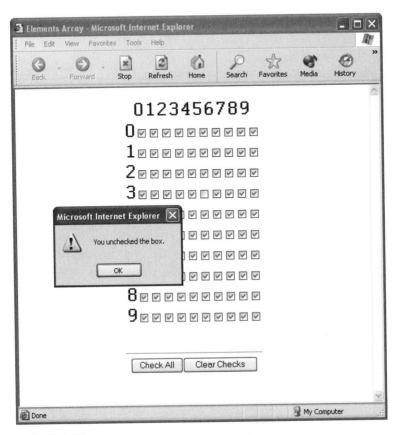

FIGURE 6-17

When the check box is unchecked, an alert box is displayed.

If you click Clear Checks, then all the check boxes are cleared (see Figure 6-18).

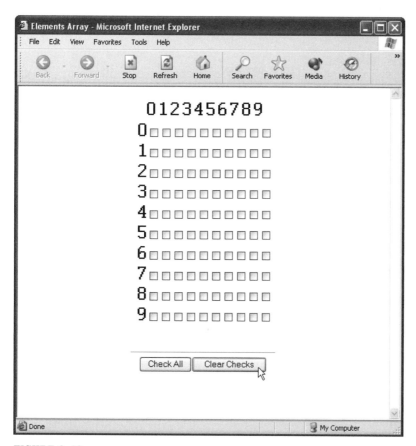

FIGURE 6-18

When the Clear Checks button is clicked, the form elements array is used to uncheck all the check boxes.

LISTING 6-14

Using the HTML Form Elements Array

```
<HTML>
   <HEAD>
   <TITLE>
   Elements Array
   </TITLE>
   </HEAD>
   <BODY>
   <SCRIPT>
   function uClicked (theBox){
      if (!theBox.checked)
         alert ("You unchecked the box.");
      else
         alert ("You checked the box.");
   }
   function clearChecks(form){
      for (var i = 0; i < 100; ++i) {
         form.elements[i].checked = false;
      }
   }
   function checkAll(form){
      for (var i = 0; i < 100; ++i) {
         form.elements[i].checked = true;
      }
   }
   document.write("<FORM><CENTER>")
      document.write("<font size=6 face='Courier'>");
      for (var i = 0; i < 10; ++i) {
         document.write(i);
      }
      document.write("</font> <br>");
   for (var i = 0; i < 10; ++i) {
      document.write("<font size=6 face='Courier'>");
      document.write(i);
      document.write("</font>");
      for (var j = 0; j < 10; ++j) {
         document.write('<INPUT TYPE="checkbox" ');
         document.write('onClick="uClicked(this)">');
      }
      document.write("<BR>");
```

```
        }
        document.write("<BR>");
        document.write("<HR SIZE=1 WIDTH=40%>");
        document.write('<INPUT TYPE="button" VALUE="Check All" ');
        document.write('onClick="checkAll(this.form)">')
        document.write('<INPUT TYPE="button" VALUE="Clear Checks" ');
        document.write('onClick="clearChecks(this.form)">')
        document.write("</CENTER></FORM>")
        </SCRIPT>
        </BODY>
</HTML>
```

What's It All About?

Life is about lists and tables. In programming languages, lists and tables are implemented using arrays.

The JavaScript Array object is a pretty rudimentary implementation of an array (in particular, without work arounds it's only one-dimensional). But you've learned all you need to know to build sophisticated programs with it in this chapter. Better yet, most of the information in this chapter is valid in almost any modern programming language. Naturally, there will be some changes to reflect the specifics of the programming language. But the concepts and techniques you've learned in this chapter will provide a solid starting place for programming in any language.

You should also pat yourself on the back! By the time you've reached this point, your code, and your programming knowledge, has come a long, long way from the humble beginnings in Chapter 1 of this book! I'm proud of you.

It's time to move on to the heart of modern programming. In Chapter 7, "Working with Objects," you'll learn what programmers mean by an *object* and all about how to work with objects.

7

Working with Objects

Objects, objects everywhere: But what are they and how do they work? The move to object-oriented programming—called "OO" or "OOP" when you want to use an acronym—has been one of the most important trends in the programming community over the past 10 or 20 years.

This chapter addresses a number of interrelated topics, each of which is important in its own right.

To start with, what is object-oriented programming? Why is it important? What is an object? How do objects and classes relate?

The focus of this book is about learning how to program and the craft of programming. It's definitely not about the ins and outs of JavaScript. JavaScript is used as a teaching language—because it's good to be able to see the consequences of one's work in action.

That said, it's still worth spending some time understanding how objects work in JavaScript. What are the objects built into JavaScript? How can you effectively use JavaScript objects? (I've called the section of this chapter that explicitly addresses these issues "JavaScript OO Lite.")

It turns out that JavaScript contains some OO features but isn't fully OO in the ways that languages such as C# and Java are. (For one thing, there's no explicit notion of a *class*, or object template, in JavaScript, as I explain in more detail later in this chapter.) However, it also turns out that one can program in a very OO fashion in a not-very-OO language—just as one can skip the OO and bang out straight procedural code in an OO language such as C# or Java. (By the way, I really don't recommend the latter of these practices.)

We'll take the leap with JavaScript and use its features to understand the essential points of object-oriented programming in general and specifically how to implement OO in JavaScript. How do you create and modify your own objects in JavaScript? How are objects best used in your programs?

JavaScript may not have classes, but, as I'll show you, it does have *prototypes*, which are used to manage object inheritance. How does a prototype differ from a class, and why should you care? How can you work with prototypes in JavaScript to get a good feeling for the power of classes and inheritance generally?

By the end of this chapter you'll be speaking, squeaking, dreaming, and rolling in objects—and, most important, you'll have learned to think like an object-oriented programmer.

Understanding Object-Oriented Programming

Let's start with the simple question "What is an object?" The easiest answer is that an *object* is simply an aggregation of values. Here I don't mean to use *aggregation* as a highly technical term. In this context it means no more and no less than "a bunch of." So, the simple answer is that an object is just a bunch of values.

 NOTE As you'll see later in this chapter, you implement objects in JavaScript using functions.

Don't Feel Overwhelmed!

This chapter contains a lot of information, and it may seem like a lot to chew. But don't worry—you can do it! Just take the chapter in small segments, digesting the theory of OO as you go. After you've worked your way through the theories and examples, I guarantee you'll have a good grasp of OO. Of course, if you're the kind of learner who prefers concrete examples, feel free to skip to the examples later in this chapter (the examples start with the "JavaScript OO Lite" section). Then you can refer back to the OO theory as needed. Whatever works for you!

Properties

Values associated with an object can just work like values associated with a variable, in which case the value is called a *property* of the object. For example, if you have a rectangle object, it might have height and width properties, each having numeric values.

The dot operator, which is a period (.), is used to show the relationship between an object and its values. You've already seen quite a few examples involving the dot operator in the earlier chapters of this book, so you probably are pretty familiar with it by now.

For example, taking the rectangle.width property I mentioned a moment ago, this statement:

```
rectangle.width = 75;
```

assigns the value 75 to the width property of the rectangle object. The following statement:

```
var theNum = rectangle.height;
```

retrieves the value stored in the rectangle.height property and assigns it to the variable theNum.

This simple example shows you one of the advantages of working with objects: An object serves to group conceptually related values. Conceptual grouping such as this leads to the ability to create modular programs that are easy to understand, debug, and maintain.

 NOTE So far, we've been looking at objects from the viewpoint of the programmer who is an object user rather than from the viewpoint of the programmer who is an object creator. From the viewpoint of an object creator, there's a technical difference between object fields, which are implemented exactly as you would implement a variable storing a value, and object properties, which are implemented using special property functions. To expand on this a little, an object field is simply a variable associated with an object, whereas an object property consists of a variable and special access functions used to read and write the variable.

ADVANCED

Methods

The values associated with an object can also be functions. (For more about functions, see Chapter 5, "Understanding Functions.") A function associated with an object is called a *method*. Another way of putting this is to say that object methods are implemented using functions.

The methods of an object do something. There's no absolute technical requirement that the *something* the method does be related to the object or use the property values related to the object. But most of the time, methods perform tasks that you'd expect to be related to an object.

Because methods do something, it's good practice to name them to show what they do. This means that a method should be named using a grammatical verb and a grammatical object that show the action and what's acted on. For example, taking the rectangle object, a good name for a method that calculates the area of the rectangle, using the height and width properties of the rectangle object, might be calcArea.

Events

You should also know that the values of an object can also include other objects and specialized functions called *events*. When an object causes, or *fires*, an event, code placed in an *event handler* procedure is processed. You've seen numerous examples of this already in this book, for example, the code placed in an onClick event handler that's executed when the user clicks a button. Events are important enough to have a chapter to themselves—Chapter 8, "Understanding Events and Event-Driven Programming." Because this book is primarily about learning the craft of programming, I haven't gone into great detail about the specific event handlers that are available in JavaScript when working with a document loaded in a Web browser. You'll find much more information about these events in Chapter 8.

Members

Collectively, the fields, properties, methods, and events of an object are called the object's *members*.

Classes and Objects

Let's sit back for a moment and consider the concept of a class and how it relates to objects. It's likely you've heard the term *class* before (and I don't mean something you attend, snooze through, and try for a good grade!). A class is a blueprint for an object. It's a central concept in object-oriented programming.

> A class is a blueprint for an object.

There are a number of metaphors used to say the same thing, but it may be helpful to repeat some of them. A class is a blueprint, and the object is a building built from it. A class is a cookie cutter, and the object is the cookie. Yum!

> A class is a cookie cutter; the object is a cookie.

When all is said and done, this boils down to the notion that you can roll out many objects based on one class. The objects have in common prebuilt characteristics, such as the properties and methods supplied by the class (the blueprint). One advantage of this is that you don't need to re-create these properties and methods each time—because they're specified in the blueprint (the class).

An object that's based on a class is called an *instance* of the class. When one creates a new object, one is said to *instantiate* the object.

> An object that's based on a class is called an instance of the class.

Constructors

When you create a new instance of an object, as you might suspect, you're actually calling a function. This kind of specialized function, whose job is to create and initialize new object instances, is called a *constructor*. (Perhaps this goes along with the blueprint metaphor: You need a constructor to actually build the house.)

At this point, the picture you should have in your head is of a number of objects based on a class. These objects all have the same properties and methods although of course the value of these properties and the action of these methods are different for the different instances of the objects.

Now let's run through some other concepts related to OO programming.

> The function used to create a new instance of an object is called a constructor.

Shared Members

There's a significant distinction to be made between instance members of a class and *shared* members of the class. Instance members are associated with an object created from a class. To use an instance member, you must first instantiate an object. The values of the members of different instantiated objects (even though they're based on the same class) will differ.

In contrast, shared members of a class don't require object instantiation for access. These values are called *shared* because they can be shared by all objects in a program and are associated with a class rather than objects based on a class. For example, in JavaScript, the Math.random method, used in the Rocks, Scissors, and Paper program example in Chapter 3, "Using Conditional Statements," doesn't require the creation of a Math object. You just use the expression Math.random() in a statement.

Inheritance

It's likely that the single most important concept in OO is *inheritance*. This is a concept that's intuitively easy to grasp. When one class inherits from another class, it "gets" all the members of the class from which it inherits. In other words, all the code associated with the original class is now part of the inheriting class.

It's easy to see why inheritance is powerful. Once you've created your original class, you can, in a single statement, give all its functionality to the classes that inherit from it, which may then extend this functionality with their own capabilities.

> *The single most important concept in OO is inheritance.*

You should also know some vocabulary that's sometimes used with inheritance. When a class inherits from another class, the inheriting class is said to be a *subclass* of the class from which it inherits. The original class is said to be a *superclass* of its subclass. *Subclass* is sometimes also used as a verb, as in "I've subclassed the Widget class by creating a RotaryWidget class that inherits from it." (In this example, the Widget class is a superclass of the RotaryWidget class.)

> *"I've subclassed the Widget class by creating a RotaryWidget class that inherits from it."*

As we'll discuss in detail later in this chapter, in JavaScript you don't really have classes; instead, you have prototypes, which for the most part you can think of as classes. So, somewhat more generally, whether the language you're using implements classes or prototypes, one can look at inheritance as the practice of organizing objects into a hierarchy in which objects are categorized according to their common characteristics and purpose. This practice makes programming easier and more intuitive because you can easily find objects based on their classification in the hierarchy. You can also create new *child* objects that inherit the prebuilt characteristics of their *parent*.

In everyday life, you deal with a great many objects (for example, this book). Sometimes your things are messy, which isn't fun and makes it hard to find things. Disorganized code is a huge problem, and organizing your programs using objects and object hierarchies helps to produce "neatnik" programs that have great clarity.

Class Interfaces

A class *interface* is a kind of contract for classes. The interface specifies the members (properties, methods, and so on) that a compliant class must have. A class is said to implement an interface when each of the members specified in the interface is present in the class. Generally, if you add code that states that a class implements an interface and then don't include the members required by the interface, you'll get a syntax error when you attempt to compile (or run) the code.

Class interfaces are important in multideveloper team projects to help create uniform class designs. They're also useful in helping to pinpoint the crucial points of a class. For example, classes that do comparisons might be required to implement a Comparison interface. The Comparison interface might specify a compareTo method, which provides a way to compare, and order, two objects based on the class. So, any class that implements the Comparison interface would have to provide a compareTo method, which would compare any two objects based on the class.

OO and Modeling

Sure, programming in an object-oriented fashion encourages code that's modular and reusable (and I'll have more to tell you about this in a bit). But for me, the great virtue of OO is that it allows programmers to build systems that closely model the real world. In these systems, if the classes— blueprints for the objects in the systems—have been designed correctly, then programs that unleash these objects will have great power. In fact, one can use OO systems of this sort to create programs that have a virtual life of their own.

This makes OO particularly effective for dealing with situations that involve complex interactions and when you don't really know how things will turn out. Examples include modeling financial markets and forecasting weather. One interesting (and highly OO) program that I've written used ideas found in Jared Diamond's Pulitzer Prize–winning book *Guns, Germs, and Steel* (W. W. Norton & Company, 1999) to model the progress of human cultures. As you might suppose, each culture was implemented as an object based on a class that represented a template for human societies. The program, written in C#, tracked the progress of each culture over time and

You can use OO to create systems that have a virtual life of their own!

showed the results of culture clashes, such as the one between the Spanish and the Incas discussed in Professor Diamond's book (see Figure 7-1).

This was a reasonably easy program to write once I became clear about the classes, objects, and relationships involved—and it would, I believe, have been close to impossible to write in a non-OO fashion.

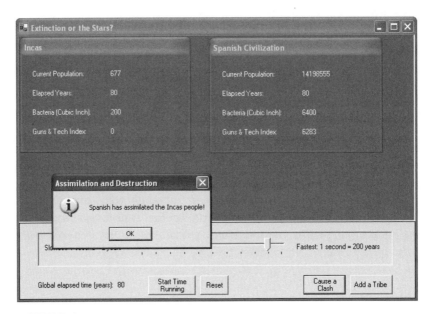

FIGURE 7-1

Each human society is implemented as an object using a general class as a template.

Key OO Concepts

The following are some of the most important concepts related to the practice of object-oriented programming:

Abstraction: *Abstraction* means filtering out the extraneous properties and attributes of objects so that users of the object can focus on the core properties that matter. Good OO practice encourages the appropriate use of abstraction.

Aggregation: *Aggregation* means the ability to create an object that's a composite of other objects by extending or combining existing objects. Aggregation, sometimes also called *containment*, is a powerful way to model real-life processes and to simplify coding.

Encapsulation: *Encapsulation* is the process of hiding (or *encapsulating*) the data used by an object and granting access to it only through specific interactions with the object. This grouping of related attributes and methods is used to create a cohesive entity that's opaque to the outside except for the specified access methods.

There are lots of real-life analogies to encapsulation. Think, for example, about requests for information from the president of the United States. If all requests for information from the president must be directed to the Press Office, then the Press Office is practicing encapsulation.

Controlling access via encapsulation is a good way to create maintainable code that has fewer bugs.

Polymorphism: From an OO viewpoint, *polymorphism* means the ability of two different objects to respond to the same request in their own unique ways. For example, a print text message might cause a printer object to print the text. The same message, when received by a screen object, might cause the text to be displayed on the screen.

Oh, No, an OO Mini-Review

When I was in college, I took an advanced mathematics class with a pretty peculiar rule for the final exam. Each student was allowed to bring in an 8½×11 sheet of paper to the final with whatever notes on it they'd like (otherwise, the final was "closed book"). Yes, in case you're curious, you could write on both sides of the sheet of paper!

I thought the concept was pretty bogus, but who was I to buck the system? I got a pen with the finest tip I could find and filled both sides of my sheet of paper with what I thought would be the answers to the questions on the final.

I don't really remember how much my "cheat sheet" matched what was on the final, but I do know that I learned a great deal by creating the cheat sheet. The teacher was actually pretty smart!

In that spirit, because I've thrown a great deal of OO theory at you in this section, I'd like to provide summary definitions of the key concepts as if there were going to be a final exam.

My suggestion to you is that at this point you shut this book and create your own OO cheat sheet. See how many OO concepts you can define. After you've spent 5 or 10 minutes thinking about this, you can, of course, open the book and look at my answers!

TRY THIS
AT HOME

Here's the OO cheat sheet:

A **class** is a template, or pattern, for objects.

An **object** is an aggregation of values.

To use an object, it first must be instantiated, which means that an **instance** of the object must be created and initialized using the **constructor** provided by the class.

Once you have an instance of an object, you can use the **properties**, **methods**, and **events** that the object provides.

A **property** is used to save and retrieve a value, just as variables are.

A **method** is used to do something, just as a function is used to do something.

An **event** is a special kind of function that's triggered, or **fired,** in response to a specific condition, such as a button being clicked. An **event handler** is a placeholder that gives you a chance to execute code when the event is fired.

The key benefits of object-oriented programming include clarity, reusability, and modularity. OO techniques are particularly helpful in situations that involve complex systems that may mimic real-life processes.

These benefits are partially obtained through **abstraction**, which helps the programmer to focus on object characteristics that matter and to filter out unimportant details; **encapsulation**, which hides internal object data and only allows gated access to objects; and **polymorphism**, which lets different objects implement the same task but each in their own way.

See how many OO concepts you can define.

JavaScript OO Lite

Let's turn from OO theory to OO as it's practiced in JavaScript.

The creator of JavaScript, Brendan Eich, who worked for a company then known as *Netscape Communications* at the time he gave birth to JavaScript in 1995, has written "JavaScript was born out of a desire to let HTML authors write scripts directly in their documents."

JavaScript has come to be used in some unanticipated ways—for example, as a server-side scripting language (a programming language processed on a server and not in a client such as a browser) and to create stand-alone programs. But the original primary purpose—and thing the language does best—was to work with objects, and object members, exposed by a document in a Web browser. (JavaScript is also very capable as a scripting language for gluing together *applets,* or stand-alone programs, created in Java, once again by using the objects and object members exposed by the applets.)

This brings to our attention the two faces of Eve, oops, I mean OO. OO can be used to create objects. But a language such as JavaScript that may not be world class in its ability to create objects (as Java, for example, is) may be very strong in its ability to manipulate objects created by others. This kind of object manipulation, the other face of OO, is extremely important and can be viewed as "OO lite."

Our discussion of OO and JavaScript will start by showing you how to use object-oriented programming to manipulate HTML documents in a Web browser. You've already seen many examples of this presented in an ad-hoc fashion in the earlier chapters of this book, but this chapter presents this material, which you can think of as "client-side OO," in a more orderly way.

> *The original and primary purpose of JavaScript was to work with objects exposed by a document in the browser.*

The Dot Operator

We've already talked about the dot operator (.), and you've seen many examples of its use throughout this book. But let's talk again explicitly about its role in JavaScript.

In JavaScript, the dot operator is used in three ways. First, it's the glue that allows you to refer to *sub-objects* in the object hierarchy. For example:

```
window.document
```

refers to the document sub-object of the window object.

The JavaScript window object, window, is at the top of the client-side object hierarchy of documents in a browser, as I'll explain in a little bit. It can be omitted without consequences, so this:

```
window.document
```

can also be written just as this:

```
document
```

But when you write *document*, what you really mean is window.document, and the dot operator is used to glue together a parent object (window) with its child (document). This can get even more hierarchic. For example, the following expression:

```
window.document.theForm.theButton
```

could be used to refer to an HTML button named theButton, itself part of a form named theForm, in the HTML document currently loaded in the browser.

The dot operator is also used to access object property values. For example, to assign the value of the length property of a String object to a variable, you could use the dot operator as follows:

```
var strLen = theString.length;
```

Finally, the dot operator is used to invoke object methods. For example, in this book I've used the write method of the document object to display text, like so:

```
window.document.write("Make it so!");
```

or, more often, abbreviated with the window object implied:

```
document.write("I did it my way!");
```

In short, without the dot operator, there would be no way to work with objects in JavaScript!

JavaScript Properties

As you know by now, a property is a setting that describes something about an object. (This is a slightly different way of looking at the fact, which we've discussed, that an object property contains data, just like a variable.) Some properties are read-only, meaning you can access the value the property contains but not modify that value. It's less common but not impossible to have a property that's write-only, meaning you can set its value but not retrieve the value. Still other properties are read-write, meaning you can set them and retrieve them.

The following is an example of using the read-only length property of the String object that's built into JavaScript to display the number of characters in the string (spaces do count as characters).

To Read and Display the Length Property:

1. Use the constructor of the JavaScript String object to create a new variable of type String:

```
var theString = new String();
```

2. Use the window.prompt method to get a string from the user (see Figure 7-2):

```
var theString = prompt("Enter a string: ","");
```

3. Use the string.length property of the string to display the number of characters in the string (see Figure 7-3):

```
document.write('The string "' + theString +  '" is ' +
    theString.length + ' characters long.');
```

See Listing 7-1 for the complete code for displaying the length of a string.

FIGURE 7-2

The user enters a string in a prompt box.

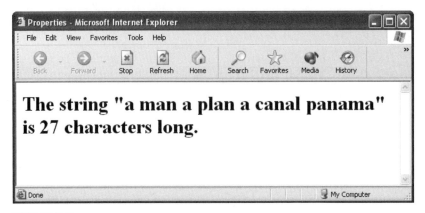

FIGURE 7-3

The length of the string the user entered is displayed.

The window.location property contains the Uniform Resource Locator (URL) of the current location of the HTML document loaded in the browser. Assigning a URL to the property causes the browser to go to that location. Let's put this into action to move the current browser to a specific location.

To Set the Location Property (and Move the Browser to a Specific URL):

1. Use the window.confirm method to allow the user to confirm that they really want to go to the new location (see Figure 7-4):

```
window.confirm("Do you want to go to Apress today?")
```

2. Embed the confirmation method within a conditional statement that places the new location value in the location property:

```
if (window.confirm("Do you want to go to Apress today?"))
    window.location = "http://www.apress.com";
```

When the user clicks OK, the browser will open the specified URL (see Figure 7-5). See Listing 7-1 for the complete code for displaying the length of a string.

FIGURE 7-4

The user is asked to confirm the URL.

FIGURE 7-5

The document.location property is set to open the URL.

 NOTE The confirm method evaluates to `true` if the user clicks OK and `false` if the user clicks Cancel.

It's important to understand that properties, such as location, can be objects in their own right as well as properties. You should also know that there's an alternative way to reference object properties. You can use the object's properties array and refer to a specific property by index number or name. Instead of this:

```
window.location
```

you can write this:

```
window["location"]
```

Furthermore, you could refer to the location property by index number if you knew the index value for the location property in the window array. We'll further discuss the issue of the correspondence in JavaScript between arrays and objects later in this chapter.

LISTING 7-1

Using the String Object's Length and the Document.Location Properties

```
<HTML>
<HEAD>
   <TITLE>Properties</TITLE>
</HEAD>
<BODY>
<H1>
   <SCRIPT>
   var theString = new String();
   theString = prompt("Enter a string: ","");
   document.write('The string "' + theString +  '" is ' +
      theString.length + ' characters long.');
   if (window.confirm("Do you want to go to Apress today?"))
     window.location = "http://www.apress.com";
     </SCRIPT>
</H1>
</BODY>
</HTML>
```

Methods

Methods operate on or with an object to do something. As you've already seen, methods are implemented as functions, and you can pretty much think of them as functions. This means that you can recognize object methods because they're always followed by parentheses, with or without enclosed parameters.

For example, the window.close() method will close the current browser window. Let's see how this works!

To Close the Browser Using the window.close() Method:

1. Use the confirm method to create a condition that checks to make sure the user wants to close the browser window:

```
window.confirm("Do you want to close the browser?")
```

2. Create a conditional statement that embeds the confirm condition and invokes the close method if the condition is true:

```
if (window.confirm("Do you want to close the browser?"))
    window.close();
```

3. Save the code and open it in a browser. The user will be prompted for confirmation (see Figure 7-6). If the user clicks OK, the browser window will shut. Listing 7-2 shows an HTML page that uses this code to close a window just as it opens.

 NOTE Note that in some browsers, depending on your security settings, you may see a second prompt box, asking if you really want to close the browser.

FIGURE 7-6

The window.close() method is used to close the browser window following a confirmation from the user.

LISTING 7-2

Using the window.close() Method to Close a Browser Window

```
<HTML>
<HEAD>
    <TITLE>Methods</TITLE>
</HEAD>
<BODY>
<H1>
I'm not even fully opened yet!
    <SCRIPT>
    if (window.confirm("Do you want to close the browser?"))
      window.close();
    </SCRIPT>
</H1>
</BODY>
</HTML>
```

 CAUTION For security reasons, some browsers will not allow JavaScript code to close a window it hasn't opened. If you find that the code shown in Listing 7-2 doesn't close the window, you're probably running a browser such as Mozilla that doesn't allow JavaScript code to shut a window. As an exercise, why not modify the code shown in Listing 7-2 to first open a window and then close it? (This will work because the code is closing a window it has opened.)

Events

In JavaScript, code that handles events fired in an HTML page that's loaded in the browser is assigned to the event handler function within the HTML element that fires the event. For example, code that responds to a button click event is assigned to the onClick event handler with the HTML <input type=button> form tag that creates the button. (As I've mentioned, Chapter 8, "Understanding Events and Event-Driven Programming," discusses event-driven programming in much greater detail.)

 NOTE Note that the event handler functions for HTML events are case sensitive. The event handler is named *onClick*, not *onclick* or *Onclick*. If you assign code to an onclick event, it will never get fired.

Because we've already seen many examples in this book that use an onClick event handler, let's take a quick look at another event, the onMouseOver event.

Some HTML elements, including links (represented by the <A> tag) and images (denoted by an <IMG> tag), fire an onMouseOver event when the user passes the mouse over a hyperlink.

JavaScript code assigned to the onMouseOver handler function in the tag will be executed when the event is fired.

Let's take as a really simple example a Web page that just doesn't want to let go. This is one really codependent piece of HTML!

Joking aside, the actual functionality—or more aptly, dysfunctionality—is to change the URL pointed to by the link when the mouse passes over the link. (As you'd expect from a snippet of dysfunctional code, the URL is changed to something that isn't a valid destination.) The URL is changed by setting the href property of the link object.

To Change the href Property of a Link in the Link's onMouseOver Event:

1. In an HTML document, create a link with a valid HREF attribute:

   ```
   <A HREF="http://www.apress.com" > Please do not leave me!</A>
   ```

2. Within the link tag, add an onMouseOver event handler:

   ```
   <A HREF="http://www.apress.com"  onMouseOver= >
   Please do not leave me!</A>
   ```

3. Assign code within quotes to the onMouseOver event that changes the value of the link object's href property:

```
<A HREF="http://www.apress.com"
    onMouseOver='this.href="I cannot let you go.";'>
    Please do not leave me!</A>
```

The code for the codependent link is shown in a codependent HTML page in Listing 7-3. If you open this page in a Web browser and hover the mouse over the hyperlink (as shown in Figure 7-7), the actual URL the link points to changes from a valid Internet destination (`http://www.apress.com`) to something that can't be opened in a browser ("I cannot let you go."), as you can see in the status bar in Figure 7-7.

FIGURE 7-7
The value of the HREF attribute (the URL that the link points to) changes when the onMouseOver event is fired.

LISTING 7-3
Codependent Link Tag and the onMouseOver Event

```
<HTML>
<HEAD>
    <TITLE>onMouseOver Event</TITLE>
</HEAD>
<BODY>
<H1>
<A HREF="http://www.apress.com" onMouseOver='this.href="I cannot let you
go.";'>
```

```
    Please do not leave me!</A>
</H1>
</BODY>
</HTML>
```

 TIP You can put as many JavaScript statements as you'd like in the event handler, provided the statements are separated by semicolons. If you have more than one or two statements, you should put them in a function and simply call the function from the event handler.

The HTML Document Object Hierarchy

HTML documents that are loaded in a Web browser expose an object hierarchy that can be manipulated using JavaScript programs. The objects in this hierarchy are connected to each other by parent-child relationships. This isn't saying anything more than the child object is accessible as a property of the parent object. For example, you'd use the expression `window.document.theForm` to reference a form named `theForm` in a loaded HTML document.

Sibling objects are all properties of the same parent and populate the array of properties of the parent object.

The document object and its children are used to manipulate elements of a document. In contrast, the window object (and some of its children other than the document object) is used to manipulate the window and frame of the document, in other words, the context of the document in the browser.

The first-level "children" of the window object are as follows:

- **navigator**: The navigator object contains properties that tell you about the browser in use.

- **frames[ ]**: The frames property is an array of references to window objects, one for each HTML frame included in the parent window.

- **location**: This is the location object for the window, which stores its URL.

- **history**: The history object stores the URLs the browser has visited.

- **document**: The document object and its child objects are used to work with the document displayed in a browser window. Children of the document object include HTML forms and controls such as buttons.

Sometimes the objects representing an HTML page exposed to JavaScript can feel like a soap opera with a complex plot (perhaps *All My Children* starring the document object). Actually, the issues are pretty simple from the developer's viewpoint: understanding what tools are available in each circumstance.

The Window Object

The window object is the "mother" of all HTML document objects, meaning it's the parent (or ancestor) of all built-in objects that can be manipulated using client-side JavaScript. As I've mentioned before, because the window object is at the top of the hierarchy, it can be referenced implicitly:

```
document
```

which is the same as writing this:

```
window.document
```

Similarly, you don't need to type the following:

```
window.onFocus
```

because onFocus refers implicitly to the window object. You can just use the expression onFocus.

Essentially, the window object serves two roles:

- It's the top of the object hierarchy of a document loaded in a Web browser via the window.document object and its children

- It's used to control the browser window and frames (through the frames array).

The JavaScript for/in statement can be used to iterate through the properties array associated with any object, sometimes called the object's *associative* array. (Chapter 4, "Working with Loops," explained this variant of the for statement for use with objects.)

NOTE JavaScript as a programming language has a Global object that provides properties, provides members, and tracks global variables (those available to all functions in a program). When a JavaScript program is seated on an HTML page and executed in a Web browser, the Global object and the window object are the same thing. (JavaScript programs executing outside a Web browser most likely don't have a window object, but they do have a Global object.)

ADVANCED

The following shows how to use the for/in statement to cycle through and display all the properties of the window object.

To Display All the Properties of the Window Object:

1. Create the framework for a for/in statement using an index variable to cycle through the object properties:

```
for (var i in window) {

}
```

2. Add code that displays each property name (expressed using the index variable, i) and the value of the property (expressed using the properties array of the object, window[i]):

```
for (var i in window) {
    document.write ("Window property(" + i +  "): " +
        window[i] + "<br>");
}
```

3. Save and run the page containing the code (see Listing 7-4). The window object's properties—and the values of the properties that are primitive JavaScript types—will be displayed as shown in Figure 7-8.

TIP You don't have any way to know in which order the `for/in` statement will go through the object's associative array.

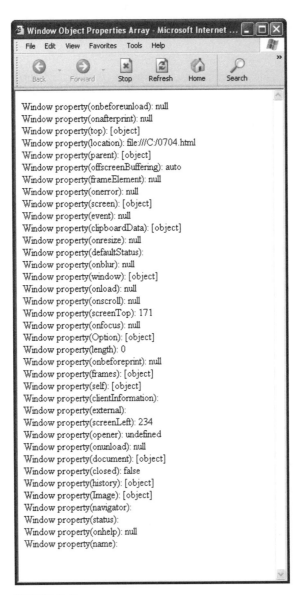

FIGURE 7-8

The associative array of the properties of the window object is displayed.

LISTING 7-4

Displaying the Associative Properties Area of a Window Object

```
<HTML>
<HEAD>
   <TITLE>Window Object Properties Array</TITLE>
</HEAD>
<BODY>
<SCRIPT>
for (var i in window) {
  document.write ("Window property(" + i +  "): " +
     window[i] + "<BR>");
}
</SCRIPT>
</BODY>
</HTML>
```

If you look through the properties and values shown in Figure 7-8, you'll see that many of the values are shown as objects, like this: [option]. This is an opaque and not terrifically useful representation, but at least you know that the property exists in the associative array and that it's an object as opposed to a primitive type such as a number or text string.

By the way, it's interesting to watch some of the values shown in Figure 7-8 change. For example, if you move and resize the Web browser, then refresh the document shown in Listing 7-4, both the screenLeft and screenTop values will change (because these represent the current location of the browser window in reference to the screen).

 TIP In Mozilla, as opposed to Internet Explorer, the screenLeft property is known as screenX, and screenTop is screenY.

Displaying an Object's Associative Array

It's easy to generalize the code shown in Listing 7-4 and come up with a general function that displays an object's associative array. Listing 7-5 shows you how you could write this function.

LISTING 7-5

A General Function for Displaying an Object's Associative Array

```
function showProperties (theObject){
    for (var i in theObject) {
        if (theObject[i] != null) {
            document.write(i + " : " + theObject[i] + "<br>");
        }
        else {
            document.write(i + "<br>");
        }
    }
    return;
}
```

If you place the showProperties function shown in Listing 7-5 in the
<HEAD> section of an HTML page and call it with the navigator object as
shown in Listing 7-6, you'll get a display like that shown in Figure 7-9.

LISTING 7-6

Displaying the Navigator's Associative Array

```
<HTML>
<HEAD>
    <TITLE>Associative object arrays</TITLE>
<SCRIPT>
function showProperties (theObject){
    for (i in theObject) {
        if (theObject[i] != null) {
            document.write(i + " : " + theObject[i] + "<br>");

        }
        else {
            document.write(i + "<br>");
        }
    }
    return;
}
</SCRIPT>
</HEAD>
<BODY>
<SCRIPT>
showProperties(window.navigator);
// showProperties(window.document);
</SCRIPT>
</HTML>
```

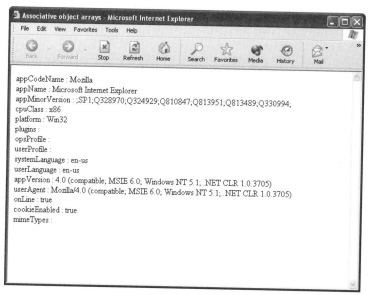

FIGURE 7-9

The navigator object associative array

TIP The navigator object is important if you're writing Web applications that must run on different browsers and operating systems. In that case, your code will likely need to inspect the navigator object's properties and branch conditionally depending on the values of the navigator's properties.

It's easy to view the document object's associative array instead of that belonging to the navigator object. In the code shown in Listing 7-6, simply replace the following statement:

```
showProperties(window.navigator);
```

with this statement:

```
showProperties(window.document);
```

When you open the HTML page in a Web browser, the properties of the document object will now be displayed (see Figure 7-10).

The showProperties function is written in a general enough way that it can be used to show the contents of the associative properties array of custom objects that you create (in addition to the arrays associated with the objects in the window object hierarchy). I show you how to do this later in this chapter after I show you how to create your own custom objects.

namespaces : [object]
lastModified : 05/03/2003 12:23:46
parentNode
nodeType : 9
fileCreatedDate : 05/02/2003
onbeforeeditfocus
bgColor : #ffffff
oncontextmenu
onrowexit
embeds : [object]
scripts : [object]
onactivate
mimeType : HTML Document
alinkColor : #0000ff
onmousemove
onselectstart
oncontrolselect
body : [object]
protocol : File Protocol
onkeypress
onrowenter
onmousedown
vlinkColor : #800080
URL : file://C:\Documents%20and%20Settings\Harold%20Davis\My%
20Documents\APress\Learn%20How%20to%20Program\Programs\0705.html
onreadystatechange
doctype
onbeforedeactivate
applets : [object]
fileModifiedDate : 05/03/2003
onmouseover
dir :
media :
defaultCharset : windows-1252
firstChild : [object]
plugins : [object]
onafterupdate
ondragstart

FIGURE 7-10

The document object associative array (shown partially)

Predefined JavaScript Objects

Now that we've had a good look at programming the objects exposed by the document object, let's have a look at the objects defined within the JavaScript programming language. These are pretty different from the objects exposed *to* JavaScript when a document is loaded in a Web browser.

JavaScript provides a number of built-in object types. Table 7-1 briefly describes the built-in objects that are standard across most JavaScript implementations. Of course, you're already familiar with some of them, such as the Array and Number objects. You should also know that, in keeping with its informal style, in JavaScript you create an object simply by using a value of the type of the object—for example, using a number creates a Number object. However, if you prefer, you can explicitly create objects based on the built-in object types using the constructor for the object. For example:

> *JavaScript the Programming Language has its own objects to play with!*

```
var theNum = new Number(42);
```

TABLE 7-1

Built-in JavaScript Object Types

Object	Description
Array	Used to work with arrays and to create new Array objects, as explained in Chapter 6, "Programming with Arrays."
Boolean	Used to work with Boolean (or logical) objects and to create new Boolean objects.
Date	Manipulates dates and times. Date() can be called as a function without the new operator, in which case it behaves in the same way as a Date object.
Error	Used to work with errors and exceptions and to create new Error objects, as explained in Chapter 10, "Error Handling and Debugging."
Function	Used to work with functions and to create new Function objects, as explained in Chapter 5, "Understanding Functions."
Global	The Global object contains built-in JavaScript methods and provides a context for global variables (those available to all code in a given application). When JavaScript is being executed in a document in a Web browser, the Global object is the window object described in "The Window Object" a little earlier in this chapter.
Math	The Math object contains constants and functions for performing mathematical operations. Note that the Math object can't be instantiated (another way of saying that you can't create objects based upon the Math object) and functions as a shared class.
Number	Used to work with numbers and to create new Number objects.
Object	Provides common functionality for all JavaScript objects; see "The Object Object."
RegExp	Used to work with, and to create, RegExp, or *regular expression* objects, which are used to match patterns and are explained in Chapter 9, "Manipulating Strings."
String	Used to work with strings and to create new String objects. Working with strings is examined in Chapter 9, "Manipulating Strings."

No, the Object
object isn't the
root of all evil!
It's the root of
all objects in
JavaScript.

DO IT RIGHT

Say "The
Object object
is the super
prototype of all
objects" 10
times quickly!

The toString
method
returns
a string
conversion
of an object
as best it can.

The Object Object

The Object object is the root of all objects in JavaScript.

Put in class terminology, it's a *superclass* of all classes in JavaScript. More accurately, because, as we've discussed, JavaScript doesn't really have classes—but rather prototype objects and instance objects—the Object object is the superprototype of all objects in JavaScript. Say that one 10 times quickly!

 NOTE   You'll become clearer about prototypes after working through a couple of examples later in this chapter.

What this boils down to is that the way of the Object object is the way of all objects in JavaScript. The examples in the remainder of this chapter should help give you a feeling for what this means.

Somewhat more specifically, the methods of the Object object are present in all objects in JavaScript. The Object method you're most likely to encounter is the toString method, present (although sometimes undefined) in all objects. The toString method returns a string conversion of an object as best it can. For example, the toString method of a number returns a string representation of a number.

The following statements:

```
var theNum = new Number(42);
var theStr = theNum.toString();
```

store a string representation of theNum in the variable theStr, namely 42, which you can then display:

```
document.write(theStr);
```

You can also write this more compactly, like so:

```
var theNum = new Number(42);
document.write(theNum);
```

Under the covers, theNum is being converted to a string just the same, using the Number object's toString method even if it isn't explicitly invoked.

It's a good idea to define the toString method for any custom objects you create, as I show you in the "Creating Objects" section of this chapter.

If the toString method hasn't been defined for an object, it generally returns the string *[object]*—which isn't really very useful!

NOTE The valueOf method is also a method of the Object object and is used when JavaScript needs to convert an object to a primitive type that isn't a string, most often a number. You can define your own valueOf methods for your own objects, and it makes sense to do so in some circumstances.

ADVANCED

Creating Objects

ADVANCED

The first section in this chapter, "Understanding Object-Oriented Programming," explained OO in a fairly language-independent fashion. (The dot operator (.) discussed at the beginning of that section and used to reference a value associated with an object is pretty much universal across programming languages.) The next section, "JavaScript OO Lite," explained how to work with the objects that are exposed by an HTML document in a Web browser. I also showed you the objects that are provided by the JavaScript programming language.

It's time to turn to the task of creating custom objects in JavaScript that use some of the OO concepts I've explained so far.

The most crucial issue is to understand the role of prototypes, which are the JavaScript analog to classes and which play the same role as classes in providing a template for objects.

The main limitation of a JavaScript prototype as opposed to the more general concept of a class is that only one generation of inheritance is available with a prototype. With a prototype, you create many instances of objects based on the prototype. But with classes, you can have one class that inherits from another class that inherits from another class (and so on), finally creating instances of objects from the class that's the remote descendent of the original class. This can be very powerful. But other than the ability to inherit multiple generations from a blueprint, you should think of a JavaScript prototype as a class.

I'll explain how prototypes work as we go along. But, first, let's look at two JavaScript keywords related to objects, new and this. The new keyword, which you've seen used in many examples in earlier chapters of this book (for example, you used new to create instances of Array objects in Chapter 5, "Understanding Arrays"), calls a constructor to create a new instance of an object.

The this keyword is used to refer to the current instance of an object.

A custom object means an object of your own.

I don't want a room of my own; I want an object of my own!

If you named a movie Something About this*, it might not sound as interesting as Something About Mary, but there are some very interesting things you can do with the* this *keyword!*

 NOTE The keywords new and this are used quite widely in OO languages for the same purposes as in JavaScript although there are some variations. For example, me is used instead of this in Visual Basic .NET.

As I've indicated, JavaScript has no explicit concept of a class, which makes it less than an ideal choice as a language to teach OO. But please keep the general concept of a class in mind as we go over what JavaScript does have, namely, *prototype* objects. Each object has a prototype object, and an object *inherits* all the members of its prototype. By *inherits*, I mean that all the members defined for the prototype can be found in any instance object that's based on the prototype. So in this way, a prototype object functions exactly like a class. The prototype object is the blueprint, or cookie cutter, and all the instance objects based upon it are the buildings (or cookies).

By the way, whether you're talking classes or prototypes, it's conventional to name a class (or prototype) starting with an initial capital letter. Objects instantiated from the class (or prototype) are named with an initial lowercase letter. For example, you could have a Car class and an object based on it named theJaguar.

You could have a Car class and an object based on it named theJaguar.

Let's look at an example that demonstrates some of these concepts using JavaScript code. Because this is our first example that shows how to create and use our own custom objects in JavaScript, what we'll do will be relatively simple so that you can see the bare-bones concepts at work. Our task will be to create a Rectangle prototype. The Rectangle prototype will have a constructor function that takes as arguments the height and width of a rectangle instance. You can also set height and width values as properties of rectangle instances. Finally, the Rectangle prototype will supply a method, calcArea, that calculates the area of a given rectangle instance.

Here goes!

Let's start with the constructor function that's used to create a Rectangle object. As noted, it accepts two arguments, one for the height and the other for the width of the instance of the Rectangle object. Within the constructor function, the this keyword is used to assign the value passed to the function to the instance property:

```
function Rectangle(height, width){
    this.height =  height;
    this.width = width;
}
```

Next, we'll create the function that will be used to implement the calcArea method:

```
function calc_Area () {
    return this.height * this.width;
}
```

This function returns the value of the instance height multiplied by the instance width. Note that I've named it slightly differently than the method (calc_Area rather than calcArea). This is to emphasize that the name used to call the method, using an instance of the prototype, is distinct from the underlying function that implements the method.

Now, let's assign the function we've just created to the value of the Rectangle prototype, using the prototype keyword, so that we can call it as an instance method:

```
Rectangle.prototype.calcArea = calc_Area;
```

Our simple Rectangle prototype is now complete. Let's instantiate an object, named theRectangle, based upon it:

```
var theRectangle = new Rectangle (3, 5);
```

To show we can, let's set a property value of the instantiated theRectangle object (replacing the original value of five set in the constructor when theRectangle was instantiated):

```
theRectangle.width = 10;
```

Finally, we can display theRectangle object's current property values and call its calcArea method to display its area as shown in Figure 7-11:

```
document.write("The rectangle instance height is: " +
    theRectangle.height + "<br>");
document.write("The rectangle instance width is: " + theRectangle.width +
"<br>");
document.write ("The calcArea method returns: " +
theRectangle.calcArea());
```

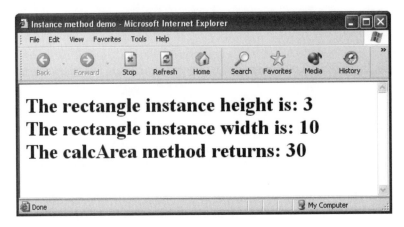

FIGURE 7-11
The object instance's values of its height and width properties and the return value for its calcArea method are displayed in the browser.

Listing 7-7 shows the complete code for creating the Rectangle proto-type, instantiating theRectangle object based on the prototype, displaying property values, and invoking an object method.

LISTING 7-7
Creating an Object and Using Object Instance Properties and Methods

```
<HTML>
<HEAD>
<TITLE>Instance method demo</TITLE>
</HEAD>
   <BODY>
   <H1>
   <SCRIPT>
   function Rectangle(height, width){
   // constructor function
      this.height =  height;
      this.width = width;
   }
   // create the function
   function calc_Area () {
      return this.height * this.width;
   }
   // turn the function into an object method
   Rectangle.prototype.calcArea = calc_Area;
```

```
// instantiate the object
var theRectangle = new Rectangle (3, 5);

// set an instance property
theRectangle.width = 10;

// call and display the instance properties and method return
document.write("The rectangle instance height is: " +
    theRectangle.height + "<br>");
document.write("The rectangle instance width is: " +
    theRectangle.width  + "<br>");
document.write ("The calcArea method returns: " +
theRectangle.calcArea());
</SCRIPT>
</H1>
</BODY>
</HTML>
```

Earlier in this chapter I explained to you the concept of shared members of a class. The code in Listing 7-7 showed how to work with instance members of a class (or, more accurately, because we're inhabiting JavaScript land, instance members of a prototype). An instance member requires that an object be instantiated, and it can have different values for each object based on a prototype (or class).

As opposed to instance members, to access a shared member you're neither required (nor can) instantiate an object instance. The best way of thinking of shared members is that they're a kind of constant value. You can also think of them as class (or prototype) variables rather than instance variables. Here are two examples of shared members in JavaScript using our Rectangle prototype:

```
Rectangle.frodo = 12;
Rectangle.Pi = 3.1415;
```

Here is an assignment statement that uses these shared members (note that no instantiation of a Rectangle object is required):

```
var theRing = Rectangle.Pi * Rectangle.frodo * Rectangle.frodo;
```

Custom Objects As Arrays

In the "Displaying an Object's Associative Array" section earlier in this chapter, I showed you how to display the array associated with the window object and other objects such as document and navigator.

You can just as easily display the members of your own objects using their associative arrays. As an example, take the Rectangle prototype and instance objects created in the previous section. If you pass the instance object to the function I showed you for displaying the elements of an object's associative array, you'll see the method and properties of the instance of the Rectangle object displayed, as shown in Figure 7-12.

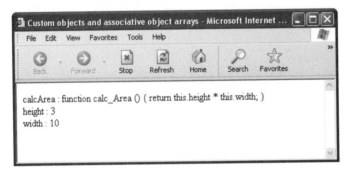

FIGURE 7-12
The properties of a Rectangle instance shown using its associative array

 TIP Because there's no way to know the order a **for/in** statement will go through an associative array, when you run this program, your display may not match that shown in Figure 7-12.

Listing 7-8 shows the HTML page that defines the Rectangle object prototype, creates an object instance based upon it, and uses the **for/in** statement to iterate through the associative array of the object instance.

LISTING 7-8
The Associative Array of a Rectangle Object Instance

```
<HTML>
<HEAD>
    <TITLE>Custom objects and associative object arrays</TITLE>
<SCRIPT>
function showProperties (theObject){
```

```
      for (i in theObject) {
        if (theObject[i] != null) {
            document.write(i + " : " + theObject[i] + "<br>");

        }
        else {
            document.write(i + "<br>");
        }
    }
    return;
}
</SCRIPT>
</HEAD>
<BODY>
<SCRIPT>
function Rectangle(height, width){
    // constructor function
        this.height =  height;
        this.width = width;
    }

    // create the function
    function calc_Area () {
       return this.height * this.width;
    }
    // turn the function into an object method
    Rectangle.prototype.calcArea = calc_Area;

    // instantiate the object
    var theRectangle = new Rectangle (3, 5);

    // set an instance property
    theRectangle.width = 10;
showProperties (theRectangle);
</SCRIPT>
</BODY>
</HTML>
```

Defining a Custom toString Method

As I mentioned earlier, it's a good idea to define a custom toString method for your own objects. This custom toString method will be used when JavaScript needs to convert an instance of your object to a string type—often for the purpose of displaying a string representation of your object instance.

It's easy to add a custom toString method to your objects. In fact, it works just like adding any other method to the prototype for object instances.

Let's take our Rectangle prototype and object instance as an example to see how to do this.

First, write a new function that returns a string. The function can be named anything, but usually it should be named to show that it's related to the toString method. The function that implements a toString method for a prototype will often use instance values of objects based on the prototype when generating a return value.

Here's my somewhat silly function for objects based on the Rectangle prototype:

```
function to_String() {
    return "I am a funny rectangle short and stout: " +
        this.height + " by " +
        this.width + "."
}
```

Next, assign the function that implements the toString (to_String) method to the toString method of the prototype object:

```
Rectangle.prototype.toString = to_String;
```

Instantiate an object based on the prototype:

```
var theRectangle = new Rectangle (2, 42);
```

And finally, write code that invokes the toString method of the Rectangle prototype on the instance of the Rectangle object and display it (the results are shown in Figure 7-13).

```
document.write(theRectangle);
```

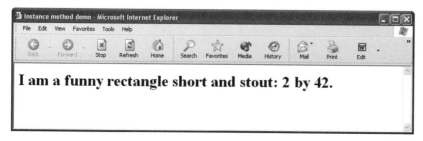

FIGURE 7-13

The custom toString method of the Rectangle object returns some cute text.

This is kind of like magic, almost spooky. The statement
`document.write(theRectangle);` would look like something that
shouldn't give intelligible results. (In fact, what you get without the
custom toString method implementation is [object Object], which isn't
indeed very intelligible.)

> *This is like magic!*

By adding the toString method to the Rectangle prototype, coders can
then casually involve instances of the Rectangle object in string conversions—and get reasonable results without worrying about it. Listing 7-9
shows an appropriate implementation of a toString method for the
Rectangle object.

> *You can get reasonable results when you do a conversion to String type without worry.*

LISTING 7-9

Implementing a toString Method

```
<HTML>
<HEAD>
<TITLE>Instance method demo</TITLE>
</HEAD>
   <BODY>
   <H1>
   <SCRIPT>
   function Rectangle(height, width){
   // constructor function
      this.height =  height;
      this.width = width;
   }
   function calc_Area () {
      return this.height * this.width;
   }
```

```
function to_String() {
    return "I am a funny rectangle short and stout: " +
        this.height + " by " +
        this.width + "."
}
Rectangle.prototype.calcArea = calc_Area;
Rectangle.prototype.toString = to_String;

var theRectangle = new Rectangle (2, 42);
document.write(theRectangle);
</SCRIPT>
</H1>
</BODY>
</HTML>
```

Creating an OO Auction

Picture yourself at Sotheby's dressed formally and ready to hold up a bidding paddle. Well, if that's too much to contemplate, think of bidding for your favorite tchatshke on eBay.

Because a tchatshke is a thing, or an object, what's a more fitting demonstration of object-oriented programming than an application that implements a tchatshke, or "thing," auction?

> **tchatshke**, n. [Yiddish] A thing as in a tourist souvenir; a tacky object displayed in one's house; a small gift; something for sale on eBay; a bauble or trinket.

ADVANCED

Real Programs Can Be Tough and Tricky

A program that actually does something substantive can be a tricky thing to write. Complexity adds up quickly, and there are usually many different possibilities you have to take into account. A fully realized program needs to be able to appropriately respond to any possible user input or action, and that can be a pretty tall order. (Who the heck knows what people are going to do, anyway?)

The JavaScript Tchatshke Gulch program I'm about to explain includes some of the features of an eBay-style auction. (I'll detail exactly what the program implements in the text.) Even though only a small subset of the features of a "real" auction application such as the eBay site are included, and there's little in the way of user input validation, it's still a complex program, by far the most complicated in this book so far. (The runner up for complexity so far is the Rock, Scissors, and Paper program in Chapter 3, "Using Conditional Statements.") This leads to a couple of points we should discuss.

Don't worry if you don't get everything about how this program works at this point. I've tried to explain it as best I can, and the fact that the program is object-oriented makes its underlying structure clearer (one of the great benefits of OO!). However, this is just not that easy a program. So, read through the text and code! You'll get something out of it, even if you don't "get" absolutely everything.

Another suggestion is that you come back later—perhaps after you've worked through the rest of this book. I'll bet just about anything that you'll find it much easier to understand the Tchatshke Gulch program!

As I've previously said, I'm a great believer in learning by doing. So my last suggestion is that you modify Tchatshke Gulch to make it yours—and learn about the program in the process. My thinking is that the process of modifying and extending the code will ensure that you learn how the program works. Learning by changing existing program code has worked well for me in my career as a professional programmer. You'll find some suggestions for extending Tchatshke Gulch in the penultimate section of this chapter.

On a slightly different topic, it's also the case that JavaScript code written using Notepad (or SimpleText on the Mac) is neither the best programming language nor the best programming environment for writing a program as complex at Tchatshke Gulch. This has both good and bad implications.

The main problem is the programming editor. In a sophisticated, modern programming editor, syntax errors are highlighted as they're made. Additionally, object hierarchies and their members are usually available via drop-down lists as you create code—so you don't have to remember, look up, or (fate forefend) misspell identifiers.

The moral here is that when you start to create serious production programs, you'll want to do so in a serious programming environment.

However, in the meantime, there are some benefits to working in a "primitive" programming environment. True, it's easier to make mistakes and harder to find them when you do. But to get things right, you'll need to understand them fully. It's a little bit like what some people believe

Who the heck knows what people are going to do?

Tchatshke Gulch is a complicated program.

OO makes the underlying structure of Tchatshke Gulch clearer!

Learning by changing works for me!

about driving: Learning to drive a shift car makes you a better driver because you understand the car better, even if you only drive automatics in "real life."

You'll find techniques and tips to help you debug JavaScript code written under "primitive" conditions in Chapter 10, "Error Handling and Debugging."

What Tchatshke Gulch Does

What a program does is sometimes called its *specifications*. Creating rigorous and useful program specifications is an important and difficult task that's one part art and one part science. Getting the specifications right is an important condition precedent to successfully writing programs that perform complex tasks. Indeed, creating a written specification document is usually the first deliverable in large-scale commercial software projects.

In brief, here's what our Tchatshke Gulch program will do. (Even a brief look at buying or selling something on eBay should give you an idea of how much it doesn't do!)

To start with, the user can create an auction by supplying a lot number, a description, a starting bid, and a bid increment as shown in the upper left of Figure 7-14. By the way, it's common to show pictures of the user interface as part of a formal program specification.

Once an auction has been started, a new one can't be created until the current one is closed. This is implemented in the user interface shown in Figure 7-14, which is shown in mid-auction because the Create Auction button is disabled. The Create Auction button is enabled when the user discovers the winner and ends the current auction by clicking Close Auction.

With an auction active, a bidder can enter a bid by supplying a name and maximum amount as shown in the upper right of Figure 7-14.

The auction uses a system called *proxy bidding* by eBay, in which the user enters a maximum that they're willing to pay, but the system bids the least amount necessary to win the object for the user. To take an example, if a bidder enters a maximum bid of $200, and the highest other bid is $100 with a $5 bidding increment, then the bidder wins the auction for $105.

Note that, as at eBay, bids can only be entered if they're greater than the current bid (or the starting bid) plus the increment.

Getting a program's specifications right is an important and difficult job.

Even a brief look at eBay should give you an idea of how much Tchatshke Gulch doesn't do!

Proxy bidding means that the computer will bid up to your maximum but no higher than necessary.

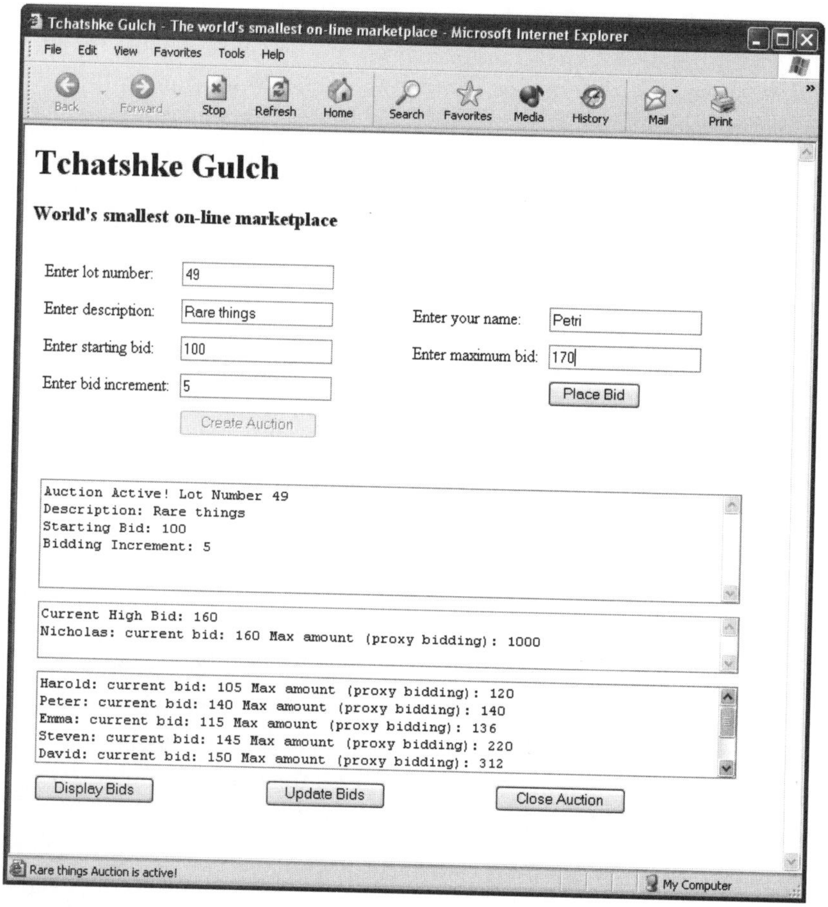

FIGURE 7-14

The Tchatshke Gulch user interface

Bids can only be entered if they're greater than the current bid.

The three large horizontal boxes at the middle and bottom of the interface shown in Figure 7-14, created using HTML <textarea> form elements, are used to display information about the auction. The top box shows general information about the auction. The middle box shows the current high bid.

When the Display Bids button is clicked, it displays the bids entered in the bottom <textarea> box. These are shown as entered, not as subsequently updated resulting from proxy bids.

When the Update Bids button is clicked, each bid is updated once to reflect the fact that an initial bid may have a higher proxy bid value than a later bid. However, the ultimate auction winner isn't determined until the Close Auction button is clicked, which also is used to set the interface up so another auction can be started. The formula used for determining the amount paid by the high bidder is that the bidder with the highest proxy value wins. This bidder pays either the proxy value or the second highest proxy value plus the bidding increment, whichever is less.

Tchatshke Gulch Objects

I think you'll agree that implementing the functionality behind the interface I just described as a bunch of functions and procedures without an OO framework would be a daunting task. Okay, so go ahead—put down this book and try if you don't believe me.

Putting together the functionality without an OO framework would be tough! Try to do it if you don't believe me.

The problem really is that you can have many bids, all of which have to be repeatedly compared to each other. There has to be a way to generalize these bids so that once you've learned how to treat two of them, you more or less know how to treat an arbitrary number of them. This insight makes plain what the OO structure behind Tchatshke Gulch ought to be: We'll need an Auction object and Bid objects. One of the properties of the Auction object should be an array containing all the extant Bid objects, providing a convenient way to manipulate bids. Figure 7-15 shows this relationship.

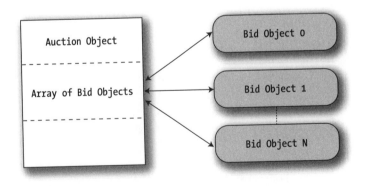

FIGURE 7-15
The Auction object contains an array of Bid objects.

The Auction object will also need properties to track the initial bid and the bidding increment for the auction.

Each Bid object will have a property for its current bid value and its maximum proxy bid value.

We will need constructors for both Bid and Auction objects. In addition, the Auction object will require methods for displaying bids, updating bids, and closing the auction to declare a winner.

If we can cleanly design the prototypes for these simple objects and their members, it shouldn't be too big a deal to write the code that glues them together to create—ta dah!—Tchatshke Gulch.

Implementing the Bid Object

Listing 7-10 shows the Bid object constructor, which establishes a name, a maximum amount (or proxy bid), and a property for the current amount of any bid. In addition, it's nice to implement a toString method for the Bid object prototype so that bids can be displayed with the required information simply by calling a Bid object's toString method.

I've also included a valueOf method to make comparison between two Bid objects easy. Using the valueOf method on Bid objects, you can use the numerical comparison operators to see if the current value of one bid is greater than another.

LISTING 7-10

The Bid Object Constructor and Prototype

```
function Bid (name, max_amount, curr_amount) {
    this.name = name;
    this.max_amount = max_amount;
    this.curr_amount = curr_amount;
}
Bid.prototype.toString = function(){
    return this.name + ": current bid: " + this.curr_amount +
    " Max amount (proxy bidding): " + this.max_amount;
}
Bid.prototype.valueOf = function() { return this.curr_amount;}
```

It's worth noting that the functions used to implement both the toString and valueOf methods are never named and are what's called a function *literal*, or *lambda*, explained in the sort function discussion in Chapter 6, "Programming with Arrays."

The Auction Object

The Auction prototype object is conceptually almost as simple as the Bid object. However, the methods that actually "run" the auction are part of the Auction object. These methods—makeBid, displayBids, updateBids, and endAuction—involve a bit of complexity.

Let's start by looking at the code for the Auction object, as shown in Listing 7-11.

LISTING 7-11

The Auction Prototype Object

```
function Auction (lot_num, desc, start_bid, increment){
    this.lot_num = lot_num;
    this.desc = desc;
    this.start_bid = start_bid;
    this.increment = increment;
    this.bidArray = new Array();
    this.status = "";
    this.currBid = start_bid;
}

function display_Bids (){
    var displayStr = "";
    for (var i = 0; i < this.bidArray.length; i++){
        displayStr += this.bidArray[i].toString() + "\r\n";
    }
    window.document.resultForm.txtBids.value = displayStr;
}

function update_Bids () {
    var winnerIndex = 0;
    for (var i = 0; i < this.bidArray.length; i++){
        if (Number(this.bidArray[i].curr_amount) < Number(this.currBid)){
            if (Number(this.bidArray[i].max_amount) >=
                Number(this.currBid) + Number(this.increment)){
                this.bidArray[i].curr_amount = Number(this.currBid) +
```

```
                    Number(this.increment);
                this.currBid = this.bidArray[i].curr_amount;
                winnerIndex = i;
            }
        }
    }
    window.document.resultForm.txtCurrentHighBid.value =
        "Current High Bid: " + this.currBid + "\r\n" +
        this.bidArray[winnerIndex].toString();
    this.displayBids();
}


function end_Auction () {
    var winnerIndex = 0;
    var highBid = 0;
    for (var i = 0; i < this.bidArray.length; i++){
        if (Number(this.bidArray[i].max_amount) > Number(highBid)){
            highBid = Number(this.bidArray[i].max_amount);
            winnerIndex = i;
        }
    }
    var runnerUpIndex = 0;
    var runnerUpBid = 0;
    for (var i = 0; i < this.bidArray.length; i++){
        if (Number(this.bidArray[i].max_amount) >
            Number(runnerUpBid) && (i != winnerIndex)){
            runnerUpIndex = i;
        }
    }
    var winningBid =
Math.min(Number(this.bidArray[runnerUpIndex].max_amount) +
        Number(this.increment),
Number(this.bidArray[winnerIndex].max_amount));
    this.bidArray[winnerIndex].curr_amount = winningBid;
    window.document.resultForm.txtCurrentHighBid.value =
        "The winner is " +
        this.bidArray[winnerIndex].name + "\r\n" +
        "Detail: " +  this.bidArray[winnerIndex].toString();
    this.displayBids();
    window.document.createForm.btnCreateAuction.disabled = false;
}
```

```
function make_Bid (name, max_amount, curr_Bid) {
    var thisBid = new Bid (name, max_amount, curr_Bid);
    this.bidArray [this.bidArray.length] = thisBid;
}

Auction.prototype.displayBids = display_Bids;
Auction.prototype.updateBids = update_Bids;
Auction.prototype.endAuction = end_Auction;
Auction.prototype.makeBid = make_Bid;
Auction.prototype.toString = function(){
    return this.desc;
}
```

The Auction object constructor defines the properties of an Auction object instance. It also creates a new array to be used to store Bid objects.

The makeBid Method

Let's have a look at Auction object methods! The makeBid method is implemented with the function make_Bid, as you can see from this prototype assignment:

```
Auction.prototype.makeBid = make_Bid;
```

The make_Bid function is simplicity itself. It simply creates a new Bid object, using the Bid object constructor, and then adds the newly created Bid instance onto the end of the bid array associated with the Auction object instance:

```
function make_Bid (name, max_amount, curr_Bid) {
    var thisBid = new Bid (name, max_amount, curr_Bid);
    this.bidArray [this.bidArray.length] = thisBid;
}
```

The displayBids Method

Here's the function that implements the Auction object's displayBids method:

```
function display_Bids (){
    var displayStr = "";
    for (var i = 0; i < this.bidArray.length; i++){
        displayStr += this.bidArray[i].toString() + "\r\n";
    }
    window.document.resultForm.txtBids.value = displayStr;
}
```

This is also not terribly complicated code (and, gee, haven't you come a long way?). If you need a refresher on working with arrays, please review Chapter 6, "Programming with Arrays."

This code simply iterates through the array of bids associated with the instance of the Auction object. For each Bid object instance, its toString method is used to concatenate it to a display string.

 NOTE The escape characters \r\n are used to add a line break to the text string used for display, as I explain further in Chapter 9, "Manipulating Strings."

Finally, after the array loop is complete, the string containing all the Bid object instance information, one bid per line, is assigned to a <textarea> box in the HTML form. (Don't worry, I'll get to the HTML in a bit!)

The updateBids Method

We're going up in the complexity world. The function that implements the updateBids method iterates through the array of bid instances:

```
function update_Bids () {
 var winnerIndex = 0;
 for (var i = 0; i < this.bidArray.length; i++){
     if (Number(this.bidArray[i].curr_amount) < Number(this.currBid)){
        if (Number(this.bidArray[i].max_amount) >=
           Number(this.currBid) + Number(this.increment)){
             this.bidArray[i].curr_amount = Number(this.currBid) +
                Number(this.increment);
             this.currBid = this.bidArray[i].curr_amount;
             winnerIndex = i;
        }
       }
    }
   window.document.resultForm.txtCurrentHighBid.value =
      "Current High Bid: " + this.currBid + "\r\n" +
       this.bidArray[winnerIndex].toString();
   this.displayBids();
}
```

If a bid's current amount is less than the current high bid, and the bid's proxy maximum is greater than or equal to the current high bid plus the increment, then the bid's current amount is adjusted upward accordingly, and the value of the variable referencing the current high bidder is changed.

Finally, the winner is displayed, and the displayBids method (which we've already discussed) is called to display all the bids (this is an example of not having to do the same work twice, or code *reusability*).

 TIP The displayBids method is reused in a number of places in the auction application. After all, once you have it written and working, why bother to do it again? The moral is to try to generalize so that your code can be easily reused.

This is an example of not having to do the same work twice, or code reusability.

The endAuction Method

Here's the function that implements the endAuction method:

```
function end_Auction () {
    var winnerIndex = 0;
    var highBid = 0;
    for (var i = 0; i < this.bidArray.length; i++){
        if (Number(this.bidArray[i].max_amount) > Number(highBid)){
            highBid = Number(this.bidArray[i].max_amount);
            winnerIndex = i;
        }
    }
    var runnerUpIndex = 0;
    var runnerUpBid = 0;
    for (var i = 0; i < this.bidArray.length; i++){
        if (Number(this.bidArray[i].max_amount) >
            Number(runnerUpBid) && (i != winnerIndex)){
            runnerUpIndex = i;
        }
    }
    var winningBid =
Math.min(Number(this.bidArray[runnerUpIndex].max_amount) +
        Number(this.increment),
Number(this.bidArray[winnerIndex].max_amount));
    this.bidArray[winnerIndex].curr_amount = winningBid;
    window.document.resultForm.txtCurrentHighBid.value =
        "The winner is " +
        this.bidArray[winnerIndex].name + "\r\n" +
        "Detail: " + this.bidArray[winnerIndex].toString();
        this.displayBids();
        window.document.createForm.btnCreateAuction.disabled = false;
}
```

What this does is first identify the bid with the highest proxy bid value. Next, in another iteration through the array of bid instances, the second highest proxy bid value is found (by finding the highest value that doesn't have an index equal to the first highest value!).

With the first and highest proxy values in hand, the amount the winning bidder pays is calculated using the min, or minimum, method of the Math object built into JavaScript and mentioned earlier in this chapter. The amount the winning bidder pays is the minimum of the runner up's proxy value plus the increment and the winner's proxy value. (Normally, this will be the runner up's proxy value plus the increment.)

Finally, the results of the auction are displayed, and the CreateAuction button is enabled.

The HTML Form

So far, I've shown you straight program code for creating object prototypes and their members. You'd place all this within <SCRIPT> tags in the <HEAD> section of your HTML document so the objects, method, and properties are ready, willing, and able when you've loaded the document in your Web browser.

This is a book about the craft of programming and about teaching people to learn how to program, so I don't want to get too bogged down in the specifics of HTML.

But without an HTML form to go with the objects, there won't be an auction application for you to run. What? No Tchatshke Gulch? Perish the thought!

Before I show you the HTML, you should know that in this section I've removed the HTML <TABLE> tags for the sake of clarity. So, what you'll see in Listing 7-12 is HTML form code. Including the <TABLE> tags would just be confusing. But if you run the code shown in the listings and wonder why it doesn't look like the figures, it's because the <TABLE> formatting codes are missing. You can have a look at these codes, which are solely used in this document for formatting, in Listing 7-13, which is the complete code and HTML for Tchatshke Gulch.

> *I don't want to get bogged down in the specifics of HTML!*

LISTING 7-12

The Tchatshke Gulch HTML Form (Table Tags Omitted)

```
<BODY bgcolor="#FFFFFF" link="#0000FF">
<H1>Tchatshke Gulch</H1>
<H3>World's smallest on-line marketplace</H3>
<form name="createForm">
Enter lot number:<input type=text name="txtLotNum">
Enter description:<input type=text name="txtDesc">
Enter starting bid:<input type=text name="txtStartBid">
Enter bid increment:<input type=text name="txtIncrement">
<input type=button name="btnCreateAuction"
   value="Create Auction" onClick="createAuction(txtLotNum.value,
   txtDesc.value, txtStartBid.value, txtIncrement.value);">
</form>

<! -- end of form for creating the auction -->
<!-- bid form -->

<form name="bidForm">
Enter your name:<input type=text name="txtName">
Enter maximum bid:<input type=text name="txtMaxBid">
<input type=button value="Place Bid"
 onClick="placeBid(txtName.value, txtMaxBid.value);">
</form>

<!-- end of bid form -->
<! -- auction results form>

<form name="resultForm">
<textarea name="txtAuctionStatus" cols=80 rows=6></textarea>
<textarea name="txtCurrentHighBid" cols=80 rows=4></textarea>
<textarea name="txtBids" cols=80 rows=5></textarea>
<input type=button value="Display Bids"
   onClick="if (theAuction != null) theAuction.displayBids();"></TD>
<input type=button value="Update Bids" name="btnUpdate"
   onClick="if (theAuction != null) theAuction.updateBids();"></TD>
<input type=button value="Close Auction"
   onClick="if (theAuction != null) {theAuction.endAuction();
      theAuction = undefined;}">
</form>
<!-- end of auction results form -->
</BODY>
```

Gluing the Application Together

Oh, the ties that bind! There are a few more pieces we need to look at to tie this application together although we're almost there.

Creating an Auction

First, if you look at the HTML code shown in Listing 7-12, there's code assigned to each onClick event handler for the five buttons in the user interface (shown empty, or without any values entered, in Figure 7-16).

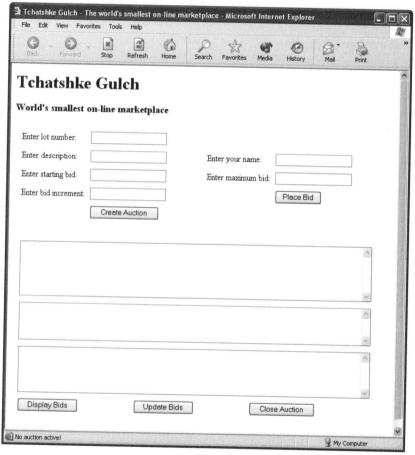

FIGURE 7-16

The Tchatshke Gulch user interface (with no values)

When the Create Auction button is clicked, the following code in its onClick event gets processed:

```
createAuction(txtLotNum.value, txtDesc.value,
    txtStartBid.value, txtIncrement.value);
```

This calls a function, createAuction, which isn't the Auction object's constructor. Instead, it takes care of some housekeeping and then calls the Auction constructor. Here's the createAuction function:

```
function createAuction(lot, desc, startBid, inc) {
  if (lot == "" || desc == "" || startBid == "" || inc == "" ) {
      alert ("You are missing a required value!");
  }
  else {
     theAuction = new Auction (lot, desc, startBid, inc);
     window.status = theAuction + " Auction is active!";
     window.document.createForm.btnCreateAuction.disabled = true;
     var displayStr = "Auction Active! Lot Number " + lot + "\r\n" +
         "Description: " + desc + "\r\n" +
         "Starting Bid: " + startBid + "\r\n" +
         "Bidding Increment: " + inc + "\r\n";
     window.document.resultForm.txtAuctionStatus.value = displayStr;
     window.document.resultForm.txtCurrentHighBid.value = "";
     window.document.resultForm.txtBids.value = "";
  }
}
```

The variable used to hold an instance of the Auction object, theAuction, is declared outside of any function so that it can be used by all the functions on the HTML page.

This code checks to see that the user actually entered values in the text boxes in the HTML form. If the user did, the next (and crucial) step is to invoke the Auction object constructor:

```
theAuction = new Auction (lot, desc, startBid, inc);
```

By the way, there's an important step I should point out. We'll need to declare the variable to hold an instance of the Auction object, theAuction, outside of any function:

```
var theAuction;
```

By declaring the instance variable outside of all the functions, its *scope*, or the context in which it can be used, extends to all the functions in the HTML document.

A variable that can be used by all the functions in an application is sometimes called a *global* variable. Good programming practice is to have as few global variables as possible, both because having a lot of global variables violates the OO objective of object encapsulation and because global variables consume more system resources than local variables.

Placing a Bid

When the Place Bid button is clicked, the following code in the onClick event handler is processed:

```
placeBid(txtName.value, txtMaxBid.value);
```

Just as with creating an auction, the placeBid function does a few things besides invoking the Bid object constructor. Let's have a look! Here's the code for the placeBid function:

```
function placeBid (name, max_value){
    if (theAuction == undefined) {
        alert ("You must first create an auction before bids can be
placed!");
        return;
    }
    if (name == "" || max_value == "" ) {
        alert ("You must enter your name and your highest bid!");
        return;
    }
    if (Number(max_value) < Number(theAuction.start_bid)) {
        alert ("Sorry, bid less than minimum. Please try again!");
        return;
    }
    if (Number(max_value) < Number(theAuction.currBid) +
        Number(theAuction.increment)){
        alert ("Sorry, your bid is less than the current bid " +
theAuction.currBid +
            " plus the auction increment amount " +
            theAuction.increment  + ". Please try again!");
        return;
    }
    var curr_Bid = Number(theAuction.currBid) +
Number(theAuction.increment);
    theAuction.currBid = curr_Bid;
    theAuction.makeBid (name, max_value, curr_Bid);
```

> *Using too many global variables violates the OO principle of encapsulation.*

```
    window.document.bidForm.txtName.value = "";
    window.document.bidForm.txtMaxBid.value = "";
    window.document.resultForm.txtCurrentHighBid.value = "Current High Bid:
" +
    curr_Bid + "[" + name + "]\r\n" +
    "Note that this does not reflect proxy bidding and maximum bids
submitted. "
    + "\r\n" +
    "Click Update Bids to progress the auction.
    Click Close Auction to determine the winner.";
    }
```

This function first checks to see that an auction has been created. Good thinking! Without an auction, you can't make a bid. It then checks to see that the user entered a name and the highest amount the user was willing to bid. Finally, the function checks to see that the bid is higher than the start price for the tchatshke being auctioned and also that the bid is higher than the current bid plus the increment.

If these conditions are met, the current bid amount is updated and the makeBid method of the Auction object instance is called:

```
theAuction.makeBid (name, max_value, curr_Bid);
```

Finally, the current bid is displayed.

The Other Auction Methods

The remaining three Auction object methods—displayBids, updateBids, and endAuction—are called directly from the onClick event handlers of the related buttons. So that you don't have to go back and look at Listing 7-12, here's the relevant HTML form code:

```
<input type=button value="Display Bids"
    onClick="if (theAuction != null) theAuction.displayBids();"></TD>
<input type=button value="Update Bids" name="btnUpdate"
    onClick="if (theAuction != null) theAuction.updateBids();"></TD>
<input type=button value="Close Auction"
    onClick="if (theAuction != null)
      {theAuction.endAuction(); theAuction = undefined;}">
```

There's not too much to say about the code in these onClick events because they call the Auction object methods pretty directly. But do note that they each, as a sanity check, test to see that an Auction object instance has been created:

```
if (theAuction != null) ...
```

You don't want to go around calling the methods of an object instance when the instance hasn't been created!

If you look at the onClick code for the Close Auction button, you'll see that it "undefines" theAuction object after the auction has been completed for a last step, or finishing touch, in this application:

```
onClick="if (theAuction != null)
    {theAuction.endAuction(); theAuction = undefined;}"
```

Finally, it may be helpful to show all the parts of this program in one fell swoop so you can see how they fit together. Listing 7-13 shows the entire Tchatshke Gulch.

Calling the methods of an object that hasn't been created is like, well, asking an unborn child to play the violin!

LISTING 7-13

Tchatshke Gulch (a Program for Implementing an Auction)

```
<HTML>
<HEAD>
<TITLE>Tchatshke Gulch - The world's smallest on-line marketplace</TITLE>
 <SCRIPT>
 // Bid prototype object
function Bid (name, max_amount, curr_amount) {
    this.name = name;
    this.max_amount = max_amount;
    this.curr_amount = curr_amount;
}
 Bid.prototype.toString = function(){
    return this.name + ": current bid: " + this.curr_amount +
      " Max amount (proxy bidding): "
        + this.max_amount;
}
Bid.prototype.valueOf = function() { return this.curr_amount;}

// Auction prototype object
function Auction (lot_num, desc, start_bid, increment){
  this.lot_num = lot_num;
```

```
        this.desc = desc;
        this.start_bid = start_bid;
        this.increment = increment;
        this.bidArray = new Array();
        this.status = "";
        this.currBid = start_bid;
    }

    function display_Bids (){
        var displayStr = "";
        for (var i = 0; i < this.bidArray.length; i++){
            displayStr += this.bidArray[i].toString() + "\r\n";
        }
        window.document.resultForm.txtBids.value = displayStr;
    }

    function update_Bids () {
        var winnerIndex = 0;
        for (var i = 0; i < this.bidArray.length; i++){
            if (Number(this.bidArray[i].curr_amount) < Number(this.currBid)){
                if (Number(this.bidArray[i].max_amount) >=
                    Number(this.currBid) + Number(this.increment)){
                        this.bidArray[i].curr_amount = Number(this.currBid) +
                            Number(this.increment);
                    this.currBid = this.bidArray[i].curr_amount;
                    winnerIndex = i;
                }
            }
        }
        window.document.resultForm.txtCurrentHighBid.value = "Current High Bid:
" +
            this.currBid + "\r\n" +
            this.bidArray[winnerIndex].toString();
        this.displayBids();
    }

    function end_Auction () {
        var winnerIndex = 0;
        var highBid = 0;
        for (var i = 0; i < this.bidArray.length; i++){
            if (Number(this.bidArray[i].max_amount) > Number(highBid)){
                highBid = Number(this.bidArray[i].max_amount);
```

```
                winnerIndex = i;
            }
        }
    var runnerUpIndex = 0;
    var runnerUpBid = 0;
    for (var i = 0; i < this.bidArray.length; i++){
        if (Number(this.bidArray[i].max_amount) >
            Number(runnerUpBid) && (i != winnerIndex)){
                runnerUpIndex = i;
            }
    }
    var winningBid =
 Math.min(Number(this.bidArray[runnerUpIndex].max_amount) +
        Number(this.increment),
 Number(this.bidArray[winnerIndex].max_amount));
        this.bidArray[winnerIndex].curr_amount = winningBid;
        window.document.resultForm.txtCurrentHighBid.value = "The winner is " +
        this.bidArray[winnerIndex].name + "\r\n" +
            "Detail: " + this.bidArray[winnerIndex].toString();
    this.displayBids();
    window.document.createForm.btnCreateAuction.disabled = false;
}


function make_Bid (name, max_amount, curr_Bid) {
    var thisBid = new Bid (name, max_amount, curr_Bid);
    this.bidArray [this.bidArray.length] = thisBid;
}


Auction.prototype.displayBids = display_Bids;
Auction.prototype.updateBids = update_Bids;
Auction.prototype.endAuction = end_Auction;
Auction.prototype.makeBid = make_Bid;
Auction.prototype.toString = function(){
    return this.desc;
}
window.status = "No auction active!";
var theAuction;


function createAuction(lot, desc, startBid, inc) {
    if (lot == "" || desc == "" || startBid == "" || inc == "" ) {
        alert ("You are missing a required value!");
```

```
        }
        else {
            theAuction = new Auction (lot, desc, startBid, inc);
            window.status = theAuction + " Auction is active!";
            window.document.createForm.btnCreateAuction.disabled = true;
            var displayStr = "Auction Active! Lot Number " + lot + "\r\n" +
                "Description: " + desc + "\r\n" +
                "Starting Bid: " + startBid + "\r\n" +
                "Bidding Increment: " + inc + "\r\n";
            window.document.resultForm.txtAuctionStatus.value = displayStr;
            window.document.resultForm.txtCurrentHighBid.value = "";
            window.document.resultForm.txtBids.value = "";
        }
}

function placeBid (name, max_value){
    if (theAuction == undefined) {
        alert ("You must first create an auction before bids can be
placed!");
        return;
    }
    if (name == "" || max_value == "" ) {
        alert ("You must enter your name and your highest bid!");
        return;
    }
    if (Number(max_value) < Number(theAuction.start_bid)) {
        alert ("Sorry, bid less than minimum. Please try again!");
        return;
    }
    if (Number(max_value) < Number(theAuction.currBid) +
        Number(theAuction.increment)){
        alert ("Sorry, your bid is less than the current bid " +
theAuction.currBid +
            " plus the auction increment amount " + theAuction.increment +
            ". Please try again!");
        return;
    }
    var curr_Bid = Number(theAuction.currBid) +
Number(theAuction.increment);
    theAuction.currBid = curr_Bid;
    theAuction.makeBid (name, max_value, curr_Bid);
    window.document.bidForm.txtName.value = "";
```

```
      window.document.bidForm.txtMaxBid.value = "";
      window.document.resultForm.txtCurrentHighBid.value =
          "Current High Bid: " + curr_Bid + "[" + name + "]\r\n" +
    "Note that this does not reflect proxy bidding and maximum bids submitted. "
          + "\r\n" +
      "Click Update Bids to progress the auction.
      Click Close Auction to determine the winner.";
}
</SCRIPT>
</HEAD>
<BODY bgcolor="#FFFFFF" link="#0000FF">
<H1>Tchatshke Gulch</H1>
<H3>World's smallest on-line marketplace</H3>
<! -- Outer table -->
<TABLE>
<TR><TD>

<! -- table and form for creating the auction -->
<form name="createForm">
<TABLE cellspacing=8>
<TR><TD>Enter lot number:</TD><TD><input type=text
name="txtLotNum"></TD></TR>
<TR><TD>Enter description:</TD><TD><input type=text
name="txtDesc"></TD></TR>
<TR><TD>Enter starting bid:</TD><TD><input type=text
name="txtStartBid"></TD></TR>
<TR><TD>Enter bid increment:</TD><TD><input type=text
    name="txtIncrement"></TD></TR>
<TR><TD></TD><TD><input type=button name="btnCreateAuction" value="Create
Auction"
    onClick="createAuction(txtLotNum.value,
txtDesc.value, txtStartBid.value, txtIncrement.value);"></TD></TR>
</TABLE>
</form>
<! -- end of table and form for creating the auction -->
</TD><TD>

<!-- bid table -->
<form name="bidForm">
<TABLE cellspacing=8>
```

```
<TR><TD>Enter your name:</TD><TD><input type=text
name="txtName"></TD></TR>
<TR><TD>Enter maximum bid:</TD><TD><input type=text
name="txtMaxBid"></TD></TR>
<TR><TD></TD><TD><input type=button value="Place Bid"
    onClick="placeBid(txtName.value, txtMaxBid.value);"></TD></TR>
</TABLE>
</form>

<!-- end of bid table -->
</TD></TR><TR>
<TD colspan=2>
<! -- auction results table>

<form name="resultForm">
<TABLE cellspacing=8>
<TR><TD colspan=3><textarea name="txtAuctionStatus" cols=80
    rows=6></textarea></TD></TR>
<TR><TD colspan=3><textarea name="txtCurrentHighBid" cols=80
    rows=4></textarea></TD></TR>
<TR><TD colspan=3><textarea name="txtBids" cols=80
rows=5></textarea></TD></TR>
<TR><TD><input type=button value="Display Bids" onClick="if (theAuction !=
null)
    theAuction.displayBids();"></TD>
<TD><input type=button value="Update Bids" name="btnUpdate"
onClick="if (theAuction != null) theAuction.updateBids();"></TD>
<TD><input type=button value="Close Auction"
onClick="if (theAuction != null)
  {theAuction.endAuction(); theAuction = undefined;}">
</TD></TR>
</TABLE>
</form>

<! end of auction results table -->
</TD></TR>
</TABLE>
<! -- end of outer table -->

</BODY>
</HTML>
```

Taking Tchatshke Gulch for a Test Drive

Enough talk! Enough code! Let's take Tchatshke Gulch for a spin.

Open up the HTML document containing the Tchatshke Gulch code in your favorite browser. Enter some values to create an auction (see Figure 7-17).

FIGURE 7-17
Creating an auction at the Tchatshke Gulch

With an auction created, you can now place a bid, as shown in Figure 7-18.

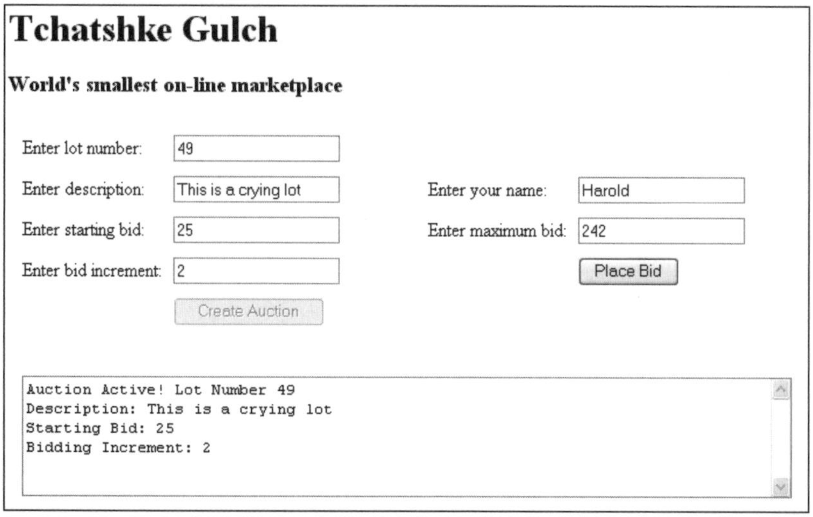

FIGURE 7-18
Placing a bid at the Tchatshke Gulch

The "vital stats" for the bid are displayed, as shown in Figure 7-19.

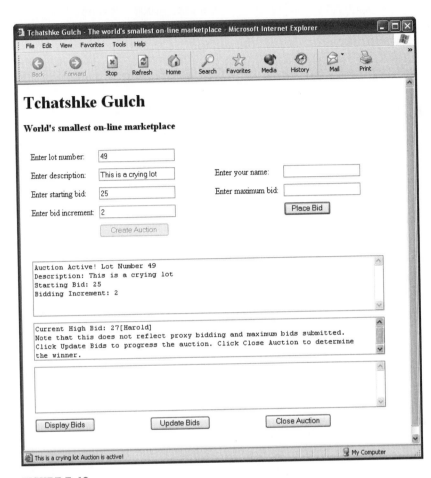

FIGURE 7-19

The bid value is shown in the Tchatshke Gulch user interface.

Go ahead! Enter some more bids! The more, the merrier (see Figure 7-20).

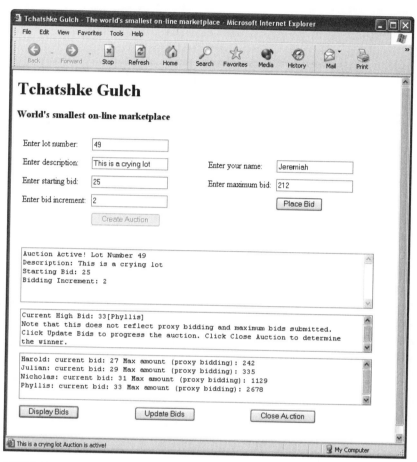

FIGURE 7-20

Bids are shown together with the associated maximum proxy bid.

When you click the Close Auction button, the bidder with the highest proxy value wins (see Figure 7-21).

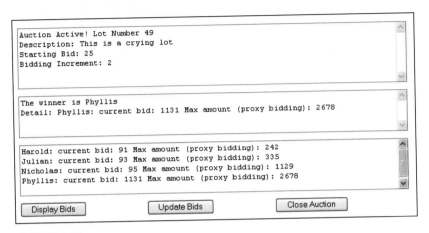

```
Auction Active! Lot Number 49
Description: This is a crying lot
Starting Bid: 25
Bidding Increment: 2
```

```
The winner is Phyllis
Detail: Phyllis: current bid: 1131 Max amount (proxy bidding): 2678
```

```
Harold: current bid: 91 Max amount (proxy bidding): 242
Julian: current bid: 93 Max amount (proxy bidding): 335
Nicholas: current bid: 95 Max amount (proxy bidding): 1129
Phyllis: current bid: 1131 Max amount (proxy bidding): 2678
```

[Display Bids]   [Update Bids]   [Close Auction]

FIGURE 7-21

And the winner is...

Note that the winner shown in Figure 7-21, Phyllis, pays $1,131, which is the correct amount: $2 (the increment) higher than the next-highest proxy bid ($1,129 bid by Nicholas).

WAY COOL

TRY THIS
AT HOME

NOTE See what you can do to extend the Tchatshke Gulch application. This is the best way to learn about the objects that comprise this program. Can you add a reserve auction feature? Can you add a way to make bidders anonymous but keep track of them? What about changing the update function to take into account maximum proxy bids (in the current application this only happens when an auction is closed). All of these, and anything else you can think of, are great exercises to help speed you down your path toward becoming a totally awesome programmer!

What's It All About?

Programming these days is largely about objects (just as eBay is largely about tchatshkes!). Within the limitations imposed by the JavaScript language and development environment, this chapter has exposed you to the crucial concepts and techniques involved in object-oriented programming. The examples in the chapter have also helped give you a "real-life" appreciation for the benefits (and necessity) of learning to think in an OO fashion.

Let's move on and take a closer look at an important aspect of OO that I haven't covered all that much: events and event-driven programming.

8

Understanding Events and Event-Driven Programming

As I explained in Chapter 7, "Working with Objects," events are a mechanism, usually associated with an object, for responding to actions such as the user clicking a button or a page being loaded. When the action occurs, an *event handler* is triggered (this is also called *firing an event*). This is the opportunity for you, the programmer, to place code that the event handler invokes.

Event-driven programming is important because most of the computer environments in use have a great deal going on. As a user, you initiate some of these "things going on" by clicking a button (or whatever), in other words, firing an event. As a user, you also use the functionality provided by program code that's processed once you (or something) have fired an event by moving a mouse, clicking a button, or performing any of the myriad things that a user can do. If you've ever worked in a windowing environment—such as, well, Microsoft Windows—or an application such as Microsoft Word, or clicked around a Web browser, why, then you've fired a great many events!

In addition, events that you're not responsible for triggering are firing all around you all the time! These events might be time-based, or they might have to do with resources available to a computer.

The right picture is of thousands of events, flying around, implemented as kinds of messages.

From the viewpoint of the programmer, managing all these events, and managing the code needed to "respond" to the events, sounds like a royal headache.

At first blush, the straight-ahead, linear response to a world full of thousands of events is to embed a giant conditional statement at the top of each and every program that checks to see what event is being responded to. This conditional statement would loop through all the possible events each time the program started processing code (for example, when that famous button was clicked).

There's some logic to this, but it's cumbersome and procedural top-down thinking, inappropriate in an event-driven world.

Conceptualizing your programs as responses to events (and only the events you care about) greatly simplifies things. For one thing, you don't have to embed your programs within a gigantic <u>if</u> statement.

As I'll show you in the second half of this chapter, it also makes sense to design many programs so that, in addition to responding to events, they fire their own custom events.

Clearly, if you think about how an event must be implemented, an event handler is a function. But there also must be a mechanism for associating the event handler with the triggering object and event. In most development environments, this amounts to a "publication" and "subscription" mechanism: By publishing (and registering) the event function, the system learns that a specialized function (the event handler) is associated with an object. Other objects that subscribe to the event invoke the event handler function when an appropriate condition occurs (the event is fired).

Objects that are prebuilt, such as the JavaScript objects shown in Table 7-1 in Chapter 7, "Working with Objects," or the HTML form elements that are programmable using JavaScript, have the ability to provide prebuilt events in a kind of scaffolding, sometimes called an *event framework*. It's also usually possible in most development environments to add your own custom events to custom objects.

Most powerful development environments (which, of course, JavaScript in a code editor is not) provide easy access to the event framework so that it's no big chore to add event handling code that's processed when an event is fired.

For example, Figure 8-1 shows the Visual Studio .NET development environment loaded with a Visual Basic .NET source code project.

In Figure 8-1, a Button control has been placed on a form (as shown in the left side of the figure). This kind of form is the basis for a window in a Windows program. The right side of the figure shows the Code Editor window. The programmer can select an event associated with the Button control from the drop-down list that's shown (each event is marked with a lightning bolt). When an event is selected, the declaration code for the event handling function is automatically created, and all the programmer has to do is add whatever code needs to be processed when the Button's event is fired.

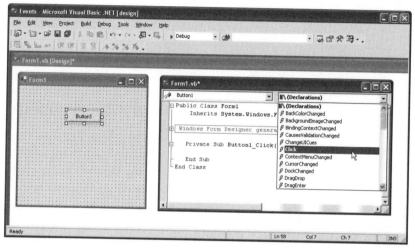

FIGURE 8-1

The Visual Studio .NET development environment loaded with a Visual Basic .NET project

We don't have it quite so easy in JavaScript in a text editor because there's no visual development environment provided. Then again, we don't really need a fancy development environment!

There are two parts to this chapter. First, we'll look at using the prebuilt events provided by an HTML form in a document loaded in a Web browser—which can be programmed using JavaScript.

You've already seen a fair amount of material that uses event-driven programming techniques to make examples work. In particular, the onClick event associated with a button HTML form element has got a lot of play. But if you need a refresher on events and the basic mechanics of events and JavaScript objects, you can turn back to "JavaScript OO Lite" in Chapter 7, "Working with Objects."

This chapter will be a little more rigorous. I'll show you how to work with the most common JavaScript events, which objects provide event handlers, and which actions fire these events. In addition, I'll show you how to "trap" events—so that your code can act to show you for yourself what is fired when.

Using Different Browsers

The predominant Web browser at this time is Microsoft Internet Explorer. However, as you may know, the first commercial Web browser was the Netscape product. Mozilla is another important browser, which is an open-source offshoot of Netscape. You can find more information about Mozilla at `http://www.mozilla.org`.

In the second part of this chapter, I'll discuss how to add custom event handlers to your own custom objects. In other words, how can you effectively fire and respond to events when these events aren't provided pre-built by the objects in your code? Some full-featured programming languages provide more extensive ways to create your own events than does JavaScript. But this chapter should give you an idea of how to work with events.

Different Event Models

For the most part, the programs in this book have used generic JavaScript code that will run in any modern Web browser. However, in this chapter we run up against a sad fact of life: The way events work in relation to objects is slightly different in Internet Explorer than in most other major browsers (for example, Mozilla and Netscape). The same code often just won't work for both kinds of browsers. Don't worry: Simple button onClick events work the same way everywhere.

Although this book isn't about Web browsers, in this chapter I'll show you how to write code related to events that runs on Internet Explorer, Mozilla, and Netscape. I'll also show you how to automate a test in a Web page to check which Web browser is running—so that your program can pick the appropriate code to process accordingly.

The moral of this story is that you have to carefully scrutinize the object and event model of any platform you're targeting. This is a good lesson to bear in mind whether you're writing code to run in a Web browser or have targeted specific applications (or operating systems).

Therefore, it's more important for you to understand the general pattern of how events work than memorizing the details of each of the JavaScript event models—because the event and object model is likely to be different in subtle and not-so-subtle ways each time you target a new application or operating system.

JavaScript Objects and Event Handlers

So far in this book, when an event has been used, mostly it has been the onClick event of an HTML form in a document loaded in a Web browser. (An exception to this was the example in the "Events" section of Chapter 7, "Working with Objects," which showed the onMouseOver event of the Link object.)

I've used the button's onClick event in all these examples to keep things simple. For the most part in these examples, the demonstration code launches when the user clicks the button. This book is about programming, not the specific events that apply to the object model exposed by a document loaded in a browser window, so I haven't gone into much detail about events. But it's worth getting a more general feeling for the kind of events that are likely to be associated with objects. You should know that the name for an event may vary depending on the application exposing the events, and, as I mentioned in the sidebar "Different Event Models," it's worth looking carefully at the event model exposed by each and every application. They're all likely to be at least somewhat different.

Table 8-1 shows the most common events associated with objects exposed to JavaScript by HTML pages loaded in a Web browser.

It's worth getting a feeling for the kind of events that are likely to be associated with objects.

TABLE 8-1.

Objects and Associated Event Handlers

Object	Event Handler
Button	onClick, onDblClick, onMouseDown, onMouseOut, onMouseOver
Document	onDblClick, onKeyDown, onKeyPress, onKeyUp, onMouseDown, onMouseOut, onMouseOver
Form	onReset, onSubmit
Image	onAbort, onDblClick, onError, onKeyDown, onKeyPress, onKeyUp, onLoad, onMouseOut, onMouseOver
Layer	onMouseOut, onMouseOver
Link	onClick, onKeyDown, onKeyPress, onKeyUp, onMouseOut, onMouseOver
Select	OnChange
Text input elements	onBlur, onChange, onFocus, onKeyDown, onKeyPress, onKeyUp
Window	onBlur, onFocus, onLoad, onResize, onUnload

Event Triggers

The names of some event handlers clearly describe what actions trigger the event. (It doesn't take rocket science to figure that an onClick event is fired when something is clicked.) Other events are a little less intuitive.

Remember, also, that event names change in different environments. For example, the JavaScript onBlur event is called the LostFocus event in most Windows programming environments.

Table 8-2 shows JavaScript event handlers and the actions that fire them.

TABLE 8-2

Events and Their Triggers

Event	Action That Fires the Event
onAbort	The loading of an image is interrupted.
onBlur	The object loses input focus—typically because the user moves to another screen element using the mouse or keyboard.
onChange	In a select list, the user selects or deselects an element. In a text box, the user enters or changes text and causes focus to move to another object.
onClick	The user clicks once. You can return false in code to cancel a default action.
onDblClick	The user clicks twice.
onError	An error occurs while loading an image.
onFocus	The object gains input focus—usually because the user has moved to the object using the mouse or keyboard.
onKeyDown	The user presses a key. You can return false in code to cancel.
onKeyPress	The user presses or releases a key. (onKeyPress is the same as onKeyDown or onKeyUp.)
onKeyUp	The user releases a key.
onLoad	A document or image finishes loading.
onMouseDown	The user presses a mouse button.
onMouseOut	The mouse is moved off an element.
onMouseOver	The mouse is moved over an element. (For links, to prevent the URL from appearing in the status bar, return true.)
onMouseUp	The user releases a mouse button.
onReset	A form reset is requested.
onResize	A window is resized.
onSubmit	A form submission is requested.
onUnload	A document is unloaded.

An Example Using the Event Object

The JavaScript event object is used to access details about an event that has just occurred. This information is stored in the properties of the object (it has no methods or events).

In this section, to learn how to work with the event object, we'll use the event object to learn what key the user pressed in a text box. The code in this example is processed when the onKeyDown event of the text box is fired. The program is also able to distinguish a specific letter—a lowercase or uppercase *t*—and take specific action when that letter is entered.

Of course, the "actions" this program takes don't amount to much: The program displays an alert box showing the letter pressed and, in case of the letter *t*, a special, different alert box. But in the "real world," you could take significant action depending on the letter entered by the user, and that's one of the points of this exercise.

Let's get started constructing the example that displays an alert box intercepting keystrokes, displaying the key pressed, and not allowing the letter *t* to be entered. To do this, we'll use the keyCode property of the event object, which stores a number representing the key pressed when an

> *In the "real world," you could take significant action depending on the letter entered by the user.*

Internet Explorer, Mozilla, and Netscape

This example involves another wrinkle we haven't dealt with so far. The object and event model of Internet Explorer is slightly different from the model for other browsers. For example, Mozilla and Netscape share a common object and event model, which you'd expect if you knew that the Mozilla and Netscape ancestry is the same. However, the Mozilla and Netscape models do differ from that of Internet Explorer.

The examples in this chapter run on the three main browsers (Internet Explorer, Mozilla, and Netscape). (For all I know, they also work on other, more obscure browsers. I just haven't tested to find out for sure.) I don't want to get too bogged down in this stuff because it's really not that directly related to the primary topic of this book, learning to program. But, as I'll show you, there are two steps you need to take to make the examples in this chapter work on both object and event models:

• Your program needs to determine which browser is running the code.

• Your program needs to contain separate code for the two different models.

onKeyDown event is fired. You should know that the number 84 represents the Unicode number, or character encoding, for the letter *t*.

 TIP You can find out more about Unicode, which is a way to universally refer to letters and other characters, on the Unicode home page, http://www.unicode.org.

Creating this application involves a number of steps. We'll need to:

- Understand how to use the event object in an event handler
- Access the keyCode property of the event object
- Use the String object's fromCharCode method to display the letter represented
- Determine if the browser running the code is Internet Explorer or Netscape/Mozilla (see the previous sidebar for more information)
- Intercept the letter *t* and delete it, using differing code depending on the object model

The event object, and its properties, can be used directly in the code assigned to an event in an HTML element. Usually, however, you'll want to do the actual programming work in a function that's called from a statement assigned to the event. In our case, we'll call the function that does the work checkKey. To make the properties of the event object, which is to say the properties of the most recently fired event, available to the checkKey function, we must pass the event object as an argument to the function.

To Use the Event Object in an Event Handler:

1. Pass the keyword event, which means the JavaScript event object, as an argument to the call to the function that will be processing the event. For example:

   ```
   <INPUT type=text name="theText" onKeyDown="checkKey(event);">
   ```

2. Use the properties of the event object as you would the properties of any other event object.

The keyCode Property

The Unicode representation of a character key that has been pressed using the keyboard is contained in the keyCode property of the event object. You can use this property to respond to individual keystrokes. For example, suppose you have something against the letter *t* and refuse to allow it in a text box.

I just picked *t* at random. Really, I don't have anything against this letter! But I did want to demonstrate how easy it is to pick out particular letters.

> *Really, I don't have anything against the letter t!*

To Display the Key Pressed:

1. Create a simple form that includes a text box:

```
<FORM name="theForm">
   <INPUT type=text name="theText">
</FORM>
```

2. Add an onKeyDown event handler to the text input:

```
<INPUT type=text name="theText" onKeyDown=" ">
```

3. Add a call to a function named checkKey to the event handler:

```
<INPUT type=text name="theText" onKeyDown="checkKey();">
```

4. Pass the event object to the checkKey function by using the event keyword as an argument:

```
<INPUT type=text name="theText" onKeyDown="checkKey(event);">
```

5. Create a function named checkKey with a parameter e that represents the event object:

```
function checkKey(e){

}
```

By the way, I could have used any legal identifier for the parameter e. Naming it e helps remind me that it contains event information.

6. Check to see if the keyCode property contains the number 84 (which means that it's a *t*):

```
function checkKey(e){
    if (e.keyCode == 84){

    }
    else {

    }
}
```

7. If the key pressed isn't a *t*, display it (see Figure 8-2):

```
function checkKey(e){
    if (e.keyCode == 84){

    }
    else {
        alert ("You entered the character " +
            String.fromCharCode(e.keyCode) + ".");
    }
}
```

This code uses the String.fromCharCode method to convert the Unicode number that represents the key to its alphabetic equivalent. Note that fromCharCode is a shared (or static) member of the String class, so you don't (and can't) instantiate a String object to use it.

8. If it's a *t*, display an alert box (see Figure 8-3):

```
function checkKey(e){
    if (e.keyCode == 84){
        alert("You have dotted those eyes, ↵
            but you can't put any Tees in the box!");
    }
    else {
        alert ("You entered the character " +
            String.fromCharCode(e.keyCode) + ".");
    }
}
```

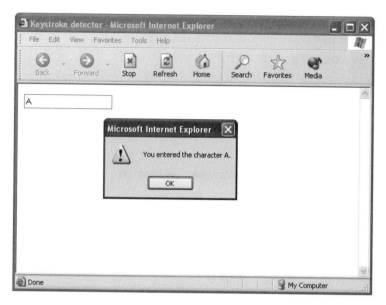

FIGURE 8-2
The letter entered by the user in the text box is displayed in an alert box.

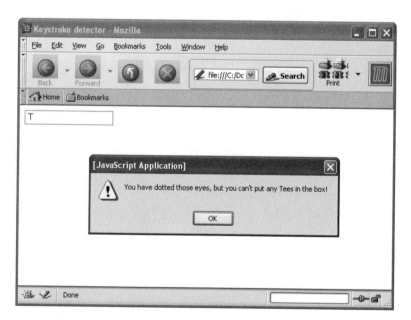

FIGURE 8-3
The letter *t* is singled out for unfair treatment.

The next thing we want to do is to delete the letter *t* from the text box. As it turns out, this is easier in Internet Explorer than in the other browsers.

We can check to see which browser is running by inspecting the appName property of the Netscape object.

To Check to See Which Browser Is Running the Code:

1. Check to see if the appName property of the Netscape object is *Microsoft Internet Explorer*:

```
...
if (Netscape.appName == "Microsoft Internet Explorer")
...
else {
    // deal with Netscape or Mozilla
}
```

 NOTE This is really a pretty crude test. The properties of the Navigator object will give you much more detailed information, should you ever need it.

In Internet Explorer, you can remove the letter from the text box simply by setting the returnValue property of the event object to false.

To Remove the *t* from the Text Box in Explorer:

1. In Microsoft Internet Explorer, cancel the results of the user's key down action by setting the event returnValue property to false:

```
e.returnValue = false;
```

This makes sure that in Internet Explorer the *t* never appears in the text box.

Because the event object in Mozilla/Netscape doesn't have a returnValue property, another strategy must be used to remove the letter from the text box. You have to go ahead and reach through the object model to find the text box on the form. When you've "got" the text box, you can take the string representing its value and use string manipulation techniques, namely the String object's substr method, to remove the last (most recently entered) letter from the value string. This is more cumbersome than the process with Internet Explorer but not difficult.

You'll find more information about manipulating string values in Chapter 9, "Manipulating Strings."

 NOTE The technique shown for Mozilla/Netscape works in Internet Explorer as well. But I wanted to show you how to use the handy-dandy returnValue property of the event object, only available in Explorer.

To Remove the Letter in Mozilla/Netscape:

1. First, check to see which browser is running:

```
if (Netscape.appName == "Microsoft Internet Explorer")
   e.returnValue = false;
else {
   // deal with Mozilla/Netscape

}
```

2. Next, add code to delete the letter *t* if it has appeared in the Mozilla/Netscape text box:

```
if (Netscape.appName == "Microsoft Internet Explorer")
   e.returnValue = false;
else {
   str = document.theForm.theText.value;
   if (str.length == 1)
      newstr=" ";
   else {
      newstr = str.substring(0, str.length -1);
   }
   document.theForm.theText.value = newstr;

}
```

You may notice that this little program works a little differently under Netscape than Internet Explorer. With Netscape (or Mozilla), the *t* does appear in the text box (see Figure 8-3) before being deleted by the checkKey function. In Internet Explorer, setting the event object returnValue to false canceled the impending action, and the *t* never appeared in the text box. So, the Mozilla/Netscape variant can be thought of as going back in time to erase something that happened while the Explorer version makes sure that it never happened in the first place.

Listing 8-1 shows the complete code for the program.

LISTING 8-1
Intercepting an onKeyDown event, Displaying the Key Pressed, and Taking Action If It's a Specific Key

```
<HTML>
<HEAD>
    <TITLE>Keystroke detector</TITLE>
</HEAD>
<BODY>
<SCRIPT>
function checkKey(e){
    if (e.keyCode == 84){
        alert("You have dotted those eyes, but you can't put any Tees in the
box!");
        if (navigator.appName == "Microsoft Internet Explorer")
            e.returnValue = false; //works with Explorer
        else {
            //deal with Netscape or Mozilla
            str = document.theForm.theText.value;
            if (str.length == 1)
                newstr=" ";
            else {
                newstr = str.substring(0, str.length -1);
            }
            document.theForm.theText.value = newstr;
        }
    }
    else {
        alert ("You entered the character " + String.fromCharCode(e.keyCode)
+ ".");
    }
}
</SCRIPT>
<FORM name="theForm">
    <INPUT type=text name="theText" onKeyDown="checkKey(event);">
</FORM>
</BODY>
</HTML>
```

Canceling a Form Submission

As you can see in the previous example, Internet Explorer's version of the event object can be used to cancel certain actions by returning a value of false (technically, setting the value of the event object's returnValue property to false). This can be used to control important aspects of browser behavior, for example, to determine whether an HTML form should be submitted.

As an example, let's use the returnValue property of an event object associated with a form submission to cancel the submission of a form. Typically, the submission of a form occurs when the user clicks the submit button provided by the form.

The way an HTML form is submitted to a Web server is controlled by the <FORM> tag. The <FORM> tag can include a number of attributes.

The value of the action attribute is a URL, normally that of the server-side program that's executed when the form is submitted. In the example I'm about to show you, the value of the action attribute is simply an HTML page (actually the HTML page developed in the first example in this chapter). This is because I really don't want anything to happen when the form is submitted.

As you may know, the method attribute determines how form values are passed to a server, but we're really not going to get into that here. It has more to do with the specifics of Web programming than it does with understanding events.

In any case, in Internet Explorer, when a form is submitted, the form object fires an onSubmit event. In Internet Explorer, as you saw in the example in the previous section, you can use the properties of the event object when an event has been fired. Setting the value of the returnValue property of the event object to false simply cancels the submission of a form. This makes, at least in Internet Explorer, a form a pretty good place to perform chores such as validating the inputs to a form (meaning making as sure as possible that there are no required fields left empty and that they actually are phone numbers, email addresses, or whatever).

 NOTE Performing validation when possible in an onSubmit event on the client side is good because it takes a load off the server and because users don't have to "hurry up and wait" for the server to tell them their input is "no good." If you've ever submitted a form on the Web, waited for a response, and received a message back eventually along the lines of "You left the hoody-doody required field empty," you'll know exactly what I mean.

ADVANCED

Listing 8-2 shows using the form onSubmit event in Internet Explorer to let the user cancel a form submission. Form submission is canceled by setting the event object returnValue property to false, as explained in the previous example. Using an <INPUT> tag of type=submit creates a submission button that submits the form when it's clicked.

LISTING 8-2
Using the onSubmit Event to Cancel a Form Submission (Internet Explorer)

```
<HTML>
<HEAD>
   .<TITLE>On Close</TITLE>
<SCRIPT>
function checkForm(e) {
   if (!(window.confirm("Do you want to submit the form?")))
     e.returnValue = false;
 }
</SCRIPT>
</HEAD>
<BODY>
<FORM name="theForm" action="0801.html"
   onSubmit="checkForm(event);">
<INPUT type=submit>
</FORM>
</BODY>
</HTML>
```

If you open the page shown in Listing 8-2 in Internet Explorer, you'll see a single submit button.

 TIP With an input element of type submit, the browser supplies the text value for the button, usually something such as Submit Query.

Clicking the button causes the confirmation box shown in Figure 8-4 to open.

If the user clicks Cancel, the form isn't submitted, whereas if the user clicks OK, the form is submitted.

Do I have to keep writing "Mozilla/ Netscape?" I'm starting to feel like calling it Mozscape or maybe Netzilla.

FIGURE 8-4
The confirmation box asks the user whether they want to submit the form.

Let's set the bar a little higher and write code (and create an HTML page) that will work for both Internet Explorer and for the browsers without a returnValue property (meaning Mozilla and Netscape).

Doing this involves a couple of tricks. It turns out that in Mozilla/ Netscape, because we can't use the ReturnValue property, our best bet is to create a faux input button that looks like a submit input element but isn't. The onClick event of this button will mimic the functionality of the onSubmit event of a submit input element.

That's the first trick. The second trick deals with the fact that the HTML form elements are themselves different for the different browsers. It's not just that the program code differs. So, what this means is that the actual HTML for the form needs to be dynamically generated, depending on the browser that's opening the page. This is done using the document.write method.

The actual script that submits (or doesn't submit) the form is pretty simple. You've already seen it for Internet Explorer. Here it is expanded to include Netzilla as well:

```
function checkForm(e) {
   if (Netscape.appName == "Microsoft Internet Explorer") {
      if (!(window.confirm("Do you want to submit the form?")))
         e.returnValue = false;
   }
   else {
      if (window.confirm("Do you want to submit the form?"))
         document.theForm.submit();
   }
}
```

The Mozscape branch of this conditional simply uses the form's submit method (rather than the properties of the event object) to submit the form should the user so choose.

Next, here's the code that dynamically generates the HTML form for Internet Explorer:

```
...
if (Netscape.appName == "Microsoft Internet Explorer") {
   document.write("<");
   document.write("FORM name='theForm' action='0801.html'
      onSubmit='checkForm(event);'");
   document.write("><");
   document.write("INPUT type=submit");
   document.write("> <");
   document.write("/FORM");
   document.write(">");
}
...
```

Finally, here's the code that dynamically generates the HTML form for Netzilla:

```
...
else {
   document.write("<");
   document.write("FORM name='theForm' action='0801.html'");
   document.write("><");
```

```
    document.write("INPUT type=button name='theButton' value='SUBMIT QUERY'
        onClick='checkForm();'");
    document.write("> <");
    document.write("/FORM");
    document.write(">");
}
...
```

You can put these snippets together in a complete HTML page as shown in Listing 8-3. If you open the page shown in Listing 8-3 in a Mozscape browser and click the Submit Query button, a confirmation box will open (shown in Netscape in Figure 8-5).

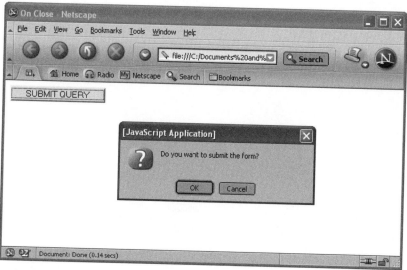

FIGURE 8-5

The cross-browser version of the application uses a button onClick event as a "faux" form onSubmit event.

Clicking Cancel cancels the form submission, and clicking OK causes the action specified in the form to take place (the page 0801.html, the first example in this chapter, is shown opened in Figure 8-6).

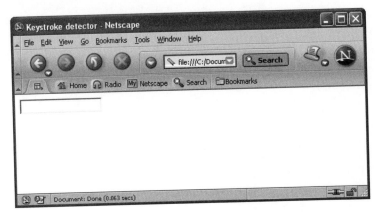

FIGURE 8-6
The action specified in the form tag takes place when the user clicks OK.

LISTING 8-3
Canceling a "Form" Submission (All Browsers)

```
<HTML>
<HEAD>
    <TITLE>On Close</TITLE>
</HEAD>
<BODY>
<SCRIPT>
function checkForm(e) {
    if (Netscape.appName == "Microsoft Internet Explorer") {
        if (!(window.confirm("Do you want to submit the form?")))
            e.returnValue = false;
    }
    else {
        if (window.confirm("Do you want to submit the form?"))
            document.theForm.submit();
    }
}
if (Netscape.appName == "Microsoft Internet Explorer") {
    document.write("<");
    document.write("FORM name='theForm' action='0801.html'
        onSubmit='checkForm(event);'");
    document.write("><");
    document.write("INPUT type=submit");
    document.write("> <");
```

```
      document.write("/FORM");
      document.write(">");
   }
   else {
      document.write("<");
      document.write("FORM name='theForm' action='0801.html'");
      document.write("><");
      document.write("INPUT type=button name='theButton' value='SUBMIT QUERY'
         onClick='checkForm();'");
      document.write("> <");
      document.write("/FORM");
      document.write(">");
   }
</SCRIPT>
</BODY>
</HTML>
```

 TIP Once again, the Netscape/Mozilla version with its faux submit button would also work for Internet Explorer. But then I wouldn't get to show you the form onSubmit button and the very useful returnValue property of the event object.

Eavesdropping on Events

ADVANCED

It's time to organize a way to delve more deeply into what happens when an event is fired. It's pretty easy to set up an application that displays events for specific HTML form elements (picking from the objects and events shown in Table 8-1 of this chapter).

In other words, the program we'll create tells you what events have been fired in response to which user actions and in what order.

For this example, let's set up a form with some text boxes—and see what events are triggered when the user enters text in them. We can also check to see what key was pressed (using the keyCode property) and whether the Alt, Control, or Shift keys were pressed.

As an exercise, you can extend the example in this section to include other objects and events.

Here's the HTML form that we'll use (table tags used for formatting have been omitted for clarity):

```
<FORM name="theForm">
Enter Your First Name: <INPUT type=text name="userFname">
Enter Your Last Name: <INPUT type=text name="userLname">
Enter Your Profession: <INPUT type=text name="userProf">
Enter Your City:            <INPUT type=text name="userCity">
<INPUT type=button name="theButton" value="Start"
   onClick="startForm();">
</FORM>
```

Note that this form contains a Start button. Clicking the Start button will start the event monitor by calling the startForm function.

Next, to manage the event monitor, we'll need a second browser window. The reason for this is that you can't receive events in a browser window without the possibility of the event reception itself triggering other events. This kind of cascading event sequence can make it difficult to see the original event. So we're better off displaying events as they're fired in a new browser window.

 NOTE Because the events we're tracking in this example are fired by four specific text boxes, we could display the events elsewhere on the page (for example, in a <textarea>) without causing events to cascade. But it's still a better practice to use a separate window as a monitor.

To do this, at the beginning of the program that will be used to monitor the events, use the window.open method to open a new window and set up a variable, doc, to refer to the document loaded in that window:

```
var newWin = window.open("","MonitorEvents","width=300, height=500");
var doc = newWin.document;
```

You can add a function that actually displays the events fired, and the event properties, with slight differences between Internet Explorer events and every other browser's event:

```
function handler(e){
    if (Netscape.appName == "Microsoft Internet Explorer"){
        e = window.event;
        doc.writeln("Event Type: " + e.type);
        if (e.keyCode) doc.writeln("Keycode: " +
String.fromCharCode(e.keyCode));
```

```
      if (e.altKey) doc.writeln("Alt Key: " + e.altKey);
      if (e.ctrlKey) doc.writeln("Ctrl Key: " + e.ctrlKey);
      if (e.shiftKey) doc.writeln("Shift Key: " + e.shiftKey);
   }
   else   {
      doc.writeln("Event Type: " + e.type);
      if (e.target) doc.writeln("Target: " +
         Object.prototype.toString.apply(e.target));
      if (e.target.name) doc.writeln("Target Name: " + e.target.name);
      if (e.which) doc.writeln("Which: " + String.fromCharCode(e.which));
      if (e.modifiers) doc.writeln("Modifiers: " + e.modifiers);
   }
}
```

You've already seen how the Explorer event object properties work, but you may be curious about the Netzilla's event properties. Some of these are shown in Table 8-3.

TABLE 8-3
Selected Non-Explorer (Mozilla and Netscape) Event Object Properties

Event Property	Meaning
modifiers	Applies to keyboard, for example, Shift, Control, and so on
target	The object that fired the event
type	The type of event fired
which	Which key or mouse button was clicked

Here's code that assigns the handler function to the specified events of an object, named, logically enough, addhandlers:

```
function addhandlers(o){
   o.onblur = handler;
   o.onchange = handler;
   o.onfocus = handler;
   o.onkeydown = handler;
   o.onkeypress = handler;
   o.onkeyup = handler;
}
```

The implication of this code is that whenever an object is passed to the addhandlers function, the specified handlers are assigned the handler function as a value. Instead of doing what the event would normally do, it's now processing the handler function and revealing itself to use. This is the perfect program for event voyeurs!

Finally, the startForm function calls the addhandlers function for each of the text boxes we want to peep at:

```
function startForm(){
    addhandlers(document.theForm.userLname);
    addhandlers(document.theForm.userFname);
    addhandlers(document.theForm.userProf);
    addhandlers(document.theForm.userCity);
}
```

You'll find the complete code for this application in Listing 8-4.

It's time to take it for a spin! Figure 8-7 shows event spying in Mozilla, Figure 8-8 shows the secret life of events in Netscape, and Figure 8-9 shows your favorite events in Explorer.

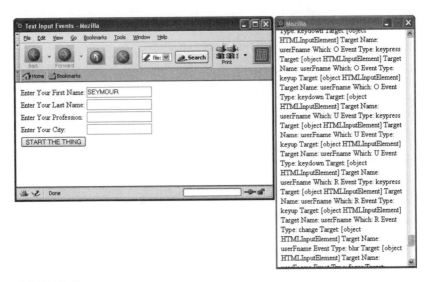

FIGURE 8-7

Watching events fired by the text boxes in Mozilla

> *This is the perfect program for event voyeurs!*

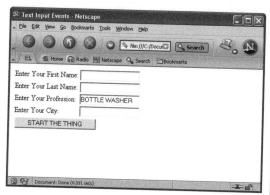
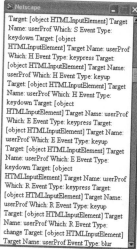

FIGURE 8-8

Watching events fired by the text boxes in Netscape

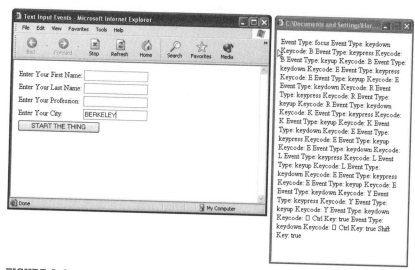

FIGURE 8-9

Watching events fired by the text boxes in Internet Explorer

LISTING 8-4
Tracking Text Box Events Using an Event Monitor

```
<HTML>
<HEAD>
   <TITLE>Text Input Events</TITLE>
</HEAD>
<BODY>
<SCRIPT>
var newWin = window.open("","MonitorEvents","width=300, height=500");
var doc = newWin.document;
function handler(e){
    if (Netscape.appName == "Microsoft Internet Explorer"){
        e = window.event;
        doc.writeln("Event Type: " + e.type);
        if (e.keyCode) doc.writeln("Keycode: " +
            String.fromCharCode(e.keyCode));
        if (e.altKey) doc.writeln("Alt Key: " + e.altKey);
        if (e.ctrlKey) doc.writeln("Ctrl Key: " + e.ctrlKey);
        if (e.shiftKey) doc.writeln("Shift Key: " + e.shiftKey);
    }
    else   {
        doc.writeln("Event Type: " + e.type);
        if (e.target) doc.writeln("Target: " +
            Object.prototype.toString.apply(e.target));
        if (e.target.name) doc.writeln("Target Name: " + e.target.name);
        if (e.which) doc.writeln("Which: " + String.fromCharCode(e.which));
        if (e.modifiers) doc.writeln("Modifiers: " + e.modifiers);
    }
}
function addhandlers(o){
    o.onblur = handler;
    o.onchange = handler;
    o.onfocus = handler;
    o.onkeydown = handler;
    o.onkeypress = handler;
    o.onkeyup = handler;
}

function startForm(){
    addhandlers(document.theForm.userLname);
    addhandlers(document.theForm.userFname);
    addhandlers(document.theForm.userProf);
```

```
    addhandlers(document.theForm.userCity);
}

</SCRIPT>
<FORM name="theForm">
<TABLE><tr><td>
Enter Your First Name:
</td><td><INPUT type=text name="userFname">
</td><td></tr><tr><td>
Enter Your Last Name:
</td><td><INPUT type=text name="userLname">
</td><td></tr><tr><td>
Enter Your Profession:
</td><td><INPUT type=text name="userProf">
</td><td></tr><tr><td>
Enter Your City:
</td><td><INPUT type=text name="userCity">
</td></tr><tr><td colspan=2>
<INPUT type=button name="theButton" value="START THE THING"
onClick="startForm();">
</td></tr></TABLE>
</FORM>
</BODY>
</HTML>
```

Firing Your Own Events

Unlike many modern development environments, the simple JavaScript environment we've been using, with completed applications running in a Web browser, doesn't provide any way to register functions as events so that there can be an easy way to respond when they've been fired. (See the sidebar "Custom Events in Visual Basic .NET" to get a sense of how easy one modern language makes it to do this.)

Even though there's no formal mechanism in our simple development environment for registering, firing, and responding to events, we can still use the concept of the event as an organizational principle for programs.

ADVANCED

Let's take a look at a simple example.

Let's suppose we have an object, which I've named *Thing*. (For a review of objects, see Chapter 7, "Working with Objects.")

The Thing object has three properties (name, text1, and text2) and a toString method implementation. Here's the constructor function and toString prototype function for the Thing object:

> *I've named the object Thing.*

```
function Thing (name, text1, text2) {
    this.name = name;
    this.text1 = text1;
    this.text2 = text2;
}
Thing.prototype.toString = function () {
    return this.name;
}
```

The idea is that if the text strings passed to the constructor of an instance of the Thing object are the same, an onSame event is fired. (In "real life," you might want to do something by executing code if two things are the same.)

Custom Events in Visual Basic .NET

In Visual Basic .NET you can add an event function to a class by declaring it with the Event keyword. Within the class, the event is fired using the RaiseEvent keyword. For example:

```
Public Event onSame ()
...
RaiseEvent onSame
```

A program that interoperates with an instance of the class needs to add the keyword WithEvents to the statement that creates the class instance. For example:

```
Private WithEvents x As New Thing
```

Then the function or procedure that handles the event is labeled with a Handles clause that names the instance and the event function. For example:

```
...
Private Sub x_onSame Handles x.onSame
...
```

That's all there is to it. You'll find similar scenarios for most modern programming languages.

Here is the method function that checks to see if the values passed to a Thing object instance are the same, along with the assignment of the function to the object prototype:

```
function check_Same() {
    if (this.text1 == this.text2) {
        this.onSame();
    }
}
Thing.prototype.checkSame = check_Same;
```

The implementation code for the onSame method just displays an alert box saying the two string properties associated with the instance are the same:

```
function on_Same () {
    alert("The two values entered in " + this.toString() +
        " are the same!");
}
Thing.prototype.onSame = on_Same;
```

To see how this works, we'll need an HTML form that allows the user to enter a name for the instance of the Thing object and two text values. Here it is (with table tags omitted for clarity):

```
<FORM>
Name your object:< input type=text name="txtName">
Enter first text: <input type=text name="txtFirst">
 Enter second text: <input type=text name="txtSecond">
<input type=button value="Do It!"
    onClick="createThing (txtName.value, txtFirst.value,
txtSecond.value);">
</FORM>
```

The Do It! button's onClick event calls a function named createThing, passing to it the information entered by the user. Here's the createThing function, which in turn invokes the object instance checkSame method:

```
function createThing (name, text1, text2) {
    var x = new Thing (name, text1, text2);
    x.checkSame();
}
```

Listing 8-5 shows the complete code in an HTML page. If you open it in a Web browser, you can try entering a name and two text strings in the text boxes and clicking the Do It! button. So long as the text strings aren't the same, nothing will happen. But if you enter two text strings that are the same, the onSame event is fired and an alert box is displayed (see Figure 8-10).

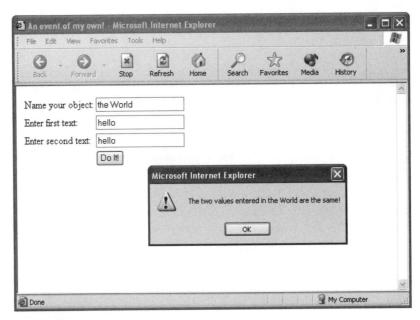

FIGURE 8-10

The custom onSame event is fired when the two text strings entered by the user are the same.

LISTING 8-5

Firing the onSame Event

```
<HTML>
<HEAD>
<TITLE>An event of my own!</TITLE>
<SCRIPT>
// Define a Thing object
function Thing (name, text1, text2) {
    this.name = name;
    this.text1 = text1;
    this.text2 = text2;
}
```

```
Thing.prototype.toString = function () {
    return this.name;
}
function on_Same () {
    alert("The two values entered in " + this.toString() +
        " are the same!");
}
function check_Same() {
    if (this.text1 == this.text2) {
        this.onSame();
    }
}
Thing.prototype.checkSame = check_Same;
Thing.prototype.onSame = on_Same;
function createThing (name, text1, text2) {
    var x = new Thing (name, text1, text2);
    x.checkSame();
}
</SCRIPT>
</HEAD>
<BODY>
<TABLE>
<FORM>
<TR><TD>Name your object:</TD><TD><input type=text
name="txtName"></TD></TR>
<TR><TD>Enter first text:</TD><TD><input type=text
name="txtFirst"></TD></TR>
<TR><TD>Enter second text:</TD><TD><input type=text
name="txtSecond"></TD></TR>
<TR><TD></TD><TD><input type=button value="Do It!"
   onClick="createThing (txtName.value,
      txtFirst.value, txtSecond.value);"></TD></TR>
</FORM>
</TABLE>
</BODY>
</HTML>
```

As Time Goes By

JavaScript provides several functions that allow you to execute code as time passes, either periodically or after a specified interval. These functions are technically methods of the Global JavaScript object, which is the same thing as the window object for JavaScript code executing against a document loaded in a browser. As usual, you don't need to reference the Window (or Global) object to use the methods because it's implied.

Table 8-4 shows the JavaScript time-related methods.

TABLE 8-4
Time–Related Methods

Method	Purpose
clearInterval	Stops the timer started using the setInterval method
setInterval	Executes specified code periodically, using the interval specified (this can be thought of as starting a timer)
setTimeout	Executes specified code following an interval

When you start a timer, you're launching an event that's handled periodically or following an interval.

These time-related methods are important in a chapter about events because essentially what you're doing when you start a timer is registering an event that's handled either periodically or after an interval (depending on whether you've used setInterval or setTimeout).

ADVANCED

NOTE Most modern programming languages provide some facility analogous to the JavaScript time–related methods. For example, in Visual Basic and C# .NET, the functionality of a timer is provided by the Timer component.

NOTE As an exercise, why not implement the functionality of the setInterval method using a loop and the setTimeout method? (It's convenient to have both methods, but you don't really need them.)

Let's work through a simple example that uses the setInterval method. In our example, the user enters a name for an object and clicks the Start button. The program then displays the object name and the current time, updated every second, in a <textarea> box (see Figure 8-11). The user also has the ability to stop the timer by clicking the Stop button shown in Figure 8-11.

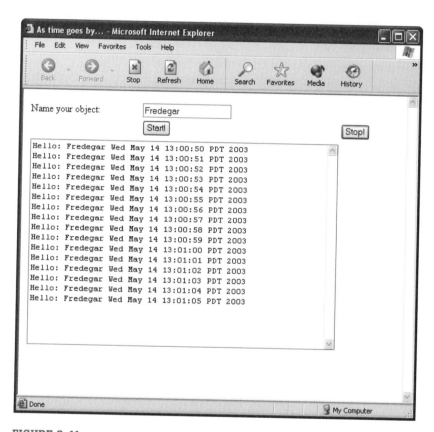

FIGURE 8-11

The setInterval method is used to display the time at one-second intervals.

Here's the HTML form used to provide the user interface for this application (the table tags used for formatting are omitted for clarity):

```
<FORM name="theForm">
Name your object: <input type=text name="txtName">
<input type=button value="Start!"
    onClick="startIt (txtName.value);">
<input type=button value="Stop!"
    onClick="stopIt();">
<textarea name="txtFired" cols = 60 rows=20></textarea>
</FORM>
```

Note that when the Start button is clicked, a function named startIt is executed. When the Stop button is clicked, the stopIt function is executed.

The program code starts by declaring two variables that will be accessible to all functions in the program, one for referencing the object that is to be created, the other for storing the timer identification (which will be needed to stop the timer):

```
var timerID;
var x;
```

Here is the constructor for the Thing object:

```
function Thing (name) {
    this.name = name;
}
```

> It's easy to imagine an application that uses many timers, which is why each timer needs its own identification so that it can be stopped.

Turning to the startIt function, what it does is to instantiate a Thing object using the name entered by the user. Next (and last) comes a call to the setInterval method:

```
function startIt (name) {
    x = new Thing (name);
    timerID = setInterval("fireIt()", 1000);
}
```

The setInterval method tells the computer to execute the code contained in the function fireIt once every 1,000 milliseconds. (As you likely know, 1,000 milliseconds is 1 second.) The return value of the setInterval method identifies the timer so that it can be stopped. It's easy to imagine an application that sets many timers, hence the need for a way to identify individual timers.

Here's the fireIt method, which creates a Date object containing the current date and time, and displays it, along with the Thing object name, each time the timer is fired:

```
function fireIt () {
   var now = new Date();
   var displayStr = window.document.theForm.txtFired.value;
   displayStr += "Hello: " + x.name +  " " + now + "\r\n";
   window.document.theForm.txtFired.value = displayStr;
}
```

All that remains is to provide the ability to stop the timer, which is accomplished in the stopIt function using the clearInterval method and the timer's identification:

```
function stopIt() {
   clearInterval(timerID);
}
```

Listing 8-6 shows the complete code for the program. If you've got the time, load it up in a browser, and go ahead and watch it fire. When the time is the last time, you can stop the process by clicking the Stop button.

I know that printing out the current time every second doesn't seem like a big deal. But bear in mind that all kinds of functionality (think animations, simulations, and automatic updating) can be accomplished using a timer.

> *Stop it! I mean, that timer is really firing me!*

LISTING 8-6

Using a Timer

> *How many applications that could be implemented using a timer can you think of?*

```
<HTML>
<HEAD>
<TITLE>As time goes by...</TITLE>
<SCRIPT>
var timerID;
var x;
function Thing (name) {
   this.name = name;
}
function fireIt () {
   var now = new Date();
   var displayStr = window.document.theForm.txtFired.value;
   displayStr += "Hello: " + x.name +  " " + now + "\r\n";
```

```
        window.document.theForm.txtFired.value = displayStr;
      }
      function startIt (name) {
        x = new Thing (name);
        timerID = setInterval("fireIt()", 1000);
      }
      function stopIt() {
        clearInterval(timerID);
      }
      </SCRIPT>
      </HEAD>
      <BODY>
      <TABLE>
      <FORM name="theForm">
      <TR><TD>Name your object:</TD><TD><input type=text
      name="txtName"></TD></TR>
      <TR><TD></TD><TD><input type=button value="Start!"
         onClick="startIt (txtName.value);"></TD>
      <TD><input type=button value="Stop!"
         onClick="stopIt();"></TD></TR>
      <TR><TD></TD><TD></TD></TR>
      <TR><TD colspan=2><textarea name="txtFired" cols = 60
      rows=20></textarea></TD></TR>
      </FORM>
      </TABLE>
      </BODY>
      </HTML>
```

Extending Tchatshke Gulch with a Timer

ADVANCED

So while we're on the topic of timers, it occurs to me that it would be helpful to see how you might use one in a more extensive way than to tell time.

Perhaps you recall Tchatshke Gulch, the "world's smallest online marketplace" application from Chapter 7, "Working with Objects." I certainly hope so!

One flaw in the original Tchatshke Gulch application is that bidding wasn't automatically updated. To update the bids, you had to click the Update Bids button (although all bids were automatically updated to their proxy maximum when the auction was closed). Even worse, the function behind the Update Bids button just updated bid amounts by one round, so if you wanted to show the true state of affairs (everyone up to their proxy maximums except the high bidder), you'd have to keep clicking away.

It's easy to fix this with a timer using the setInterval and clearInterval methods. Using a timer, the Auction.Update method currently in place can be left more or less intact. It just needs to be invoked periodically, say, once a second. After a relatively short amount of time, all bids will be correctly updated to reflect their proxy maximums except the high bidder, whose bid will be incrementally higher than the next-highest proxy bid (see Figure 8-12).

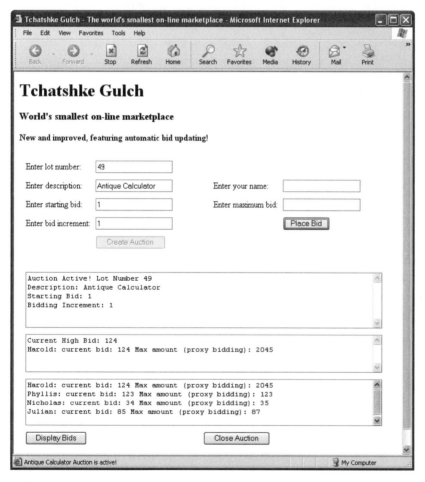

FIGURE 8-12

The setInterval method is used to automatically update proxy bids.

Because Tchatshke Gulch is a long program, I'm not going show the entire revised code listing, most of which would just be a repeat of Listing 7-13, anyhow. You can always download the revised code from the Downloads section at http://www.apress.com.

Here are the steps to take:

1. Get rid of the Update Bids button—we won't be needing it!

2. Create a variable outside any function to reference the timer identification:

   ```
   var timerID;
   ```

3. In the createAuction function, start the timer with an interval of 1 second (equals 1,000 milliseconds), tell the timer to execute the Auction instance's updateBids method and save the timer identification:

   ```
   timerID = setInterval("theAuction.updateBids()", 1000);
   ```

4. Modify the updateBids method to make sure that it doesn't do anything unless there has actually been at least one bid (otherwise, you'll get a syntax error when the program attempts to operate on the array of bids, which doesn't exist yet):

   ```
   function update_Bids () {
       if (this.bidArray.length > 0) {
       // former updateBids code goes here
         ...
       }
   }
   ```

5. Clear the timer as a first step in the endAuction method:

   ```
   clearInterval(timerID);
   ```

Demonstrably, this is not much trouble for what's really a big improvement to the program.

It's clear that it makes sense to think of a timer as a gizmo that fires events periodically (or at a specified time) rather than in response to a user action or system event. Actually, that's very cool and groovy.

This isn't much work for a big improvement to the program.

What's It All About?

Programming for the Web—or in Windows, with a small or big *W* for that matter—relies on events. You just can't expect to figure out everything in environments with today's complexity, so it makes much more sense to create programs that fire events when something happens. These same programs also must respond to, or *handle*, events as they "come in" if these events are significant to the objects in the program.

JavaScript is a great language for learning to use the events that are provided "ready to wear" by a Web browser when a document is loaded into it. Handling events in this sense, which is a little like a passive partner responding to a more active one and is also a form of what's called *client-server* programming, is pretty much the same in JavaScript as in most other modern programming languages.

There's a little less capability in the JavaScript language when it comes to registering and firing your own events. But as I showed you in this chapter, you can still use the event model in your own program architecture. In addition, it's easy and powerful to use timers to create periodic event "simulacrums." The material in the second half of this chapter should stand you in good stead when you move to a programming language with more advanced event creation facilities.

Learning to program well is largely about string manipulation. (Oddly enough, this is certainly true in a formally reductive sense.) So let's move on to Chapter 9, "Manipulating Strings."

9

Manipulating Strings

When programmers say *string* or *strings*, what they mean is a string or strings of characters (or text). Programmatically working with strings of text is a whole lot of fun: You can see instant results, and it's kind of like working though a puzzle involving words and letters.

Do the same kinds of people like crossword puzzles and creating programs that manipulate strings? I don't know, but they should: I get the same kind of pleasure out of doing each!

Strings are particularly important to computer programs because—to a great extent—people and computers communicate using strings of text. People input strings of text into the computer, for example, their name, logon, and password.

For the most part, any information that a computer program needs the user to see is also displayed as a string. You can say some things with icons or pictures, but any message of any complexity requires words—meaning, strings of text.

It's hard to imagine a program that doesn't use some text in its user interface. (For some programs, text is the *only* input and output.) Because text is such a significant part of most programs, it follows that learning to manipulate strings of text is important.

Programming languages do differ widely on the string-handling capabilities they make available to programmers. JavaScript is pretty "middle of the road" in this regard. It isn't the most sophisticated programming language when it comes to handling strings in the world. But if JavaScript isn't

Working with strings of text is great fun!

the Fred Astaire of string-handling programming languages (with Fred Astaire I'm reaching for an actor who denotes sophistication), neither is JavaScript one of the Beverly Hillbillies.

String manipulation is primarily accomplished using the methods of the String object. You'll be please to know that the skills you learn in this chapter will be portable to almost any computer language because the JavaScript String object methods pretty much work the same way (and are called the same thing) as the string manipulation methods available in every other language.

So let's go ahead and get started massaging, er, manipulating, those strings!

Learning to manipulate strings of text is very important!

Using String Methods

JavaScript isn't one of the Beverly Hillbillies when it comes to strings.

The JavaScript String object provides many handy-dandy methods. Table 9-1 shows the most important of these string methods.

Besides the string methods shown in Table 9-1, the String object has one property, length. The length property contains the number of characters in a string.

TABLE 9-1
Selected String Object Manipulation Methods

Method	Description
charAt()	Returns the character at a given position in a string
concat()	Concatenates one or more values to a string
indexOf()	Searches a string for a substring or character; returns the first occurrence of the substring or character
lastIndexOf()	Searches a string backwards for a substring or character; returns the first occurrence
split()	Splits a string into an array of strings using a specified delimiter character to make the break
substring()	Extracts a portion of a string
toLowerCase()	Converts a copy of a string to all lower case
toUpperCase()	Converts a copy of a string to all upper case

In order to use one of these String object methods, as usual you need to create a string instance based on the object. You can do this in a number of ways. We've already used many of them throughout this book.

Methods for creating String objects include the following:

- Using the String constructor, for example, `var x = new String ("Hello");`

- Using the String() conversion function

- Using an object's toString method

- Simply assigning a literal text string to a variable

Once you've created a string instance, you can use it to invoke a string method in the usual fashion (see Chapter 7, "Working with Objects," if you need a refresher course on how objects work in JavaScript).

To Use a String Object Method:

1. Create a variable containing a string. For example:

   ```
   var myStr = "Beasts of England";
   ```

2. Use the dot operator to apply a string method to the string. For example:

   ```
   var newStr = myStr.toLowerCase();
   ```

In the example, newStr would contain the string *beasts of england*.

String Methods Used to Generate HTML

You should also know that besides the methods shown in Table 9-1 there are a whole slew of methods that are used to make a copy of a string embedded in HTML tags. This makes sense because as a language JavaScript is widely used to output HTML. Table 9-2 describes these methods.

Selected HTML Generation Methods of the String Object

Method	Description
anchor()	Places a copy of the string within an HTML anchor
blink()	Places a copy of a string within <BLINK></BLINK> tags
bold()	Places a copy of the string with <BOLD></BOLD> tags
fontcolor()	Uses the color attribute of the <FONT> tag to change the color in which the string is displayed
fontsize()	Uses the size attribute of the <FONT> tag to change the font in which the string is displayed
link()	Creates a hypertext link around a copy of the string

Because these methods are pretty simple to figure out if you need to, and they're not widely useful beyond using JavaScript to build pages for the Web, I won't go into them in detail. However, I will show you a quick example so you can get the gist.

Using the Link Method

The following shows how you'd create an HTML hyperlink using the String object's link method.

To Create and Display a Link:

1. Create a string. For example:

```
linkText = "Apress";
```

2. Use the link method of the String object to add a hyperlink to the string:

```
linkText.link("http://www.apress.com")
```

3. Display the results using the document.write method:

```
document.write(linkText.link("http://www.apress.com"));
```

4. Open an HTML page containing the code, as shown in Listing 9-1, in a browser. The link will appear like any hyperlink, with the URL it points to appearing in the browser's status bar (see Figure 9-1).

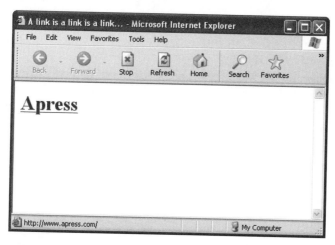

FIGURE 9-1
The String object's link method is a quick way to create a hyperlink.

LISTING 9-1
Using the String Object's Link Method

```
<HTML>
<HEAD><TITLE>
A link is a link is a link...
</TITLE></HEAD>
<BODY>
<H1>
<SCRIPT>
   linkText = "Apress";
   document.write(linkText.link("http://www.apress.com"));
</SCRIPT>
</H1>
</BODY>
</HTML>
```

It's time to move on and start having some fun playing with strings!

Converting a String to Upper Case

Suppose you want to check the user input in a text field to make sure it's a specified string. For that matter, you might also need to check the opposite—that it isn't a specified string.

In this situation, it's helpful to convert the input string to all upper case. (You could also use all lower case just as well. The important thing is that you don't have to worry about variation in cases.) If you don't convert the strings all to one case, you have to worry about things such as the string *Lawyer* not being equal to *lawyer*. So, the way to get around this is to convert the strings all to one case before you do the comparison.

Converting to all upper, or all lower, case is easy with the String object's toUpperCase and toLowerCase methods.

 NOTE This isn't a politically correct example. It's just intended for fun. Please believe me when I say that I have no desire to offend anyone!

As a perhaps somewhat silly example, suppose Saint Peter at the Pearly Gates has designed an HTML form to weed out lawyers so that they can't enter heaven. Because Saint Peter has magical powers, he can be sure that all lawyers will enter their profession in the HTML form as either *attorney* or *lawyer*. But—for whatever reason—he can't be sure that the supplicants before the gate won't vary the case of their entry to try and sneak past him. This means that he needs to write a program that converts the user's input to all upper case and makes sure it's not equal to *ATTORNEY* or *LAWYER*.

 TIP The program could just as well convert the input to all lower case and check to make sure that it's not equal to *attorney* or *lawyer*.

To Convert an Input String to All Upper Case for the Purpose of Comparison:

1. Create an input form containing the field for the value you want to compare (see Listing 9-2 for the Pearly Gates sample).

2. Name the Profession text input userProf. The toUpperCase() method will be used to check that the user doesn't enter *lawyer, attorney,* or a mixed-case version of either in the Profession field.

3. Add a button that invokes a function to check the field, passing the userProf text field as a parameter:

```
<INPUT type=button name="theButton" value="SUBMIT QUERY"
  onClick="checkLawyer(window.document.theForm.userProf.value)";>
```

4. Write the checkLawyer function to compare the input in a case-neutral fashion:

```
function checkLawyer(str) {
   if ((str.toUpperCase() == "LAWYER") ||
         (str.toUpperCase() == "ATTORNEY"))
         alert ("Lawyers are not wanted here...");
   else
      alert("Your application will be evaluated!");
}
```

5. Save the page shown in Listing 9-2 and open it in a browser. If the user enters *lawyer* or *attorney* for a profession, the comparison works no matter how idiosyncratic the capitalization that's used (see Figure 9-2).

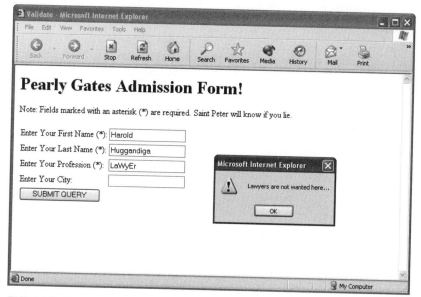

FIGURE 9-2

No lawyer will make it past Saint Peter by varying the case in a text string!

LISTING 9-2
Converting Strings to Upper Case

```
<HTML>
<HEAD>
   <TITLE>Validate</TITLE>
<SCRIPT>
function checkLawyer(str) {
    if ((str.toUpperCase() == "LAWYER") ||
        (str.toUpperCase() == "ATTORNEY"))
        alert ("Lawyers are not wanted here...");
    else
       alert("Your application will be evaluated!");
}
</SCRIPT>
</HEAD>
<BODY>
<H1>
Pearly Gates Admission Form!
</H1>
Note: Fields marked with an asterisk (*) are required.
Saint Peter will know if you lie.
<FORM name="theForm">
<TABLE>
<tr><td>
Enter Your First Name (*):
</td><td>
<INPUT type=text name="userFname">
</td><td></tr><tr><td>
Enter Your Last Name (*):
</td><td>
<INPUT type=text name="userLname">
</td><td></tr>
<tr><td>
Enter Your Profession (*):
</td><td>
<INPUT type=text name="userProf">
</td><td></tr><tr><td>
Enter Your City:
</td><td>
<INPUT type=text name="userCity">
</td></tr>
```

```
<tr><td colspan=2>
<INPUT type=button name="theButton" value="SUBMIT QUERY"
   onClick="checkLawyer(window.document.theForm.userProf.value)";>
</td></tr>
</TABLE>
</FORM>
</BODY>
</HTML>
```

Getting Playful with Strings

In this section, we're going to get down, get funky, and have some fun with strings. The example program in this section has functions that do the following:

- Capitalize all the "words" in a string.

- Count the "words" in a string.

- Reverse the "words" in a string.

- Reverse the string itself.

In order to set up a user interface for this, our program will provide two HTML <textarea> elements: one for the user to input a string, the other to display the results of the string manipulation (see Figure 9-3).

Besides the <textarea> elements for the input of a string and the display of the manipulated string, the user interface provides five buttons. Four of the buttons will activate one of the functions listed previously, and the fifth button will be used to clear the user's input string.

These buttons are also shown in Figure 9-3. The onClick event associated with each of these buttons activates the corresponding functionality.

Listing 9-3 shows the HTML used to create this user interface, along with the onClick event handler for each button. (I've omitted the <TABLE> tags for clarity—to see them, check out the complete code shown in Listing 9-7.)

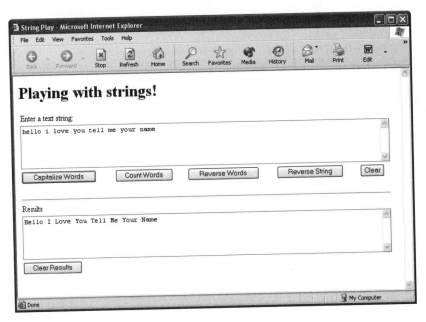

FIGURE 9-3
The Playing with Strings user interface is shown with the words in a string capitalized.

LISTING 9-3
The HTML User Interface for the Playing with Strings Application (Including onClick Event Handlers)

```
<BODY>
<H1>
Playing with strings!
</H1>
<FORM name="theForm">
Enter a text string:
<TEXTAREA name=inStr rows=5 cols=90>
</TEXTAREA>
<INPUT type=button value="Capitalize Words"
   onClick="capWords(document.theForm.inStr.value)";>
<INPUT type=button value="Count Words"
   onClick="countWords(document.theForm.inStr.value)";>
<INPUT type=button value="Reverse Words"
   onClick="revWords(document.theForm.inStr.value)";>
<INPUT type=button value="Reverse String"
   onClick="document.theForm.results.value =
revString(document.theForm.inStr.value)";>
```

```
<INPUT type=button value="Clear"
onClick='document.theForm.inStr.value=""';>
Results
<TEXTAREA name=results rows=5 cols=90>
</TEXTAREA>
<INPUT type=button name="theButton" value="Clear Results"
   onClick='document.theForm.results.value=""';>
</FORM>
</BODY>
```

Splitting a String

Let's not split hairs—instead, let's split strings!

The functions I'm about to show you that do things to the "words" in a string use the split method of the String object.

No, the split method isn't something devised to break up couples! Rather, the split method breaks a string into an array of strings, using a specified *delimiter*. The delimiter is a character or string that's used to specify where the original string splits. For example, if you had the string "Ohana means family", and the delimiter were the string " means ", then using the split method would create a two-element array with the first element containing the value "Ohana" and the second element containing the value "family".

Here's the way this little example might look in code:

```
var str = "Ohana means family";
var delim =" means ";
var strArray = new Array(str.split(delim));
```

strArray[0] would now contain the string value "Ohana" and strArray[1] would contain the value "family".

 NOTE You can also use a regular expression as the delimiter. Regular expressions are explained in the "Regular Expressions" section of this chapter.

ADVANCED

A crude way to separate the words out of a string of text is to split the string using the space character (" ") as the delimiter. The examples in this section use this recipe, which isn't perfect! There are a number of special situations that cause it to not capitalize words that should be capitalized. For example, a word immediately following a quotation will not be capitalized. Another example: A word entered following a line break will not be capitalized unless spaces were also entered.

The algorithm for splitting a text string into words using a space as the delimiter is quite crude.

Certainly, you could write code to deal with each special case that mattered to you. As a matter of fact, as an exercise, why don't you write some code to deal with each of these special situations? (Hint: The easiest thing to do to cover several cases is to use a regular expression as the delimiter.)

In the meantime, close enough is good enough! The examples in this section will use a space character (" ") as a crude way to split text strings into words. But let's just be sure that we're on the same page that this isn't a perfect way to determine the words in a text string.

Capitalizing "Words" in a String

Listing 9-4 shows the capWords function that capitalizes the first letter in each word of the string. The function also assigns its results to the value of the results <textarea> element, but alternatively you could design the function to just return a value (the string with the first letter of each word capitalized).

LISTING 9-4

Capitalizing the First Letter in Each Word of a String

```
function capWords(str){
   var words = str.split(" ");
   for (var i=0 ; i < words.length ; i++){
      var testwd = words[i];
      var firLet = testwd.substr(0,1);
      var rest = testwd.substr(1, testwd.length -1)
      words[i] = firLet.toUpperCase() + rest
   }
   document.theForm.results.value = words.join(" ");
}
```

If you open the page containing the user interface HTML and the capWords function in a browser, you can enter text as shown in Figure 9-3.

When you click Capitalize Words, the button's onClick handler calls the capWords function, which displays the results of capitalizing the first letters of each word in the results <textarea>, also as shown in Figure 9-3.

Here's how the capWords function works:

1. The input string is broken up into an array of words using a space as a delimiter.

2. The array of words is iterated through.

3. Each "word" is divided into two strings using the String object's substr method.

4. The two strings are the first letter and the rest of the word.

5. The first letter is capitalized using the toUpperCase method.

6. The capitalized first letter is concatenated back together with the rest of the word.

7. The remade word is assigned as the value in the array of words.

8. The array of words is joined together, with a space character inserted between each element.

9. The result is assigned to the value of the <textarea> (alternatively, this value could be used as the return value of the function).

Counting "Words"

Listing 9-5 shows the function used to count the words in a text string.

LISTING 9-5

Counting the Words in a Text String

```
function countWords(str){
    var count = 0;
    var words = str.split(" ");
     for (i=0 ; i < words.length ; i++){
        // inner loop -- do the count
        if (words[i] != "")
            count += 1;
    }
    document.theForm.results.value =
        "There are " +
        count +
        " words in the text string you entered!";
}
```

As with the example in the previous section that capitalizes the first letter of each word, the split method is used to save each word as an element of an array.

If you're looking at this code carefully, you might wonder at this point why we can't just assume that the length property of the array of words is the number of words in the array. However, the length property of the words array can't be used by itself to determine the number of words because some of the elements of the array may be strings without characters (spaces). It's necessary to include a test for empty words:

```
if (words[i] != "")
    count += 1;
```

As an exercise, it might be fun to see what happens without this test. Rewrite the code to simply return the length of the words array and try entering a string with multiple spaces between words. You'll find the count is inaccurate. What other ways of rewriting this code can you think of?

If you run the code in the user interface in a Web browser, enter a text string containing words, and click Count Words, the number of words in the string will be displayed (see Figure 9-4).

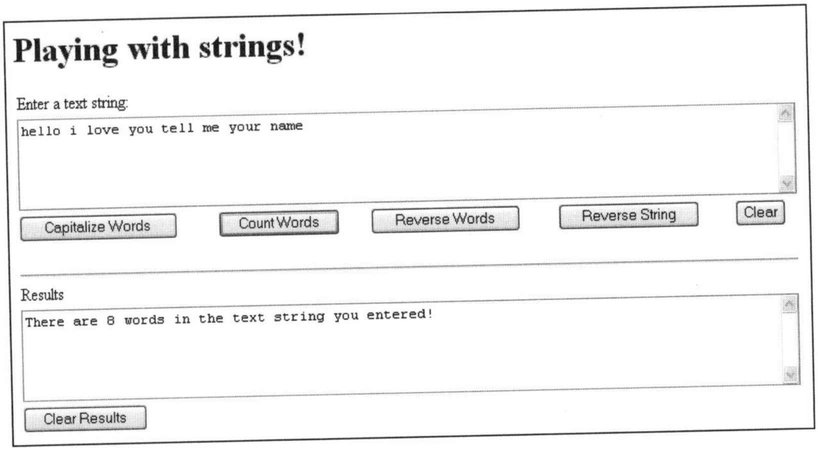

FIGURE 9-4
The function counts the number of words in a string.

Reversing the Words in a String

We'll take a slightly different tack to reverse the words in a string.

Here's how the process will work conceptually:

1. First, the input string is broken up into an array of words using the split method in the usual fashion.

2. A new array, backwards, is created to hold the words in backwards order.

3. As the original array is looped through, each word is assigned to the backwards array. However, the backwards array uses a counter that starts at the top and works its way down.

4. Finally, the elements of the backwards array are joined together and displayed as the results of the operation.

The following shows the process with the actual code that will be used.

To Reverse the Words in a String:

1. Split the string into an array of words, using a space as the delimiter:

```
function revWords(str){
   var words = str.split(" ");

}
```

2. Create a new array for the reversed string:

```
function revWords(str){
   var words = str.split(" ");
   var backWords = new Array();

}
```

3. Assign the last word of the old array to the first element of the new array. In other words, cycle backwards through the original array:

```
function revWords(str){
   var words = str.split(" ");
   var j = words.length - 1;
   var backWords = new Array();
   for (i=0 ; i < words.length ; i++){
      backWords[j] = words[i];
      j--
   }

}
```

4. Display the results:

```
function revWords(str){
   var words = str.split(" ");
   var j = words.length - 1;
   var backWords = new Array();
   for (i=0 ; i < words.length ; i++){
      backWords[j] = words[i];
      j--
   }
   document.theForm.results.value = backWords.join(" ");
}
```

5. Add the function to the user interface and open the page in a Web browser.

6. Enter some text containing words in the upper textarea box.

7. Click Reverse Words. The reversed words will be displayed in the bottom textarea box (see Figure 9-5).

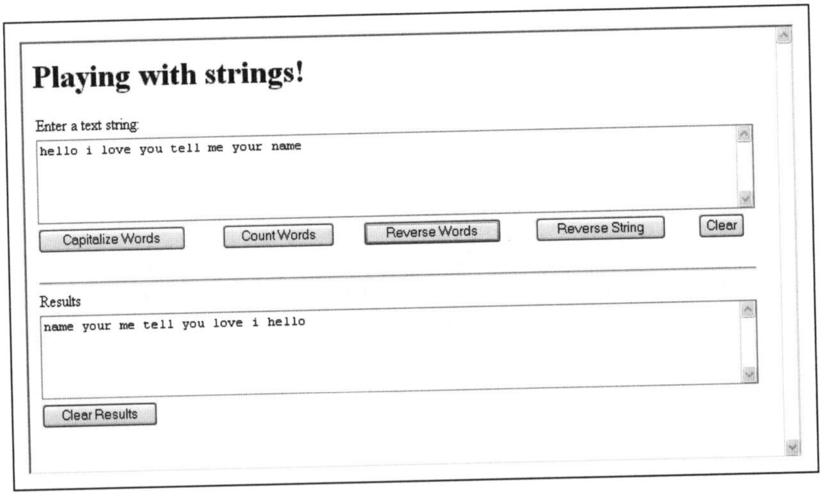

FIGURE 9-5

The words in the text string are reversed.

Reversing a String

Reversing a string is a pretty common programming task. In fact, many programming languages (but not JavaScript) have a built-in string method for reversing a string.

I'm sure you'll appreciate that reversing a string is a different operation from reversing the order of the words in a string.

The string reversal function I'll show you, revString, shown in Listing 9-6, returns the reversed string value rather than displaying the value, so it's a more generally usable function.

The idea is to iterate through the string input from the top, or last, character down. Each character is then added to the beginning of the new, reversed string using the substr method.

> *Reversing a string isn't the same as reversing the order of the words within a string.*

 TIP Remember that being "one off" is a great source of programming errors! Think carefully about the upper and lower bounds for loops such as the one used in Listing 9-6 because it's easy to be off by one.

LISTING 9-6

Reversing a String

```
function revString(str) {
    var retStr = "";
    for (i=str.length - 1 ; i > - 1 ; i--){
        retStr += str.substr(i,1);
    }
    return retStr;
}
...
<INPUT type=button value="Reverse String"
    onClick="document.theForm.results.value =
revString(document.theForm.inStr.value)";>
```

The revString function is called and passed the input value in one fell swoop in an assignment statement in the onClick handler (as shown at the end of Listing 9-6).

If you run the function within the user interface opened in a browser, you can enter a text string. Next, click the Reverse String button. The reversed string will appear in the bottom textarea box (see Figure 9-6).

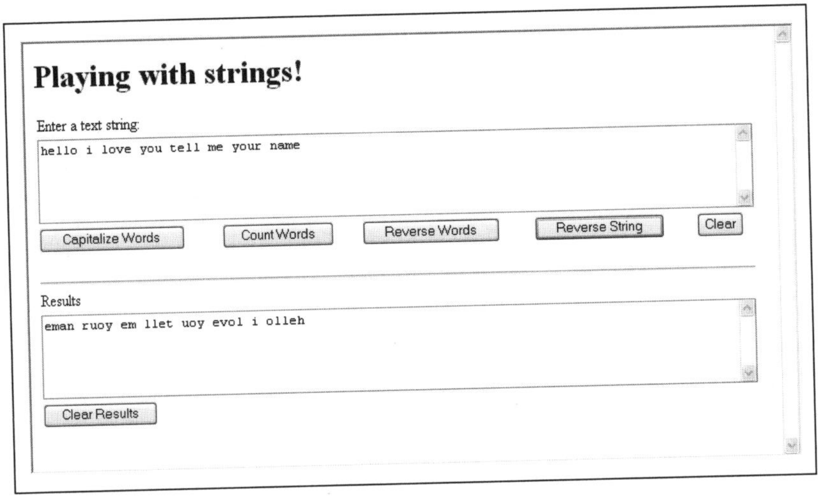

FIGURE 9-6
The string has been reversed.

You can go ahead and play with these strings, using more than one of the string manipulation functions on a given string by copying and pasting the results of an initial manipulation back into the upper box and then applying another manipulation function.

For example, Figure 9-7 shows the reversed string created in Figure 9-6 but with all the first letters of words capitalized.

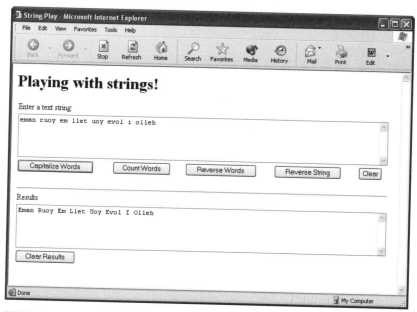

FIGURE 9-7

The first letters of the words in the reversed string have been capitalized.

Listing 9-7 shows the complete code for the Playing with Strings application.

LISTING 9-7

Playing with Strings

```
<HTML>
<HEAD>
   <TITLE>String Play</TITLE>
<SCRIPT>
function capWords(str){
   // break into an array of words,
   // using space as the delimiter
   var words = str.split(" ");
   for (var i=0 ; i < words.length ; i++){
      // inner loop -- do the capitalizing
      var testwd = words[i];
      var firLet = testwd.substr(0,1); //lop off first letter
      var rest = testwd.substr(1, testwd.length -1)
      words[i] = firLet.toUpperCase() + rest
```

```
      }
      document.theForm.results.value = words.join(" ");
   }
   function countWords(str){
      var count = 0;
      // break into an array of words,
      // using space as the delimiter
      // words.length won't work because of spaces
      var words = str.split(" ");
        for (i=0 ; i < words.length ; i++){
           // inner loop -- do the count
           if (words[i] != "")
              count += 1;
        }

        document.theForm.results.value =
           "There are " +
           count +
           " words in the text string you entered!";
   }
   function revWords(str){
      // break into an array of words,
      // using space as the delimiter
      var words = str.split(" ");
      var j = words.length - 1;
      var backWords = new Array();
      for (i=0 ; i < words.length ; i++){
         backWords[j] = words[i];
         j--
      }
      document.theForm.results.value = backWords.join(" ");
   }
   function revString(str) {
      var retStr = "";
      for (i=str.length - 1 ; i > - 1 ; i--){
         retStr += str.substr(i,1);
      }
      return retStr;
   }
   </SCRIPT>
   </HEAD>
   <BODY>
```

```
<H1>
Playing with strings!
</H1>
<FORM name="theForm">
<TABLE>
<tr><td colspan=5>
Enter a text string:
</td></tr><tr><td colspan=5>
<TEXTAREA name=inStr rows=5 cols=90>
</TEXTAREA>
</td></tr><tr><td>
<INPUT type=button value="Capitalize Words"
    onClick="capWords(document.theForm.inStr.value)";>
</td><td>
<INPUT type=button value="Count Words"
    onClick="countWords(document.theForm.inStr.value)";>
</td><td>
<INPUT type=button value="Reverse Words"
onClick="revWords(document.theForm.inStr.value)";>
</td><td>
<INPUT type=button value="Reverse String"
    onClick="document.theForm.results.value =
revString(document.theForm.inStr.value)";>
</td><td>
<INPUT type=button value="Clear"
onClick='document.theForm.inStr.value=""';>
</td></tr><tr><td colspan=5><br><hr>
Results<br>
</td></tr><tr><td colspan=5>
<TEXTAREA name=results rows=5 cols=90>
</TEXTAREA>
</td></tr><tr><td colspan=5>
<INPUT type=button name="theButton" value="Clear Results"
    onClick='document.theForm.results.value=""';>
</td></tr>
</TABLE>
</FORM>
</BODY>
</HTML>
```

ADVANCED

Regular Expressions

A *regular expression* is used to define a pattern of characters. These patterns can be used for many purposes, including string manipulation, user input validation, and searching and replacing. Typically, the pattern represented by the regular expression is matched against a string. In the simplest example, the regular expression is a literal string of characters, for example, *moth*. This simple regular expression pattern matches against a string that contains it, for example, *mothra*. The regular expression fails to match a string that doesn't contain it, such as *godzilla*.

Although this example seems simple enough, you shouldn't underestimate the importance of regular expressions, which provide access to powerful algorithms that are the natural and easy answer to many programming problems. It's also a great deal of fun to learn to program with regular expressions!

In JavaScript, regular expressions are deployed using methods of the String object and the regular expression object (the regular expression object is called RegExp). In this section, we'll only look at using regular expressions with the String object. I won't explain the methods associated with the RegExp object.

Regular expressions are literals enclosed within a pair of slash characters, for example:

```
/harold/
```

In other words, regular expressions are literals delimited by slashes in the same way that strings are delimited by quotation marks. So /moth/ is to regular expressions as "moth" is to strings.

> *The regular expression* moth *fails to match the string* Godzilla, *but* moth *would match* mothra *or* There are moths in the room.

To Create a Regular Expression:

1. Assign a pattern to a variable. For example:

```
var pattern = /mothra/;
```

Within regular expressions, alphabetic and numerical characters represent themselves. Here are some examples of this simple kind of regular expression:

```
/mothra/
/m/
/1234/
/Ma65/
```

In addition, there are many special characters that have meaning as part of the *grammar* (or rules) of regular expressions. These special characters and the rules for creating regular expressions are fairly intricate, and I'm won't go into them in great detail in this section. Instead, I'll show you a few simple examples involving regular expressions so that you can get a feel for them and begin to have some appreciation for what they can do for you and your programs.

In other words, the whole topic of regular expressions is pretty involved. I hesitated to even bring it up in *Learn How to Program*. This is a tough topic, and I don't want you to get confused. But ultimately, I decided you should at least be exposed to the concept of a regular expression and get some feeling for what it can do.

If you look at the rules for creating regular expressions presented later in this section and decide that they're too complicated to be fun, fine! You can skip the material. However, you should at least get a feeling for what regular expressions can do so that if you encounter a programming problem that cries out for their use, you can then figure out how to use them.

On the other hand, if you like regular expressions, you can go ahead and learn them in depth!

You should also know that when you've seen the regular expression engine in one language, you've pretty much seen the regular expression engine in all computer languages. Regular expressions work the same way in JavaScript as in Java as in Perl as in Visual Basic as in C#.

> *I'm a computer program crying out for a regular expression!*

> *If regular expressions tickle your fancy, go ahead and learn all about them!*

> *Regular expressions work in pretty much the same way no matter what the language.*

The Man Who Invented Regular Expressions

The concept of the regular expression was invented in the 1950s by Stephen Kleene, a lanky mathematician and logician. Kleene, who was a remarkably tall man and enjoyed mountain climbing in his spare time, was inspired in his work by Gödel and Turing.

The first use of regular expressions in computers was as part of compilers. A *compiler* is a program that converts code written in a high-level computer language to instructions that the computer can understand. Regular expressions were (and are) useful in compilers because they help the compiler to recognize the elements that it's processing and to make sure they're syntactically correct, also called *well-formed*.

String Regular Expression Methods

The String object has four methods that are used with regular expressions. Table 9-3 describes these methods.

TABLE 9-3

String Object Regular Expression Methods

Method	Description
match()	Performs pattern matching with a string.
replace()	Searches and replaces within a string using a regular expression.
search()	Searches within a string using a regular expression.
split()	Splits a string into an array using a delimiter (as explained earlier in this chapter). The delimiter can be a regular expression, which is very cool.

Basic Regular Expression Syntax

An alphanumeric character within a regular expression matches itself as in the *moth* examples at the beginning of this section. In another example, the regular expression v matches the v in the string *love*.

This basic character matching, called a *literal* character match, is at the core of the concept of a regular expression. But let's kick it up several notches! Things are about to get more complicated.

Besides alphanumeric characters, you can match many nonalphanumeric characters using escape sequences.

Table 9-4 shows regular expression literal character matches for both alphanumeric characters and nonalphanumeric characters.

Let's kick it up a notch! Things are about to get more complicated.

TABLE 9-4

Regular Expression Characters and Character Sequences, and Their Matches

Character/ Character Sequence	Matches
Alphabetic (a–z and A–Z)	Itself
Numeric (0-9)	Itself
\b	Backspace within a [] character class (character classes are discussed shortly); outside a character class but within a regular expression, it means a word boundary
\f	Form feed
\n	New line
\r	Carriage return
\t	Tab
\/	Slash (literal /)
\\	For-slash (literal \)
\.	.
*	*
\+	+
\?	?
|	|
\(	(
\ )	)
\[	[
\]	]
\{	{
\}	}
\xxx	The character specified by the octal number xxx
\xnn	The character specified by the hexadecimal number nn

Attributes

There's an exception to the rule that regular expression patterns appear with the forward slash delimiters. Two regular expression *attributes*—which may be combined—can be placed after the final forward slash. These are as follows:

- **i** means perform a case-insensitive match.

- **g** means find all occurrences of the pattern match, not just the first: This is termed a *global* match.

As an example:

```
/mOTh/i
```

matches *mothra* because the regular expression is case insensitive.

Character Classes

Individual literal characters can be combined into *character classes* in regular expressions. Character classes are contained within square brackets. A match occurs when one or more of the characters contained in the character class produces a match with the comparison string.

To Use a Character Class:

Place the characters that are the members of the class within square brackets to create a regular expresssion. For example:

```
/[1234]/
```

The characters within a class can be specified using ranges, rather than by specific enumeration. A hyphen is used to indicate a range. Here are some examples:

```
/[a-z]/           // means all lowercase characters from a to z
/[a-zA-L]/        // means all lowercase characters from a to z and all
                  // uppercase characters between A and L
/[a-zA-Z0-9]/     // means all lowercase and uppercase letters, and all
                  // numerals
```

Thus, /[a-zA-L]/ wouldn't produce a match with the string XYZ. But it would match the string *xyz*. By the way, you may have noticed that you could use the case attribute instead of separately listing uppercase and lowercase ranges. /[a-z]/i is the equivalent of /[a-zA-Z]/.

Negating a Character Class

A character class can be negated. A negated class matches any character *except* those defined within brackets.

To Negate a Character Class:

Place a caret (^) as the first character inside the left bracket of the class. For example:

```
/[^a-zA-Z]/
```

In this example, the regular expression /[^a-zA-Z]/ will match if and only if the comparison string contains at least one nonalphabetic character. *abcABC123* is a match, but *abcABC* is not.

Common Character Class Representations

Because some character classes are frequently used, JavaScript regular expression syntax provides special sequences that are shorthand representations of these classes. Square brackets aren't used with most of these special character "abbreviations."

Table 9-5 shows the sequences that can be used for character classes.

TABLE 9-5

Character Class Sequences and Their Meanings

Character Sequence	Matches
[...]	Any one character between the square brackets.
[^...]	Any one character not between the brackets.
.	Any one character other than new line. Equivalent to [^\n].
\w	Any one letter, number or underscore. Is equivalent to [a–zA–Z0–9_].
\W	Any one character other than a letter, number, or underscore. Equivalent to [^a–zA–Z0–9_].
\s	Any one space character or other white space character. Equivalent to [\t\n\r\f\v].
\S	Any one character other than a space or other white space character. Equivalent to [^ \t\n\r\f\v].
\d	Any one digit. Equivalent to [0–9].
\D	Any one character that is not a digit. This is equivalent to [^0–9].

For example, the pattern /\W/ matches a string containing a hyphen (–), but it fails against a string containing only letters (such as abc).

In another example, /\s/ matches a string containing a space, such as *mothra and godzilla*. But /\s/ fails against strings that don't contain white space characters, such as *antidisestablishmentarianism*.

Repeating Elements

So far, if you wanted to match a multiple number of characters, the only way to achieve this using a regular expression would be to enumerate each character. For example, /\d\d/ would match any two-digit number. And /\w\w\w\w/ would match any four-letter alphanumeric string such as *love* or *1234*.

This isn't good enough. In addition to being cumbersome, it doesn't allow complex pattern matches involving varied numbers of characters. For example, you might want to match a number between two and six digits in length or a pair of letters followed by a number of any length.

This kind of "wildcard" pattern is specified in JavaScript regular expressions using curly braces ({}). The curly braces follow the pattern element that's to be repeated and specify the number of times the pattern element is to be repeated.

In addition, there are some special characters that are used to specify common types of repetition.

Table 9-6 shows both the curly brace syntax and the special repetition characters.

TABLE 9-6

Syntax for Repeating Pattern Elements

Repetition Syntax	Meaning
{n,m}	Match the preceding element at least n times but no more than m times.
{n,}	Match the preceding element n or more times.
{n}	Match the preceding element exactly n times.
?	Match the preceding element zero or one times. In other words, the element is optional. Equivalent to {0,1}.
+	Match one or more occurrences of the preceding element. Equivalent to {1,}.
*	Match zero or more occurrences of the preceding element. In other words, the element is optional but can also appear multiple times. Equivalent to {0,}.

Organizing Patterns

The JavaScript regular expression syntax provides special characters that allow you to organize patterns. These characters are shown in Table 9-7 and are explained in a little more detail following the table.

TABLE 9-7
Alternation, Grouping, and Reference Characters

Character	Meaning
|	Alternation. This matches the character or subexpression to the left or right of the | character.
(...)	Groups several items into a unit, or subexpression, that can be used with repeated syntax and referred to later in an expression.
\n	Matches the same characters that were matched when the subexpression \n was first matched.

Alternation

The pipe character (|) is used to indicate an alternative. For example, the regular expression /jaws|that|bite/ matches the three strings *jaws*, *that*, or *bite*. In another example, /\d{2}|[A-Z]{4}/ matches either two digits or four capital letters.

Grouping

Parentheses are used to group elements in a regular expression. Once items have been grouped into *subexpressions*, they can be treated as a single element using repetition syntax. For example, /visual(basic)?/ matches *visual* followed by the optional *basic*.

Referring to Subexpressions

Parentheses are also used to refer back to a subexpression that's part of a regular expression. Each subexpression that has been grouped in parentheses is internally assigned an identification number. The subexpressions are numbered from left to right, using the position of the left parenthesis to determine order. Nesting of subexpressions is allowed.

Subexpressions are referred to using a backslash followed by a number. So \1 means the first subexpression, \2 the second, and so on.

A reference to a subexpression matches the same characters that were originally matched by the subexpression.

For example, the regular expression:

```
/['"][^'"]*['"]/
```

matches a string that starts with a single or double quote and ends with a single or double quote. (The middle element, [^'"]*, matches any number of characters, provided they're not single or double quotes.)

This expression doesn't distinguish between the two kinds of quotes. A comparison string that started with a double quote and ended with a single quote would match this expression. For example:

```
"Ohana means family. Nobody gets left behind or forgotten.'
```

This, which starts with a double quote and ends with a single quote, matches the regular expression pattern I just showed you, even though it isn't symmetrical in respect to the kinds of quotation marks used.

 NOTE An improved result would be to have a match depend on the kind of quote with which the match began. If it begins with a double quote, it should end with a double quote; likewise, if it starts with a single quote, it should end with a single quote. As an exercise, if you're having fun with regular expressions, go ahead and implement this!

TRY THIS AT HOME

If you've worked your way through the material I've just shown you, you now know everything you always wanted to know about regular expressions but were afraid to ask!

It's time to hit the pedal to the metal and the rubber to the road. Let's work through a few examples that show how regular expressions can be used.

This section explains everything you always wanted to know about regular expressions but were afraid to ask!

Matching a Date

Suppose you have a program that asks the user to input a date. The problem is that you need to be sure that the user has actually input a date in the format that your program requires. The answer is to use a regular expression to make sure the text string entered by the user matches the format your program needs.

NOTE In the real world, there are a number of other ways to handle this problem. The best solution might be to only allow visual inputting of dates via a calendar interface. That way, not only could you make sure that the format was right, you could also make sure that the data entered was actually a date.

To Match a Date in mm/dd/yyyy Format:

1. Use \/ to represent a slash within the pattern (see Table 9-4 for an explanation of this literal character sequence).

2. Use parentheses to group the digits that represent month, days, and year:

   ```
   (\d{2})
   (\d{2})
   (\d{4})
   ```

3. Combine the slash sequence with the month, days, and year:

   ```
   (\d{2})\/(\d{2})\/(\d{4})
   ```

4. Add a \b at the beginning and end of the regular expression to make sure that the date string starts and the fourth-year digit ends a "word":

   ```
   /\b(\d{2})\/(\d{2})\/(\d{4})\b/
   ```

5. The regular expression is now complete. To use it, first create a function to check the date format against a text string passed to the function:

   ```
   function checkDate(testStr) {

   }
   ```

6. Within the function, assign the regular expression to a variable named pattern:

   ```
   var pattern = /\b(\d{2})\/(\d{2})\/(\d{4})\b/;
   ```

7. Use the match method of the string passed to the function, with the regular expression, to check to see if there's a match and display a message accordingly:

```
var result = testStr.match(pattern);
if (result != null)
    return "Well done. This look likes a date in the specified
format!";
else
return "For shame! You didn't input a date in the specified
pattern.";
```

8. Set up an HTML form with a text box for the user to input a string to test for "dateness" and a button with an onClick event handler to launch the checking function as shown in Listing 9-8.

9. Open the HTML page that includes the regular expression and user interface, shown completely in Listing 9-8, in a Web browser.

10. Enter something that is manifestly not a date, and click Verify the Format. The appropriate message will display (see Figure 9-8).

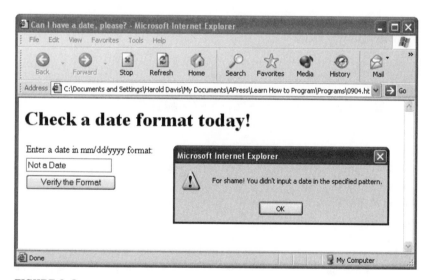

FIGURE 9-8

Using the regular expression pattern shows that the user input isn't in date format.

11. Enter a string correctly formatted as a mm/dd/yyyy date, and click Verify the Format. This time, the input will be recognized as being in "date" format (see Figure 9-9).

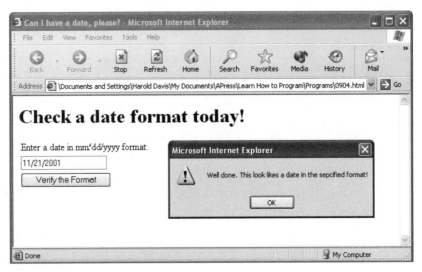

FIGURE 9-9

It's easy to use regular expressions to make sure that user input is in the proper format.

LISTING 9-8

Using a Regular Expression to Match a Date Format

```
<HTML>
<HEAD>
   <TITLE>Can I have a date, please?</TITLE>
<SCRIPT>
function checkDate(testStr) {
   var pattern = /\b(\d{2})\/(\d{2})\/(\d{4})\b/;
   var result = testStr.match(pattern);
   if (result != null)
      return "Well done. This look likes a date in the specified format!";
   else
      return "For shame! You didn't input a date in the specified
pattern.";
}
</SCRIPT>
```

```
</HEAD>
<BODY>
<H1>
Check a date format today!
</H1>
<FORM name="theForm">
<TABLE>
<tr><td colspan=4>
Enter a date in mm/dd/yyyy format:
</td></tr><tr><td colspan = 4>
<INPUT type=text name=testStr size=20 maxlength=10>
</td></tr>
<tr><td colspan=4>
<INPUT type=button name="theButton" value="Verify the Format"
onClick="alert(checkDate(document.theForm.testStr.value))";>
</td>
</tr>
</TABLE>
</FORM>
</BODY>
</HTML>
```

Trimming a String

You might think that *trimming* a string is something like trimming a tree or providing a holiday meal with all the trimmings! But no, in fact, trimming a string means to remove leading and/or trailing space characters from a string. This is an operation that often takes place within programs. In fact, it's so common that many languages (but not JavaScript) have built-in trimming functions. Fortunately, it's easy to create your own trimming functions using regular expressions.

 TIP You could create trimming functions without using regular expressions, but regular expressions make it very easy!

I don't trim Christmas trees, I trim strings!

A left trim removes leading space characters. A right trim removes trailing space characters. If you simply trim, you remove both leading and trailing spaces from a string.

I've organized the trim example so that the trim function calls both the right trim function and the left trim function, thus removing both leading and trailing blanks. Although the sample application is used for full trimming, you could easily break out the left trim or right trim functions if you needed to use them.

Here's the regular expression used for a left trim (it matches the first nonspace character and then continues to the end of the string):

```
var pattern = /[^\s]+.*/;
```

Here's the regular expression used for a right trim (it matches everything up to the trailing spaces):

```
var pattern = /.*[\S]/;
```

To understand this example, you should know that the match method of the String object, which accepts a regular expression to make the matches, returns a results array. The first element of the results array (its zero element) contains the first pattern match made with the regular expression, which is what's used in this example to return the trimmed string.

Have fun trimming!

To Trim a String Using Regular Expressions:

1. Create a form with two text inputs, one for an input string and the other for the trimmed version of the input string:

```
<FORM name="theForm">
<TABLE>
<tr><td colspan=4>
Enter string for trimming:
</td></tr><tr><td colspan = 4>
<INPUT type=text name=testStr size=60>
</td></tr>

...
<tr><td colspan=4><br><hr>
Here's the trimmed string:
<br></td></tr><tr><td colspan = 4>
<INPUT type=text name=display size=60>
</td></tr>
</TABLE>
</FORM>
```

2. Create an input button that invokes a function named trim using the input string as the function argument and displaying the trimmed result:

```
<INPUT type=button name="theButton" value="Trim"
   onClick="document.theForm.display.value =
   trim(document.theForm.testStr.value)";>
```

3. Create a trim function that returns the trimmed value using a left trim (ltrim) and right trim (rtrim) function:

```
function trim(testStr) {
   return rtrim(ltrim(testStr));
}
```

4. Create the scaffolding for the ltrim function:

```
function ltrim(testStr) {

}
```

5. Add code to ltrim() that returns an empty string if the input was empty:

```
function ltrim(testStr) {
   if (testStr == "")
      return "";
   else {

   }
}
```

Without this code, the function will generate a run-time syntax error when the pattern match is attempted against an empty string.

6. Construct the regular expression that matches anything that's not blank and then continues to the end of the string:

```
var pattern = /[^\s]+.*/;
```

7. Use the match method of the String object to match the regular expression against the input string and obtain a result array:

```
function ltrim(testStr) {
    if (testStr == "")
        return "";
    else {
        var pattern = /[^\s]+.*/;
        result = testStr.match(pattern);


    }
}
```

8. Return the string that matches the pattern (the [0] element of the result array):

```
function ltrim(testStr) {
    if (testStr == "")
        return "";
    else {
        var pattern = /[^\s]+.*/;
        result = testStr.match(pattern);
        return result[0];
    }
}
```

9. Construct the scaffolding for the rtrim function, along with the check for empty input:

```
function rtrim(testStr) {
    if (testStr == "")
        return "";
    else {

    }
}
```

10. Create a pattern that matches anything and everything up until the first of the trailing blanks:

```
var pattern = /.*[\S]/;
```

11. Use the match method to obtain a regular expression match and return the first element (result[0]) of the result array:

```
function rtrim(testStr) {
    if (testStr == "")
        return "";
    else {
        var pattern = /.*[\S]/;
        result = testStr.match(pattern);
        return result[0];
    }
}
```

12. Save the page and open it in a browser (the complete code is shown in Listing 9-9).

13. Enter a text string for trimming.

14. Click Trim. The results of trimming will appear as shown in Figure 9-10.

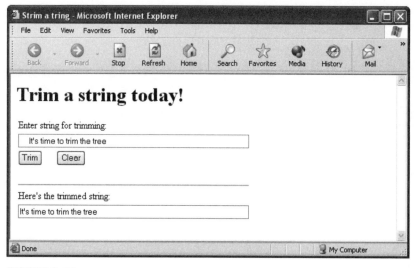

FIGURE 9-10

Regular expressions can be used to trim a string.

LISTING 9-9

Trimming a String Using Regular Expressions

```
<HTML>
<HEAD>
   <TITLE>Strim a tring</TITLE>
<SCRIPT>
function ltrim(testStr) {
   if (testStr == "")
      return "";
   else {
      var pattern = /[^\s]+.*/;
      result = testStr.match(pattern);
      return result[0];
   }
}
function rtrim(testStr) {
   if (testStr == "")
      return "";
   else {
      var pattern = /.*[\S]/;
      result = testStr.match(pattern);
      return result[0];
   }
}

function trim(testStr) {
   return rtrim(ltrim(testStr));
}

</SCRIPT>
</HEAD>
<BODY>
<H1>
Trim a string today!
</H1>
<FORM name="theForm">
<TABLE>
<tr><td colspan=4>
Enter string for trimming:
</td></tr><tr><td colspan = 4>
<INPUT type=text name=testStr size=60>
```

```
</td></tr>
<tr><td colspan=3>
<INPUT type=button name="theButton" value="Trim"
   onClick="document.theForm.display.value =
   trim(document.theForm.testStr.value)";>
</td><td>
<INPUT type=button name="theButton" value="Clear"
   onClick='document.theForm.testStr.value="";
document.theForm.display.value=""'>
</td></tr><tr><td colspan=4> <br><hr>
Here's the trimmed string:
<br> </td></tr><tr><td colspan = 4>
<INPUT type=text name=display size=60>
</td></tr>
</TABLE>
</FORM>
</BODY>
</HTML>
```

Many Other Uses for Regular Expressions!

There are many, many other uses for regular expressions.

Here are a couple of examples off the top of my head.

The following regular expression will match any URL that includes a protocol, for example, `http://www.apress.com` or `http://www.bearhome.com`:

`/\w+:\/\/[\w.]+\/\S*/`

But suppose you need to parse out the parts of a URL, for example, to determine a domain name from a URL. This kind of chore is often done to provide information about Web traffic, to analyze Web server logs, to create Web crawlers, or to perform automated navigation on behalf of a user.

How would you write a regular expression that could be used to parse out the component parts of a URL?

Another place that regular expressions are useful is in parsing words out of a text string. In the Playing with strings example earlier in this chapter, I showed you how to parse the words out of a text string using a space character as the delimiter between words. I noted that this was a pretty crude way to determine whether something was or wasn't a word and that using a space as a delimiter failed to also recognize "words." You can use a regular expression as a better way to match words in a string.

> *Can you figure out how this regular expression works?*

To Match a Word:
Use the regular expression:

```
/\b[A-Za-z'-]+\b/
```

You still have to think carefully about what exactly a "word" is. This regular expression defines a word to include apostrophes and hyphens but not digits or underscores (so *42nd* would fail the match).

Regular expressions are also powerful tools to use when you need to search for text. Most of the search engines you use in everyday life—for example, eBay, Google, and Yahoo—are largely powered by regular expressions.

What's It All About?

Well, Alfie (or Austin), you've come a long way. This chapter contained some pretty powerful and complicated material. I bet if you tell your friends and neighbors that you've learned to program using regular expressions, they'll be mightily impressed.

It's the case that coding with text strings, which with a nod to the control freaks among us is often called *string manipulation*, is important to a great many programs. If you can program well with strings, you've probably learned to be a good programmer. The material in this chapter should have you well on your way to becoming a veritable Machiavelli with strings!

The next chapter, Chapter 10, "Error Handling and Debugging," covers some very important material relating to program flaws, or bugs. What are the different kinds of program bugs? How are they best avoided in the first place? How can you test your programs to uncover bugs? How can you find and fix bugs if you have them? What's the best way to write code to "bullet proof" it against bugs?

So I'll see you in the next chapter for the big bug roundup! Yee-haw!

Calling All Readers

Regular expressions are fun. See what you can come up with! If you write a neat program in JavaScript that uses regular expressions, send it to me (use the email address `learntoprogram@bearhome.com`).

I'll publish the best examples I get in the next edition of this book. You'll receive credit for the program and a free copy of the book when it's republished.

10

Debugging and Exceptions

Economics has been dubbed "the dismal science," but there's nothing so dismal as debugging a computer program that's malfunctioning.

Before you can fix a computer program, you usually need to know the why and how of its malfunction. I've spent many frustrating hours trying to understand why a program isn't working properly.

If things really go wrong, in the process of fixing the program I make things worse. Usually, this means I don't understand the problem well enough. Be this as it may, it's human to attempt to shortcut tedious tasks—but doing so often leads to long delays!

Anyhow, if I attempt to fix a program without really first understanding the problem, I might try something and then run the program again to see if the fix worked. If I'm lucky, the fix worked! But, if not, I'm often hit with a flash of inspiration and try another "quick fix." By the time I've iterated this process half a dozen times, I may no longer even be able to get back to where I started—and the program still doesn't work right!

The moral of this sordid little tale of woe and bad working habits is that debugging a computer program is one place in which it pays to work in an organized fashion. Be calm, cool, and collected, and keep notes so that you can retrace your steps.

Perhaps the most important habit when debugging is to be methodical. It helps to think things through as though you were the computer, processing the software program. What could have caused the aberrant results? What are the possibilities? How can you rule them out one by one?

Be methodical. Think like a computer!

As I said in the first chapter of this book, to successfully program you must learn to think like a computer. Nowhere is this truer than in debugging.

The goal of this chapter is to provide you with the tools you need to deal with bugs. To that end, I'll provide an overview of the different categories of bugs you'll encounter: syntax errors, runtime errors, and logical errors. This material is language independent and applies to all programming environments. I'll also briefly describe some of the most common kinds of errors.

Next, I'll explain syntax errors in the context of JavaScript. JavaScript lacks the sophisticated debugging tools available in most modern development environments, but I'll show you how to make the best of what's available.

Testing a program is a vital step in making sure that it's bug free and in uncovering latent defects. I'll provide some guidelines for testing your programs.

Finally, I'll show you how to add *exception handling* code to your programs using the JavaScript Error object. Exception handling allows you to anticipate and deal with errors that you think might happen; it's also a good way to structure code that's more rigorous and less prone to bugs in the first place.

Why Is a "Bug" a Bug?

Supposedly, the use of the word *bug* to mean a problem or flaw in a computer program comes from a literal insect that was creating havoc inside a 1950s computer. Admiral Grace Hopper, an early programmer and one of the creators of the language COBOL, is said to have discovered that a moth was causing a vacuum tube monster to malfunction, hence the term *bug*.

These days, a bug refers to any error, problem, or flaw that causes computer software or hardware to malfunction.

In actual historical fact, *bug* was used long before the invention of the computer to mean a glitch or problem in an industrial or scientific process. (Thomas Edison is on record as having used the term this way.) However, Admiral Hopper is probably the first to use the term in connection with a computer (if the moth causing her problem had been preserved, it would no doubt be a valuable collectible today!).

The Different Kinds of Bugs

Squash those bugs today!

As a general matter, three kinds of errors, or bugs, can occur in a program: syntax errors, runtime errors, and logical errors. We want to understand the kind of bug we have so we can squash that bug!

Syntax Errors

Syntax errors, which are the most easily dealt with kind of bug, are caused by improperly constructed code. Put a little more formally, a syntax error occurs when a statement in a program fails to meet the requirements of the language definition. Therefore, the program can't be compiled or interpreted—meaning "made ready" for the machine to execute—by the program designed to convert your "high-level" statements to machine-readable code.

It's a sin to commit a syntax error!

Just as there are many ways to sin, there are also many ways to create syntax errors. The most common of these are discussed later in this chapter in the section "JavaScript Syntax Errors."

If your code contains a syntax error, it's likely that you'll get a syntax error message when you attempt to open it in a browser. I'll show you how this works later in this chapter in the section "Finding Bugs."

The point here is that usually you can't even get a program to run if it contains syntax errors. This makes things easier because you know you have a problem. As the saying goes, the first step to fixing a problem is knowing you have one.

With syntax errors, you know you have a problem!

As I'll show you, the error message you get in JavaScript with a syntax error will help you to pinpoint the error by providing a line number for the problem. This facility is relatively wimpy compared with what you'll find in a full-fledged development environment such as Visual Studio .NET, which actually flags syntax errors as you create the statement containing them.

The advantage of learning in a "primitive" language such as the one used in this book (a text editor, JavaScript, and a Web browser) is that you'll learn to program well without creating too many syntax errors by necessity.

Runtime Errors

Runtime errors occur when a program that has no syntax errors attempts to perform an illegal operation.

JavaScript in a Web browser isn't a great environment for demonstrating runtime errors because it's protected by nature and has limited access to system resources.

For example, dividing by zero is generally inadvertent. One scenario that causes a division by zero is if the user inputs a value of zero, which is used in a division. (Of course, it's far more likely that the zero divisor will be the inadvertent result of a computation.)

In most environments, attempting to divide by zero causes a runtime error. However, in JavaScript, anything divided by zero is the special value Infinity, so attempting to divide by zero doesn't cause an error (see Listing 10-1 and Figure 10-1).

LISTING 10-1
Dividing by Zero

```
<HTML>
<HEAD>
<TITLE>Don't bug me, please!
</TITLE>
</HEAD>
<BODY>
<H1>
<SCRIPT>
var theNum = new Number(42 / 0);
var theStr = theNum.toString();
document.write(theStr);
</SCRIPT>
</H1>
</BODY>
</HTML>
```

Trust me, however, when I say that in most environments attempting to divide by zero at runtime will cause an error.

Many runtime errors are caused by attempting to access resources that aren't available for one reason or another: Because the resource doesn't exist, the program doesn't have proper permissions to access it, the resource hasn't been freed, or the resource is full.

To provide examples of these kinds of errors a little more concretely—they occur when you attempt to write to a full disk, write to a file that doesn't exist or that's being used by another program, use a network resource that isn't available, or log on to a database with incorrect credentials.

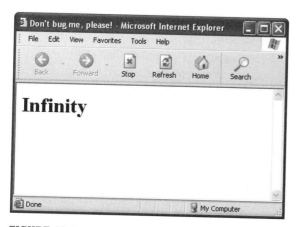

FIGURE 10-1

In JavaScript, anything divided by zero is the special value Infinity.

There's nothing syntactically illicit about any of these things; they just can't be done. They also can't all be easily anticipated.

The most embarrassing thing about runtime errors is that they often don't appear when you're testing a program. Runtime errors generally start to make themselves known only after your program is installed and someone starts using it, but good testing methodology, as I explain later in this chapter, helps obviate this possibility.

The best thing to do is to anticipate possible runtime problems and handle them using exception handling code as explained later in this chapter. If the user might enter zero causing a divide by zero flaw, handle that possibility using a catch clause. If your program depends upon access to a network drive, handle the possibility that the drive isn't available. And so on.

> *You should assume that any resource external to your program that your program depends upon might not be available and write code accordingly.*

Logical Errors

Logical errors occur when a program runs properly but produces the wrong results. This kind of error can be the hardest of all errors to debug because, unlike runtime errors, a logical error will often not produce a dramatic or obvious symptom such as a program crash. In contrast, in most environments (but not in JavaScript in a browser) there's no doubt that a program will crash if you try to perform an unhandled division by zero.

In fact, logical errors can cause inconsistent results that are sometimes correct and sometimes wrong. This situation can be particularly frustrating to debug. The subtler the problem, the harder it may be to fix (or to be sure that an error even exists).

> *Logical errors occur when a program runs properly but produces the wrong results.*

Thinking carefully about how your program works is one of the best ways to resolve logical errors. I'll show you some techniques later in this chapter for pinpointing logical errors although, frankly, the facilities available to JavaScript programmers working in a text editor are minimal.

As I've mentioned a number of times, one of the most common logical errors involves being "one off" when iterating through a loop. One-off errors are very common and quite pesky. You should always be on the lookout for one-off errors. Essentially, this error involves getting the termination condition for the loop wrong—it's off by one.

It's also easy to forget that JavaScript arrays start at zero and assume that they start at one.

Another condition that can be the source of problems is getting the termination condition of a while statement wrong.

> *It can be easy to get the termination condition in a* while *statement wrong.*

JavaScript Syntax Errors

This section discuses some common JavaScript errors. These problems may seem trivial, but the error messages generated by these bugs may point in completely different directions. So, if you're bewitched, bewildered, and baffled by a bug, double-check the pointers in this section.

Before we discuss specific syntax errors, let's look at the way you can tell in a Web browser that an error has taken place.

> *The error messages generated by these syntax errors may be confusing!*

Syntax Error Notification

If you load a page containing syntactically incorrect JavaScript into Internet Explorer, when the page loads, an error icon appears on the status bar along with a message "Done, but with errors on page," as shown in Figure 10-2. (I'll show you the comparable feature in Netscape later in this section.) One caveat is that if the syntax error is in code not processed as part of loading a page, for example, in an onClick event handler, then the syntax error may not display (until the event is fired).

To show an example of the way syntax errors are displayed, I took the Tchatshke Gulch program developed in Chapter 7 and Chapter 8, and I removed a closing parenthesis from one of its functions. When the mutilated code was saved and opened in Internet Explorer, a warning icon appeared on the left of the status bar at the bottom of the browser.

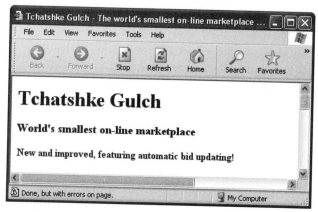

FIGURE 10-2

If there are syntax errors on the page, an error icon appears on the status bar in Internet Explorer.

Double-clicking the error icon opens a message box, which provides a line and character number for the error and describes the error (see Figure 10-3).

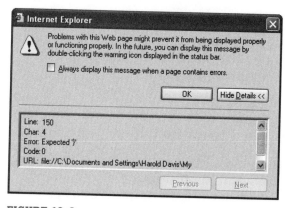

FIGURE 10-3

Double–clicking the error icon opens a message box that describes the error and provides a location.

You can use the line number provided to locate the problem by counting the number of lines in your program.

Many a happy hour have I spent counting program lines to locate a syntax error!

It's the case that the interface used to tell you about syntax errors works a little different in Netscape (and Mozilla). When you open the botched Tchatshke Gulch program in Netscape, you won't see any notification that the page contains a syntax error. You'll need to open the JavaScript console to find an error description and line number (see Figure 10-4).

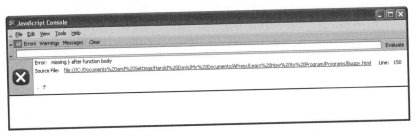

FIGURE 10-4

The JavaScript console provides information about syntax errors in Netscape and Mozilla.

NOTE To open the JavaScript console in Netscape (or Mozilla), select Tools ➤ Web Development. Then choose the JavaScript Console option from the Web Development submenu.

As I've mentioned before, by the standards of modern development environments, this is pretty crude. Generally, good programming environments don't let you make simple syntactic errors—they inform you of the error while the statement is open in the code editor.

Variance in Case in an Identifier

As I've explained, JavaScript is a weakly typed language and doesn't require explicit variable declaration. (You *can* declare variables, and it's a good idea to do so for clarity's sake, but there's no way to set your programs so that declaration is mandatory.)

This means that you can be happily using a variable named theKount with one or two references to thekount. You may know what should be stored in theKount, but thekount could contain anything—and certainly not something assigned by your design. The results are completely unpredictable. Be especially careful when you name variables to make them clearly distinguishable—and never, never use two variables with the same name whose only difference is the case of some of the letters.

Variable names being off because of case variance is probably the single biggest syntax-error issue in JavaScript—so watch out for it. However, you can also run into similar problems with function names. For example, if you try to call the function doSomething from an event handler:

```
<INPUT type=button value="Click Moi" onClick="doSomething();">
```

and the function is actually created with a lowercase *s*:

```
function dosomething() {
}
```

you'll get an "Object expected" error message in Internet Explorer when the event handler is fired because the Click Moi button has been clicked. This shows up in Internet Explorer as a warning icon in the status bar, as I described earlier in this chapter. When the warning icon is double-clicked, a message box opens that describes the error and location (see Figure 10-5).

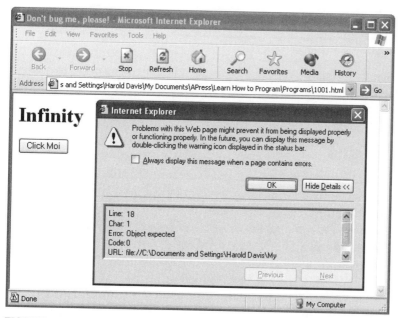

FIGURE 10-5

The error message in Internet Explorer provides a location for the error and a somewhat opaque description.

This error message "Object expected" is a little opaque. What does it really mean? What it's trying to say, in its own clumsy way, is that it looked for a function named doSomething and couldn't find it (because of the case variance).

To become an effective debugger, it helps to learn to understand the nuances of the error messages provided by the development environment.

Netscape gets the error message a little better. There's no indication of a problem when the Click Moi button is clicked. Nothing happens. But if you open the JavaScript console, as I described earlier in this chapter, the error message "doSomething is not defined" is really quite accurate and allows you to easily spot the problem (see Figure 10-6).

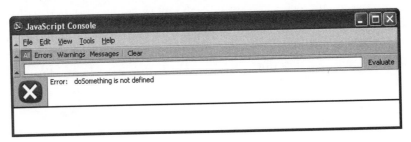

FIGURE 10-6

The JavaScript console in Netscape provides a helpful description of the error.

HTML Issues

HTML problems can "spill over" into the surrounding JavaScript code. It's wise to look your HTML over as well as your JavaScript if you have an otherwise intractable bug.

The cure for this problem? Be careful with your HTML. Make sure that it's working before you add any JavaScript code.

Weird problems that don't have any obvious solutions may indeed be HTML "spill over," and it's always worth having a hard look at them.

The good news is that, as you'll discover as you progress as a programmer, in many development environments you don't have to worry about this as an issue. If your project isn't targeting a Web page, then likely all you have to worry about is program code. In fact, it's worth knowing that some of the more sophisticated Web development environments—such as ASP.NET—go to great lengths to separate HTML and program code. This means that when you're programming in these environments, you don't have to worry about "trivial" HTML issues, such as a missing end bracket (>) on a tag.

Mismatched Parentheses

This problem of mismatched parentheses is easy to fall into and not particularly JavaScript specific. The best cure is avoidance: Lay out the parentheses and curly braces *before* adding content to the enclosed functions or expressions. If all else fails, start counting those left and right facing parentheses to make sure they add up.

> *Make sure parentheses, braces, and quotes match up!*

Missing Quotes

Missing terminating quotes can present the same kind of problems as a mismatched set of parentheses in JavaScript. Because JavaScript code can involve complex string generation (often of HTML), it's common to have nested string expressions that combine single- and double-quoted literals with variables. A missing quote could throw the whole thing off and make the JavaScript interpreter think the entire remainder of the script was a literal, creating unpredictable results.

As with parentheses, lay out the quotes before you lay in the contents. And if all else fails, count quotes to make sure they match.

> *If you use a reserved word as an identifier, the results will be unpredictable.*

Using Reserved Words As Identifiers

If you use a reserved JavaScript word such as `location` or `open` as the name of a variable or function, you're likely to generate unpredictable results. If you have a bug and can't find an apparent cause, double-check to make sure you haven't used a reserved JavaScript word as an identifier.

> *Check to make sure your comparisons are comparisons and not assignments!*

Assigning Instead of Comparing

Assignment, indicated with one equal sign (=), and comparison, denoted with two (= =), are often confused. If you can't find the cause of a bug, double-check to make sure your assignments are really assignments and your comparisons are really comparisons.

Finding Bugs

Now that we understand the different kinds of bugs and have looked at some of the most common syntax problems in JavaScript, let's move on to look at some techniques for finding bugs.

You've already seen how the syntax error message displays work in Internet Explorer and Netscape. I won't go over that ground again. But sometimes it's useful to create your own error messages to use for diagnostic purposes. These error messages can also display the value of variables at specific times. This can be particularly helpful in pinpointing logical errors.

I'll show you two techniques for displaying error messages that include the values of variables, and then I'll move on to a discussion of program testing.

Ad-Hoc Error Displays

The lowly alert statement can be your biggest ally in debugging a program. I find that I insert alert statements or their analog in other development environments, such as the MessageBox.Show method in Visual Basic .NET, even when sophisticated debugging tools are available.

It can be helpful to generate ad-hoc displays of variables and their values if you suspect that something is wrong. This technique is particularly useful within loops; alert statements are most often used.

> *The lowly alert statement is your friend!*

Using *alert* Statements

You can use alert statements to display variable values in a spontaneous fashion. In other words, this is a debugging tool that's easy to implement (and requires no special software). The only downsides are that the alert statement only provides the information you program it to display and that you may have to click OK many times to cycle through a loop. (An alert box is *modal*, meaning that you can't move on until you've clicked OK.)

Let's work through an example. You probably remember the code used in Chapter 9, "Manipulating Strings," used to count the words in a string (this was shown in Listing 9-5). Listing 10-2 shows this code again.

LISTING 10-2

Counting Words in a String (Okay Version)

```
function countWords(str){
   var count = 0;
   var words = str.split(" ");
    for (var i=0 ; i < words.length ; i++){
       // inner loop -- do the count
       if (words[i] != "")
          count += 1;
    }

   document.theForm.results.value =
      "There are " +
      count +
      " words in the text string you entered!";
}
```

Now let's intentionally mutilate the countWords function shown in Listing 10-1 so that the loop malfunctions by introducing a one-off error. If we start the loop at one rather than zero by using the iteration statement:

```
for (var i=1 ; i < words.length ; i++){
   ...
}
```

then the countWords function will give us the wrong result. Listing 10-3 shows the "broken" version of the code.

LISTING 10-3

Counting Words in a String ("Broken" Version)

```
function countWords(str){
   var count = 0;
   var words = str.split(" ");
    for (var i=1 ; i < words.length ; i++){
       // inner loop -- do the count
       if (words[i] != "")
          count += 1;
    }

   document.theForm.results.value =
      "There are " +
      count +
      " words in the text string you entered!";
}
```

If you run the code shown in Listing 10-3 in an appropriate user interface and enter some words separated by spaces, you'll see that the count of words is, indeed, one off (you can count the words entered in Figure 10-7 to verify this!).

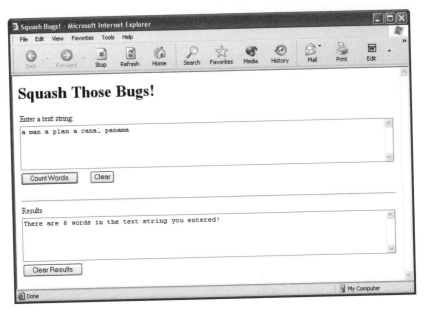

FIGURE 10-7
The count of words is one less than the actual number of words entered.

Adding an alert statement that displays the value of the iteration variable and the current word will immediately pinpoint the problem. Here's how.

To Use an *alert* Statement to Display Values:

1. Within the code where you suspect a problem (for example, the function shown in Listing 10-3), place an alert statement that displays the current iteration counter value, as well as the value of any related array elements:

```
alert("The count is " + i + " ; current word is " + words[i]);
```

2. Save the revised function (as shown in Listing 10-4).

3. Open the page containing the suspect function in a browser.

4. Run the suspect function. An alert box will be displayed for each loop iteration, showing the value of the iteration counter variable and the value of the related words array element. The first time the alert box is displayed, as you can see in Figure 10-8, it shows you that the first word has been skipped in the count, so it's easy to figure out that you have a one-off error and that your loop is starting higher by one than where it should start.

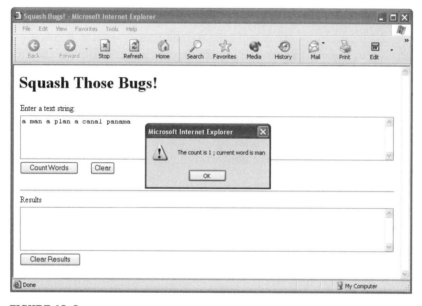

FIGURE 10-8

The alert box shows that the problem is a one-off error in the loop iteration variable.

LISTING 10-4

Broken Word Counting Function with Diagnostic alert Statement

```
function countWords(str){
   var count = 0;
   var words = str.split(" ");
    for (var i=1 ; i < words.length ; i++){
       // inner loop -- do the count
       alert("The count is " + i + " ; current word is "
```

```
            + words[i]);
        if (words[i] != "")
            count += 1;
    }

    document.theForm.results.value =
        "There are " +
        count +
        " words in the text string you entered!";
}
```

Displaying Values in a Window

Variety, as they say, is the spice of life. A simple variation on the alert box as a diagnostic tool is to display diagnostic messages in a separate window. It's easy to write the values to a separate window, and this has the advantage of not interrupting execution of the code while the diagnostic statements are executed. You can read the list of values in one fell swoop.

If you entered a sentence containing many words, you can understand why having to click through an alert box for each word is a nuisance.

If you entered a long sentence with many words in the previous example and then clicked through all the resulting alert boxes, you'll understand why this can be a good idea.

The example uses the broken word counting loop shown earlier in Listing 10-3.

To Use a Document Window to Display Values:

1. Add a statement that creates a new window:

```
var debugMe = window.open("", "debugMe",
    "height=300,width=250,resizable=yes,scrollbars=yes");
```

This statement should come before, so that it's processed before, the suspect function.

2. Within the suspect function and within the loop, add a statement that displays the iteration and array value, once for each pass through the loop:

```
debugMe.document.writeln("The count is " + i +
    " ; current word is " + words[i] + "<BR>");
```

3. Save the page containing the faulty function and diagnostic window statement (the code for both are shown in Listing 10-5).

4. Open the page in a browser and click Count Words. The function runs normally. While it's running, the separate window is populated in each pass through the loop with the counter value and the value of the corresponding word as shown in Figure 10-9. Looking at the display in the diagnostic window shown in Figure 10-9, it's easy to see that the first word has been omitted, leading to the natural diagnosis that the faulty function starts its count one too high!

Fawlty towers, yes! Faulty functions, no!

LISTING 10-5

Counting Words in a String with Diagnostic Separate Window Display

```
var debugMe = window.open("", "debugMe",
   "height=300,width=250,resizable=yes,scrollbars=yes");
function countWords(str){
   var count = 0;
   var words = str.split(" ");
    for (var i=1 ; i < words.length ; i++){
       // inner loop -- do the count
       debugMe.document.writeln("The count is " + i +
           " ; current word is " + words[i] + "<BR>");
       //debugMe.document.close();
       if (words[i] != "")
          count += 1;
   }

   document.theForm.results.value =
      "There are " +
      count +
      " words in the text string you entered!";
}
```

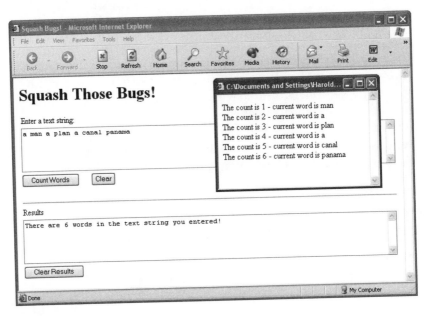

FIGURE 10-9

You can use a separate diagnostic window to review values without interrupting program execution.

"Real" Debugging Tools

Although ad-hoc debugging techniques come in handy even in the most advanced development environments, you should know that when you "graduate" to programming in a professional development environment you'll have many tools available to help you with pinpointing logical errors.

In addition to essentially real-time syntax error checking, most modern development environments provide tools that provide the ability to do the following:

Do "real" programmers use "real" debugging tools? If the tools are available, they should.

- Step through code statement by statement
- View the value of variables at any point
- Set program breakpoints so that program execution stops at a given statement
- Run statements interactively
- Modify the value of variables in a running program

- Check to see whether an *assertion* (a logical condition) is true or false while a program is running

- And much, much, more. . . .

Testing a Program

No program is complete until it has been tested. Even the simplest programs require some ad-hoc testing: Does the program run? Does it work right with some sample inputs?

> Every program must be tested.

With very short, simple programs you may be able to get away with informal testing. But the more complex (and longer) your program, the more need there is for rigorous testing.

Formal testing plans require a good bit of thought about the data (or inputs) you'll use.

Even if you don't think you need a formal testing plan, keep the following suggestions in mind when you test your programs:

- Make sure you can "backtrack," meaning retrace your steps, when correcting syntax problems.

- Don't make a problem worse when you're attempting to fix it.

- Beware of introducing new bugs, sometimes called *side effects*, when fixing the first bug.

- Rigor and discipline in the testing process are good things. You should write down the tests you're performing so that you know what you did and can run the same tests again if you need to do so.

- Be diligent in attempting to "break" your application. In real life, everything that can go wrong will. Be relentless in trying to reproduce this truism in your testing process. It's much, much better that something should break during your testing process, when you can easily fix it, than after you've released your program.

> It's far, far better that a program "break" during testing than in the real world.

- Track your testing process carefully, possibly using software designed for the testing process. Pay particular attention to the test values of variables.

- Consider bounding values (those at the upper and lower ends of the possible ranges that can be assigned to variables).

- One-off errors are a great source of problems, particularly in looping. You should suspect a one-off error in the loop counter whenever a logical error occurs and a loop is present.

- Test for runtime errors under as great a variety of operating conditions as possible.

Exception Handling

Bullet-proof programs need to be able to anticipate runtime errors if they're to work as they're supposed to work in the real world because it's inevitable that some runtime errors will occur. For example, a network resource might not be available because the network is down. Or maybe a file can't be written to disk because the disk drive is full. Even with the best code in the world, these kinds of errors can happen.

And when code isn't the best in the world, other kinds of errors can happen. For example, you may recall the code I presented near the beginning of this chapter that illustrated the pitfalls of naming a function dosomething and calling it in an onClick event using the case-variant name doSomething:

```
function dosomething() {
}
...
<INPUT type=button value="Click Moi" onClick="doSomething();">
```

When executed, as you'll recall, this code caused an "Object expected" error (see Figure 10-5 and related text).

Conceptually, the right way to deal with runtime errors, and errors such as the "Object expected" error, is by using *exception handling.*

An exception is exceptional because it's an unexpected condition, or error, in a program. It's in the nature of life that some of these unexpected conditions can't be anticipated. The point of *exception* handling is to deal with, or handle, all exceptions regardless of whether the exception can be reasonably anticipated.

In JavaScript, you accomplish exception handling by using the try and catch statement blocks and by using the properties of the JavaScript Error object.

Code placed in the try block is the main body of a function being monitored for exceptions.

Code placed in the catch block is executed in response to specific exceptions or as a general handler for all exceptions that aren't specifically handled.

An example will make this clearer, but first let me make a couple of points: Many languages (but not JavaScript) provide the ability to add a Finally code block as well as try and catch blocks. The point of the Finally block is to provide a place for code that will execute no matter what happens in the other blocks of code. So code in the Finally block can be used for cleanup purposes, such as saving data or files and closing resources.

 CAUTION JavaScript didn't implement try and catch statements until JavaScript version 1.2 (meaning Internet Explorer 5 and later and Navigator 6 and later), so if you're using a browser that's more than a few years old, there's a chance that this code will not run in it.

Let's take the dosomething function and modify it so that our click event calls a function named goodFunc, which in turn makes the call to doSomething. This will enable us to implement exception handling in the goodFunc function.

Here's what the code looks like prior to the implementation of exception handling:

```
function dosomething() {
}
function goodFunc(){
    doSomething();
}
...
<INPUT type=button value="Click Moi" onClick="goodFunc();">
...
```

If you run this code and click the button, you'll get the "Object expected" error as explained earlier in this chapter.

Here's the goodFunc function with try and catch blocks implemented:

```
function goodFunc(){
    try {
        doSomething();
    }
    catch (e) {
        if (e.description == "Object expected") {
```

```
            alert("Cannot find a function named doSomething!");
         }
         else {
            alert ("Other error" + e.description);
         }
      }
   }
}
```

Note that the `catch` statement block is passed the JavaScript Error object as an argument (e). A nice message is displayed if the error "caught" by the `catch` block is the "Object expected" error (see Figure 10-10).

All other errors are handled in a generic fashion, with their description displayed.

Listing 10-10 shows the complete code for the example.

ADVANCED

CAUTION The object models of Internet Explorer and Netscape differ in respect to their Error objects. I leave it to you as an exercise to write the code that makes this example work with Netscape. True cross-browser Web applications written in JavaScript need to check which browser is running and conditionally execute the appropriate code for that browser.

FIGURE 10-10

The "Object expected" error is caught and handled.

LISTING 10-6

Catching the "Object Expected" Error

```html
<HTML>
<HEAD>
<TITLE>Don't bug me, please!
</TITLE>
</HEAD>
<BODY>
<H1>
<SCRIPT>
function dosomething() {
}
function goodFunc(){
   try {
      doSomething();
   }
   catch (e) {
      if (e.description == "Object expected") {
         alert("Cannot find a function named doSomething!");
      }
      else {
         alert ("Other error" + e.description);
      }
   }
}
</SCRIPT>
</H1>
<FORM>
<INPUT type=button value="Click Moi" onClick="goodFunc();">
</FORM>
</BODY>
</HTML>
```

Throwing Errors

As we've discussed, it makes sense to handle exceptions for several reasons. To recap, it's better that end users don't see the often-inscrutable error messages that JavaScript interpreters provide. If you've caught an error, you can also take remedial action to fix it in code or to keep track of the problem without bringing your program to a screeching halt. Finally, by throwing an error in appropriate circumstances, you can handle exceptions that are *custom*—meaning that the programmer, not the JavaScript interpreter, devised them. (Yet another reason to throw an error is to verify that exception handling is working.)

> *Food for thought: How is throwing an error like firing an event?*

In this way, throwing custom exceptions, or errors, within a program can be used to handle extraordinary program conditions in an architecturally sane way. Actually, throwing an exception in code for this purpose is a lot like firing an event. If this is food for thought, have another look at Chapter 8, "Understanding Events and Event-Driven Programming," and compare and contrast exceptions and events. Please feel free to send me an email on the topic.

To Throw an Error:

1. Create a form containing a text box for the error message and a button to throw the error:

```
<FORM name="theForm">
Enter text for the error:
<INPUT type=text name=errText size=40>
<INPUT type=button name=btnThrow value="Throw it!">
</FORM>
```

2. Add an onClick event handler to the button that invokes a function named throwError and pass it the value entered in the error text box:

```
<FORM name="theForm">
Enter text for the error:
<INPUT type=text name=errText size=40>
<INPUT type=button name=btnThrow value="Throw it!"
   onClick="throwError(document.theForm.errText.value);">
</FORM>
```

3. Create the framework for the throwError function:

```
function throwError(errString) {

}
```

4. Create a `try...catch` structure within the function:

```
function throwError(errString) {
   try {


   }
   catch(e){


   }
}
```

The variable e is an implicit instance of the JavaScript Error object. Of course, you could use any other valid JavaScript identifier instead of e to refer to this instance of the Error object although it's conventional to use something such as e or err.

5. Create and throw the new Error instance that will be caught, providing an error number and the string passed to the function for the description:

```
function throwError(errString) {
   try {
      throw new Error (42, errString);
   }
   catch(e){


   }
}
```

6. When the error is "caught," use an `alert` statement to display the error number and description:

```
function throwError(errString) {
   try {
      throw new Error (42, errString);
   }
   catch(e){
      alert("Error number: " + e.number + "; Description: " +
e.description)
   }
}
```

7. Save the page (the complete source code is shown in Listing 10-7).

8. Open the page in a browser.

9. Enter text for the error you want to throw and click Throw it! The error text you entered will be displayed in an alert box, proving that the error has been thrown and successfully caught (see Figure 10-11).

LISTING 10-7

Throwing an Error

```
<HTML>
<HEAD>
    <TITLE>Throw that error!</TITLE>
<SCRIPT>
function throwError(errString) {
    try {
        throw new Error (42, errString);
    }
    catch(e){
        alert("Error number: " + e.number + "; Description: " +
e.description)
    }
}
</SCRIPT>
</HEAD>
<BODY>
<H1>
Throw that error!
</H1>
<FORM name="theForm">
<TABLE><TR><TD colspan=2>
Enter text for the error:
</TD><TD>
<INPUT type=text name=errText size=40></TD></TR>
<TR><TD colspan=2></TD><TD>
<INPUT type=button name=btnThrow value="Throw it!"
    onClick="throwError(document.theForm.errText.value);">
</TD></TR></TABLE>
</FORM>
</BODY>
</HTML>
```

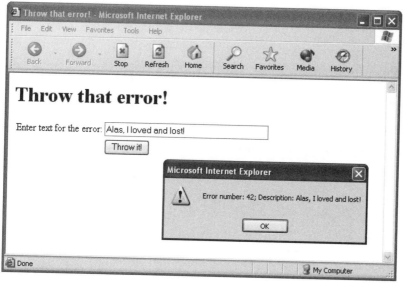

FIGURE 10-11

The "Alas, I loved and lost!" error has been thrown and caught.

Error Catching

Error catching is often used to give particular errors or conditions special handling. For example, you might want to catch the condition in which an input string is equal to 42. If the string isn't equal to 42, an exception, which isn't handled, is generated. (More realistically, you might want to catch an error when program input is outside the required range.)

To Catch an Error:

1. Create a form with a text input box and a button:

```
<FORM name="theForm">
We can handle 42:
<INPUT type=text name=errText size=40 value="42">
<INPUT type=button name=btnThrow value="Catch it!">
</FORM>
```

2. Add an onClick event handler to the button that displays an alert box containing the return value of a function named catchError:

```
<INPUT type=button name=btnThrow value="Catch it!"

   onClick="alert(catchError(document.theForm.errText.value));">
```

3. Create the framework for the catchError function:

```
function catchError(errString) {


}
```

4. Create outer try and catch statement blocks to deal with general errors and if the string isn't equal to 42:

```
function catchError(errString) {
   try {


   }
   catch (e){
      return(e + " This one not handled here!");
   }
}
```

5. Create inner try and catch statement blocks:

```
function catchError(errString) {
   try {
      try {


      }
      catch(e) {


      }
   }
   catch (e){
      return(e.description + " This one not handled here!");
   }
}
```

6. Within the inner try block, throw one error if the string is equal to 42 and a different error if it's not:

```
function catchError(errString) {
   try {
      try {
         if (errString == 42)
            throw new Error (42, "errString is 42!");
         else
            throw new Error (0, "errString is NOT 42!");
```

```
      }
      catch(e) {

      }
    }
    catch (e){
       return(e.description + " This one not handled here!");
    }
  }
```

7. In the inner catch block, check the error number:

```
...
catch(e) {
   if (e.number == 42)

}
...
```

8. If the condition is the one we're looking for—for example, the Number property of the Error object is 42—return an appropriate message. Otherwise, *rethrow* the error back up to the next highest handler (this is also called *propagating* the error):

```
...
catch(e) {
   if (e.number == 42)
      return (e.description + " Got this one!");
   else
      throw e; // re-throw the error
}
...
```

9. Save the page (the source code is shown in Listing 10-8).

10. Open the page in a browser.

11. With 42 entered in the text box, click Catch it! An alert box will display showing that this condition has been caught (see Figure 10-12).

12. With something other than 42 entered in the text box, click Catch it! An alert box will display showing that the exception has been propagated back to the general error handler (see Figure 10-13).

LISTING 10-8

Catching an Error

```
<HTML>
<HEAD>
   <TITLE>Catch that error!</TITLE>
<SCRIPT>
function catchError(errString) {
   try {
      try {
         if (errString == 42)
            throw new Error (42, "errString is 42!");
         else
            throw new Error (0, "errString is NOT 42!");
      }
      catch(e) {
         if (e.number == 42)
            return (e.description + " Got this one!");
         else
            throw e; // re-throw the error
      }
   }
   catch (e){
      return(e.description + " This one not handled here!");
   }
}
</SCRIPT>
</HEAD>
<BODY>
<H1>
Catch that error!
</H1>
<FORM name="theForm">
<TABLE>
<TR><TD colspan=2>
We can handle 42:
</TD><TD>
<INPUT type=text name=errText size=40 value="42">
</TD></TR><TR><TD colspan=2>
</TD><TD>
<INPUT type=button name=btnThrow value="Catch it!"
   onClick="alert(catchError(document.theForm.errText.value));">
</TD></TR>
</TABLE>
</FORM>
</BODY>
</HTML>
```

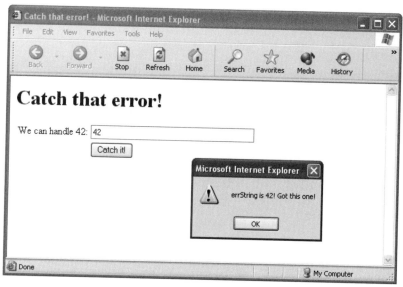

FIGURE 10-12
Error number 42 has been caught.

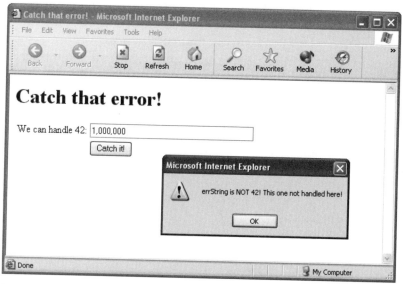

FIGURE 10-13
The non-42 error is caught by the general handler.

> ### The Error Object Across Browsers
>
> As I noted earlier in this chapter, the Error object model used in these examples is specific to Internet Explorer. I leave it to you as an exercise to write code that performs similar functionality in Netscape as well! You should know, however, that if you treat an error as a simple text string—by assigning a text value to the error and testing for a specific error by comparing against the text string—the code will run on both browsers. I've focused on the Internet Explorer model because it will give you a better sense of what programming with structured exception handling is like in modern languages, without getting bogged down in too many language-specific details.

What's It All About?

This chapter has covered a great deal of ground. You learned about the different kinds of program bugs: syntax errors, runtime errors, and logical errors.

Next, I showed you some of the most common JavaScript syntax problems for which you should be watching.

Then we moved on to techniques for finding bugs generally.

We discussed how to test your programs, and I explained why testing a program is important.

Finally, I showed you the mechanics of exception handling in JavaScript using `try` and `catch` statements and the JavaScript Error object.

So what's it all about, Alfie? (Or Austin?)

As you become a more sophisticated programmer, you'll find it increasingly important to have a deep understanding of bugs and their causes. The more complicated and interesting the program, the more important it is to rigorously test your programs and to implement an architecture that anticipates exceptional conditions.

By working through this chapter, you've laid the foundation for good programming habits in these areas.

11

Programming
with JavaScript

This book has concentrated on showing you how to program. I thought it most important to teach you the ideas and concepts behind programming and to show you the techniques used in most modern programming languages. I've also tried to inculcate good programming practices right from the start.

In this scheme of things, creating actual applications for the sake of creating applications has been a secondary goal. True, we've built some impressive applications, for example, the game of Rock, Scissors, and Paper in Chapter 3 and the Tchatshke Gulch auction in Chapter 7 and Chapter 8. But these applications were examples to illustrate techniques (Rock, Scissors, and Paper showed conditional expressions, and Tchatshke Gulch showed object-oriented programming and how to work with a timer event).

This chapter presents a few JavaScript applications for the sake of the applications. Obviously, I'll explain the techniques used as we go along. But the point of these applications is to be joyful in the act of creating the application, not in any specific programming technique. My hope is that these programs will spur you on to design and write your own (see the sidebar "Calling All Readers").

Calling All Readers

I'd love to see what JavaScript applications you create! If you write a really neat program in JavaScript, send it to me along with an email describing what the program does (use the email address learntoprogram@bearhome.com).

I'll publish the best, coolest examples I get from readers in the next edition of this book. You'll receive credit for the program and a free copy of the book when it's republished.

In this chapter, I'll show you the following:

- How to password protect a JavaScript page

- How to create *rollovers*, which is the name for a visual effect that changes the appearance of an object based on the current location of the mouse

- How to display a slide show on the Web using JavaScript

These are fun applications, and they're easy. So come on in, the water's fine; let's all have a party because . . . you're a programmer now!

Password Protecting a Page

> The technique used in this example is simple and deliciously sneaky!

Truly effective password protection is, of course, impossible in a solely client-side environment. (As you probably know, the programs in this book have all been written in client-side JavaScript.) You shouldn't regard any client-side mechanism as 100-percent secure under any conditions. Client-side password protection shouldn't be used to store state secrets such as the access codes to the Star Wars defense system or the combination to Fort Knox.

If you think about it, in a client-side environment any kind of password protection is bound to be tricky to implement because the user can view your source code. However, if you don't need really, really bullet-proof protection, and enough is good enough for your password scheme, then the example I'm going to show you for password protecting a page using only client-side programming works pretty well—and is quite sneaky!

The scheme uses a filename (without the .html extension) as the password. If the user doesn't enter the password, she is never "sent" to the protected page. The password can never be viewed by opening the source code—because it doesn't exist in code but rather as the part of a filename that comes before the file extension.

In the example, there's one password for everybody rather than individual user name and password pairs. Although limited, this could still be useful. For example, you might want to protect your confidential business plan that has been placed on the Web but have one password to give out to various possible investors.

In order to create individual name and password pairs in client-side JavaScript, you can use *cookies*. Cookies are tokens placed by Web applications on individual computers that the Web application can use to track computers, users, and choices made by individual users.

TRY THIS
AT HOME

User names and passwords—possibly encrypted—can be stored as cookies on individual systems. Why don't you see if you can create an application of your own using cookies?

You can find out more about programming cookies in JavaScript at WebReference.com (http://www.webreference.com/js/column8/) and elsewhere on the Web.

ADVANCED

NOTE Actually, it'd be far better to use a server-side database to store user names and passwords. Server-side processing could be done using a Common Gateway Interface (CGI) program or other server-side mechanism, such as server-side HTML generation.

CAUTION When using the single-password arrangement, you must take care from a Web administration viewpoint to place the protected file in a directory that contains a file named index.html. If you don't do this, a user could discover the contents of the directory (and the name of the supposedly password protected file) by entering the name of the directory followed by a forward slash (/).

To Password Protect a Home Page:

1. Create an HTML file that's to be protected by a password. The password will be the name of the file without the .html extension. In the example, it's named *LearnToProgram.html*, and the password is *LearnToProgram*.

2. Add some HTML to LearnToProgram.html, for example:

```
<HTML>
<HEAD>
<TITLE>
Learn to Program
</TITLE>
<HEAD>
<BODY>
<H1>
You made it: You're in like Flynn.
</H1>
</BODY>
</HTML>
```

3. Create a new HTML page in the same directory as LearnToProgram.html. This access page will be used to password protect LearnToProgram.html. You'll give out the URL to this access page.

4. Create an HTML skeleton within the access page:

```
<HTML>
<HEAD>
   <TITLE>
   Test that password
   </TITLE>
</HEAD>
<BODY>
...
</BODY>
</HTML>
```

5. At the top of the <BODY> section of the page, add beginning and ending <SCRIPT> tags:

```
<BODY>
<SCRIPT>

</SCRIPT>
</BODY>
```

6. At the beginning of the script block, declare a password variable and assign an empty string to it:

```
<SCRIPT>
var password = "";
```

7. Prompt the user for the password:

```
password=prompt("Please enter your password!","");
```

8. If the user entered a password, use the href property of the browser's location object to go to the file named in the password variable plus the .html file extension:

```
if (password != null) {
   location.href= password + ".html";
}
```

Of course, this will only succeed in opening a file if a file named in the password variable plus .html exists in the current directory.

9. Save the access page (you can find the complete source code for the page in Listing 11-1).

10. Open the access page in a browser. A prompt box will appear (see Figure 11-1).

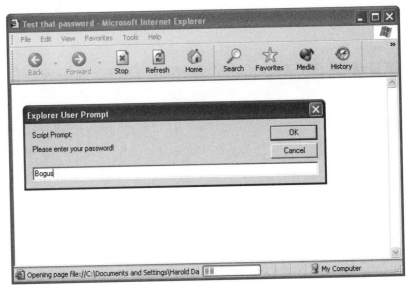

FIGURE 11-1

The user enters the password in a prompt box.

11. Enter a phony password—such as *Bogus*—in the prompt box.

12. Click OK. It's possible (but unlikely) that the file thus specified exists in the current directory serving HTML, in which case Bogus.html will open. More likely, it doesn't—in which case the server will generate an HTTP 404 "File not found" error. The resulting page served to the user will depend on the Web server and browser; most likely it will appear as shown Figure 11-2, but a blank screen is also a possible result.

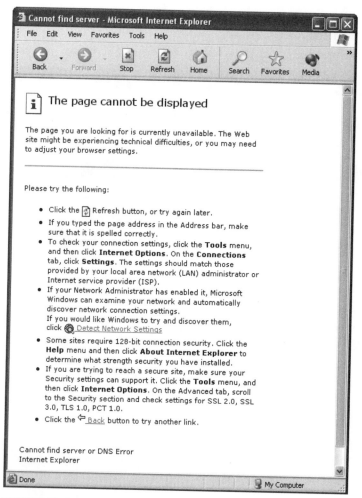

FIGURE 11-2

If the file pointed to by the password input isn't found, an HTTP 404 error is generated.

13. Open the access page again and enter the right password (see Figure 11-3).

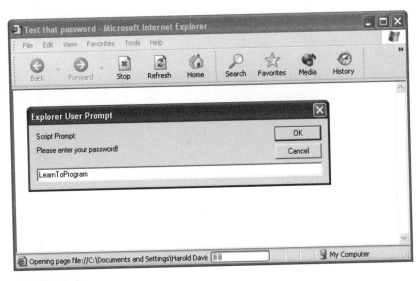

FIGURE 11-3
The password is LearnToProgram.

14. Click OK. The protected page will open (see Figure 11-4).

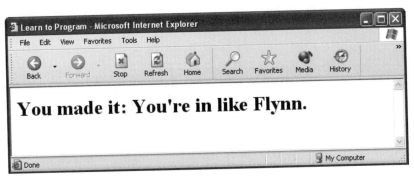

FIGURE 11-4
When the password (the name of the destination page) is correctly entered, the page will open.

LISTING 11-1

Password Protecting a Page

```
<HTML>
<HEAD>
<TITLE>
Test that password
</TITLE>
</HEAD>
<BODY>
<SCRIPT>
var password = "";
password=prompt("Please enter your password!","");
if (password != null) {
   location.href= password + ".html";
}
</SCRIPT>
</BODY>
</HTML>
```

Problems with This Password Scheme

I've mentioned quite a few problems with this password scheme if intended to protect pages that must be truly secure. Here's a summary of these problems:

- Client-side password protection should never be regarded as completely secure because users can view the source code used to create the client-side document.

- A file named index.html must be located in the directory containing the protected file, or any user can view directory information (including the name of the protected file).

- It's best to use cookies to provide individualized user logins and passwords.

- A better scheme is to use server-side processing and a database to manage user information and passwords.

- A table and form arrangement can be used to receive passwords rather than the prompt box shown in the example.

Creating a Rollover

A *rollover* is a visual effect in a Web browser page in which passing the mouse pointer over an area in the page causes another area to visually change. A good example is a Web site that sells clothing. This site could allow you to see how a garment looks using different fabric—you would see the different fabric patterns in the garment when you pass the mouse pointer over a color swatch. In fact, you'll find rollovers in use on a great many industrial-class commercial Web sites.

You can use nested rollovers fairly easily to create menus that expand when the mouse pointer rolls over a top-level menu. Why don't you try to do so? Implementing an expanding menu using rollovers is a great exercise.

TRY THIS AT HOME

The Image Object Event Model

Creating a rollover involves the simple use of the properties and events of the HTML Image object. To some degree, Image objects function like any other HTML element in a Web page, and they're manipulated using JavaScript in the same way. But there are some properties and events that only apply to image elements.

Images placed in an HTML document using the HTML <IMG> tag correspond to JavaScript Image objects. Each graphic, represented by an <IMG> tag, is referenced as a JavaScript object. The Image object can be referred to by its name or as a member of the images array of the document object. The images array of the document object stores an Image object for each image that's placed on an HTML page using an <IMG> tag.

It probably goes without saying that the major impact an image has on an HTML page isn't an issue of JavaScript, or HTML, but rather a matter of the graphic itself. As you probably know, the bulk of static graphics displayed on the Web are saved as GIF (.gif) or JPEG (.jpg or .jpeg) files.

Each JavaScript Image object is a child of the document object. Image properties are referenced hierarchically, using the name of the image or the image's position in the images array. For example, the following:

```
window.document.images[0]
```

is the first image in the images array for a given document, and the following:

```
document.theImage
```

is an <IMG> element with its name attribute set to equal theImage.

Images have some properties, in addition to name, that are useful in creating visual effects. As is usual with HTML elements, these JavaScript properties correspond to HTML attributes.

First, an Image object's src property sets (or reads) the URL of the graphic file that's to be displayed. Most JavaScript image manipulation routines use the src property as the main mechanism for creating visual special effects such as animations (for an example, see the slide show application later in this chapter).

Second, you can use the width and height properties of the Image object to dynamically generate effects having to do with the size of an image.

Image controls support the standard HTML element mouse events, which are shown again in case you don't remember them in Table 11-1. (Events were explained in Chapter 8, "Understanding Events and Event-Driven Programming.")

You can place your code in any of these event handlers. It's important that you distinguish between the different mouse events so that your JavaScript programs function as they're intended.

TABLE 11-1

Standard HTML Element (Including Image Object) Mouse Events

Event	Fires
onClick	When a user clicks on an element. A click event doesn't occur unless an onMouseDown is followed by an onMouseUp over the same element. In other words, onClick isn't the same as onMouseDown.
onMouseDown	When a user presses the mouse button while the mouse pointer is over an element.
onMouseMove	When a user moves the mouse within an element.
onMouseOut	When the mouse is moved out of an element.
onMouseOver	When the mouse is moved over an element.
onMouseUp	When a mouse button is released while the mouse pointer is over an element.

Table 11-2 shows some events that are specific to the Image object.

TABLE 11-2
Image Objects Events

Event	Fires
onAbort	If a user cancels the download of an image
onError	If an error occurs when downloading an image
onLoad	When an image finishes loading successfully

Rollovers

As I've already explained, a rollover is a commonly used and easy-to-achieve effect in which passing the mouse over one image causes a change in another image. For example, suppose you want to show your Web page audience an easy chair upholstered in the fabric selected by the user or, as in the sample project, a butterfly in the pattern the user selects. You've always wanted to dress a butterfly, haven't you?

This project shows you how to use a rollover to "try on" different patterns for a butterfly.

Take a butterfly to the virtual dressing room today!

To Create a Rollover:

1. Create nine image files to be used in the rollover. In the example, these are named as shown in Table 11-3 and can be downloaded from the Apress Web site.

TABLE 11-3
Graphics Files Used in the Rollover Example

Filenames	Contains
white.gif	Blank butterfly image that will be filled with patterns
bubble1–swatch.gif bubble2-swatch.gif check1-swatch.gif check2-swatch.gif	Swatch files that represent possible patterns
bubble1.gif bubble2.gif check1.gif check2.gif	Butterfly filled with the designated pattern

2. Place an <IMG> tag at the beginning of the <BODY> section of an HTML page. This tag will use its src attribute to reference the blank image of a butterfly that's to be filled with patterns:

```
<IMG src="white.gif" height=100 width=175 border=0>
```

3. For each of the four patterns that will be used to fill the butterfly, create an <IMG> tag that loads the swatch file as the value of the src attribute:

```
<IMG src="bubble1-swatch.gif" height=75 width=75 border=2>
```

4. For each of the four <IMG> tags that represents a pattern, add an onMouseOver event handler that loads the graphic file containing the butterfly filled with the pattern into the first <IMG> tag on the page when the mouse passes over the pattern:

```
<IMG src="bubble1-swatch.gif" height=75 width=75 border=2
    onMouseOver="document.images[0].src='bubble1.gif'";>
```

This code assigns the file bubble1.gif to the src property of the first image on the page, designating it as the zero element of the images array.

5. For each of the four <IMG> tags, add an onMouseOut event handler that returns the original blank butterfly to the first image when the mouse leaves the pattern swatch:

```
<IMG src="bubble1-swatch.gif" height=75 width=75 border=2
    onMouseOver="document.images[0].src='bubble1.gif'";
    onMouseOut="document.images[0].src='white.gif';">
```

6. Save the page (Listing 11-2 shows the complete source code).

7. Open it in a browser. As shown in Figure 11-5, the butterfly is patternless.

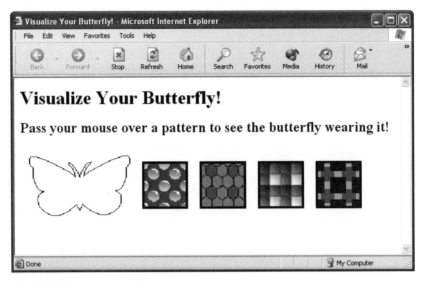

FIGURE 11-5

The butterfly has no pattern.

8. Pass your mouse over a pattern swatch. The butterfly will be "filled in" with the pattern (see Figure 11-6).

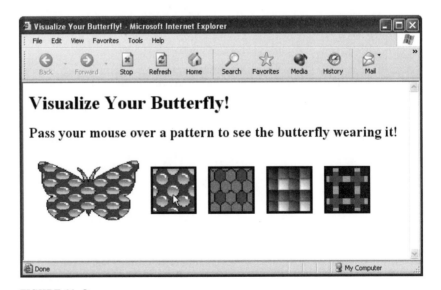

FIGURE 11-6

The butterfly is "filled in" with the first pattern.

9. Move the mouse to another pattern. The butterfly will "fill in" with that pattern (see Figure 11-7).

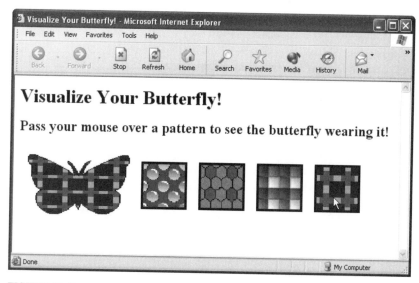

FIGURE 11-7
The butterfly is now "dressed" using the plaid pattern.

 NOTE As I've noted several times, it's obviously true that the visual benefit of the rollover effect depends more on the quality of the graphics used than on programming skill.

 TIP There's nothing to stop you from creating a rollover that changes the graphic rolled over (or clicked) rather than another graphic. This could be called an *auto-rollover*.

> *An image that changes when it's rolled over could be called an auto-rollover.*

LISTING 11-2
Creating a Rollover Effect

```
<HTML>
<HEAD>
   <TITLE>Visualize Your Butterfly!</TITLE>
</HEAD>
<BODY><H1>
```

```
Visualize Your Butterfly!
</H1><H2>
Pass your mouse over a pattern to see the butterfly wearing it!
</H2>
<TABLE cellpadding=5 cellspacing=10>
<TR><TD>
<IMG src="white.gif" height=100 width=175 border=0>
</TD><TD>
<IMG src="bubble1-swatch.gif" height=75 width=75 border=2
    onMouseOver="document.images[0].src='bubble1.gif'";
    onMouseOut="document.images[0].src='white.gif';">
</TD><TD>
<IMG src="bubble2-swatch.gif" height=75 width=75 border=2
    onMouseOver="document.images[0].src='bubble2.gif';"
    onMouseOut="document.images[0].src='white.gif';">
</TD><TD>
<IMG src="check1-swatch.gif" height=75 width=75 border=2
    onMouseOver="document.images[0].src='check1.gif';"
    onMouseOut="document.images[0].src='white.gif';">
</TD><TD>
<IMG src="check2-swatch.gif" height=75 width=75 border=2
    onMouseOver="document.images[0].src='check2.gif';"
    onMouseOut="document.images[0].src='white.gif';">
</TD></TR></TABLE>
</BODY>
</HTML>
```

Creating a Slide Show

Creating a "slide show" is simply a matter of using a timer to display a series of images. When the timer is "fired," a new image is loaded into an HTML <IMG> object using its src property.

This example shows you how to create a slide show that displays images either in a specified order or by choosing random images from those available. Generating random numbers using the random and floor methods of the JavaScript Math object are reviewed in the sidebar "Generating Random Numbers." (Chapter 3, "Using Conditional Statements," also explained the Random method in the context of the Rock, Scissors, and Paper application.)

Generating Random Numbers

In the slide show example, two methods of the JavaScript Math object, Math.floor and Math.random, are used to generate a random slide pick. As you've already seen, random numbers are useful in many other contexts, such as interactive games.

Math.floor returns the nearest rounded-down integer to its argument.

Math.random returns a pseudorandom number between zero and one. (*Pseudo* because, as you may know, there's no such thing as a method that truly generates a random number—there are only random number generators that meet various statistical tests for randomness.)

The expression used in the slide show example

```
Math.floor(Math.random() * 11)
```

picks a number at random between zero and 10 (corresponding to the elements of the picture array).

The images used for the slide show happen to be hosted on my personal Web site, http://www.bearhome.com. But you could substitute any images you like, provided they're accessible via a Web URL or a local path.

 NOTE The slide show program uses the setTimeout method to provide timer functionality. Timers were explained in Chapter 8, "Understanding Events and Event-Driven Programming."

To Create a Slide Show:

1. In an HTML page, create a form containing a button to start the show in sequential order, a button to start the show in random order, and a button to stop the show followed by an <IMG> element (to display the slide show):

```
<H1>View a slide show of our garden today!</H1>
<FORM>
<TABLE cellpadding=20 cellspacing=20>
<TR><TD>
<INPUT type=button value="Show in Order"
    name=theButton onClick="inOrder();">
</TD><TD>
<INPUT type=button value="Random and Repeat"
```

```
       name=theButton onClick="showRandom();">
</TD><TD>
<INPUT type=button value="Stop" name=theButton
       onClick="clearTimeout(timeOutId);">
</TD></TR>
</TABLE><BR>
</FORM>
<IMG name=slideshow
     src="http://www.bearhome.com/garden/images/gard6.jpg"
     width=500 border=5>
```

When this page is loaded, it'll display a single image as shown in
Figure 11-8. The buttons include onClick event handlers that will be
used to start and stop the show.

FIGURE 11-8

The slide show page loads showing a single, static image.

2. Load the photographs that will be displayed in the slide show into a JavaScript array:

```
<SCRIPT LANGUAGE=JAVASCRIPT TYPE="TEXT/JAVASCRIPT">
<!-- Hide that code from very old browsers
var gardenPix = new Array
("","http://www.bearhome.com/garden/images/gard1.jpg",
"http://www.bearhome.com/garden/images/gard2.jpg",
"http://www.bearhome.com/garden/images/gard3.jpg",
"http://www.bearhome.com/garden/images/gard4.jpg",
"http://www.bearhome.com/garden/images/gard5.jpg",
"http://www.bearhome.com/garden/images/gard6.jpg",
"http://www.bearhome.com/garden/images/gard7.jpg",
"http://www.bearhome.com/garden/images/gard8.jpg",
"http://www.bearhome.com/garden/images/gard9.jpg",
"http://www.bearhome.com/garden/images/gard10.jpg");
```

Note that element zero of the array is set to contain an empty string rather than an image.

3. Create a variable to store the index number of the displayed image:

```
var whichPic = 1;
```

4. Create a variable to store the timeout identifier:

```
var timeOutId;
```

5. Create a function, inOrder, that uses the setTimeout method to call the showPic function in index order, one picture every second, continuously looping:

```
function inOrder() {
    showPic(whichPic);
    whichPic ++;
    if (whichPic > 10)
        whichPic = 1;
    status = whichPic;
    timeOutId=setTimeout("inOrder();",1000);
}
```

The variable timeOutId now refers to the return value of the setTimeout method, and it can be used to stop the timer from firing.

6. Create a function, showRandom, that uses the JavaScript random number generator to call the showPic function in random order:

```
function showRandom() {
    whichPic = Math.floor(Math.random() * 11);
    if (whichPic == 0)
        whichPic = 1;
    showPic(whichPic);
    status = whichPic;
    timeOutId=setTimeout("showRandom();",1000);
}
```

Note that because there's no image stored in the zero element of the array, if the random generator returns zero, it's replaced with the value 1. This is done to make sure that the random generator is used to pick a slide between one and 10.

7. Create the showPic function, which actually displays a single image by assigning the array element with the value passed to the function to the src attribute of the image control:

```
function showPic(i) {
    document.images[0].src=gardenPix[i];
}
```

Note that the image element is referred to as the first (zero element) of the images array associated with the loaded document object.

8. Save the HTML page (Listing 11-3 shows the complete source code).

9. Open the page in a browser (Figure 11-8).

10. Click Show in Order or Random and Repeat to start the slide show (see Figure 11-9).

NOTE You can use the slide show technique to create animations that use graphics rather than photographs.

TIP The example shows the index number of the currently displayed image in the status bar so you can see what's going on "under the hood" better. For example, the image shown in Figure 11-9 is the sixth image in the image array.

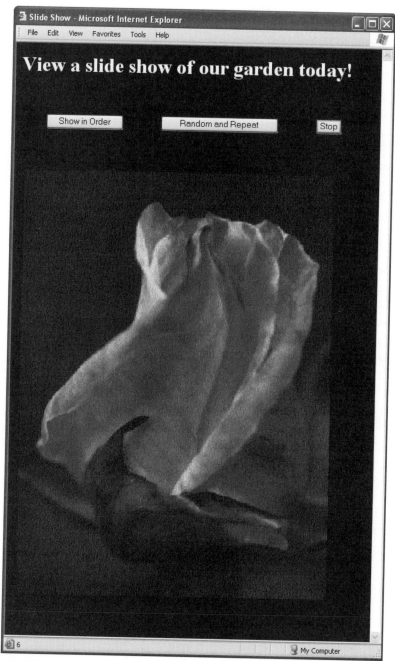

FIGURE 11-9

The slide show displays images in index order or at random; in either case, the index value of the image is displayed on the status bar.

LISTING 11-3

Creating a Slide Show Using a Random Number Generator

```html
<HTML>
<HEAD>
   <TITLE>Slide Show</TITLE>
</HEAD>
<BODY bgcolor=black text=white>
<SCRIPT>
var gardenPix = new Array
("","http://www.bearhome.com/garden/images/gard1.jpg",
"http://www.bearhome.com/garden/images/gard2.jpg",
"http://www.bearhome.com/garden/images/gard3.jpg",
"http://www.bearhome.com/garden/images/gard4.jpg",
"http://www.bearhome.com/garden/images/gard5.jpg",
"http://www.bearhome.com/garden/images/gard6.jpg",
"http://www.bearhome.com/garden/images/gard7.jpg",
"http://www.bearhome.com/garden/images/gard8.jpg",
"http://www.bearhome.com/garden/images/gard9.jpg",
"http://www.bearhome.com/garden/images/gard10.jpg");
var whichPic = 1;
var timeOutId;
function inOrder() {
   showPic(whichPic);
   whichPic ++;
   if (whichPic > 10)
      whichPic = 1;
   status = whichPic;
   timeOutId=setTimeout("inOrder();",1000);
}
function showRandom() {
   whichPic = Math.floor(Math.random() * 11);
   if (whichPic == 0)
      whichPic = 1;
   showPic(whichPic);
   status = whichPic;
   timeOutId=setTimeout("showRandom();",1000);
}
function showPic(i) {
   document.images[0].src=gardenPix[i];
}
// End code hiding from ancient browsers -->
```

```
</SCRIPT>
<H1>View a slide show of our garden today!</H1>
<FORM>
<TABLE cellpadding=20 cellspacing=20>
<TR><TD>
<INPUT type=button value="Show in Order" name=theButton
onClick="inOrder();">
</TD><TD>
<INPUT type=button value="Random and Repeat"
name=theButton onClick="showRandom();">
</TD><TD>
<INPUT type=button value="Stop" name=theButton
onClick="clearTimeout(timeOutId);">
</TD></TR>
</TABLE><BR>
</FORM>
<IMG name=slideshow src="http://www.bearhome.com/garden/images/gard6.jpg"
    width=500 border=5>
</BODY>
</HTML>
```

Where Do You Go from Here?

You've come a long way! I think I can safely call you *Programmer, Gear Head, Propeller Head,* or even *Geek* rather than Alfie or Austin. . . .

If you've worked through this book, you've learned a great deal about programming. You understand enough about the syntax and structure of programming so that you should pretty easily be able to pick up the details of any modern programming language—and use it to great effect! Best of all, you've learned the right way to think about programming and code. Along the way, you've also learned to "think like a computer."

The concepts you've learned in this book will stand you in good stead as you start programming for the rest of your life. Best of all, you've learned the habits of good, consistent, methodical programming—so there's nothing you'll have to "unlearn" as you continue programming.

As I've said repeatedly in this book, the best way to learn programming is by doing it.

To learn more about programming and to keep the skills you've learned in this book from getting rusty, you need to keep programming.

You've learned to "think like a computer."

The best way to learn programming is by doing it!

To keep from getting rusty, you need to keep programming.

As the joke goes, "How do you get to Carnegie Hall?" Practice, practice. The same thing is as true for programmers as it is for musicians. If you keep practicing programming, you'll become a virtuoso.

The *Star Wars* character Yoda might have said, "Programmer you must be. There is no other way." Once a programmer, always a programmer. By reading and working through this book, your life has changed. It's up to you to internalize the change, to continue thinking like a programmer, and to add to your programming skills.

There are many paths you can take to continue programming, and which you choose largely depends upon your needs, situation, and interests. Here are some suggestions (also please see the "For Further Information" sidebar):

- You can keep on programming in JavaScript. For example, an interesting exercise that I mentioned earlier in the chapter is to write a JavaScript program that saves and retrieves user information, such as a name and password, using a cookie.

- You can write macros for Microsoft Office applications such as Word or Excel.

- You can learn to create programs for applications that display graphics on the Web, such as Macromedia Flash.

- You can explore languages such as C and Java.

- You can learn more about Visual Studio .NET and the .NET languages including Visual Basic .NET and C#.

Good luck in your journey as a coder!

Finally, as I've said, I'm personally interested in your progress. Please send me a note from time to time at the special email address learntoprogram@bearhome.com and let me know how you're progressing as a programmer.

For Further Information

With a sound conceptual understanding of programming and programming languages, you'll find many good sources for information about programming topics.

You'll find many great books about programming available from Apress (the publisher of this book) at http://www.apress.com.

Microsoft Developer Network (MSDN) provides tons of useful information about programming in Microsoft Office, Visual Studio .NET, Visual Basic .NET, and C#. You'll find the MSDN home page at http://msdn.microsoft.com.

If you're interested in learning to program in Visual Basic .NET, you'll find my book *Visual Basic .NET for Windows: Visual QuickStart Guide* (Peachpit Press, 2003) helpful. This book is, in part, the continuation of *Learn How to Program*; it picks up from where *Learn How to Program* ends.

If you're interested in learning to program in C (and JavaScript, by the way, is basically a stripped-down variant of C, so this is a reasonable choice), the GNU C compiler is a good bet. It's available for no cost, along with a lot of good information about C, at
http://www.gnu.org/software/gcc/gcc.html.

You can download a version of Java, also at no cost, and learn tons about the Java programming language at Sun's Java site at http://java.sun.com.

Programming Macromedia Flash is very cool and a good way to apply your new programming skills. A good book on the topic is William Drol's *Object-Oriented Macromedia Flash MX* (Apress, 2002).

Index

Symbols

-- (Decrement operator) 37
! (Not) operator 39
!= inequality operator 40
!== nonidentity operator 40
% (Modulus operator) 37
&& (And) operator 39
(%=) modulo assignment operator 37
(.) dot operator
   introduction to OOP 193
   ways of using 201
(|) alternation regular expression 328
(+) addition operator 25
(+) additive operator
   mistaken for string concatenation
     operator 109
(+) string concatenation operator 24
   mistaken for plus operator 109
(++) increment operator
   adds 1 to its operand 96
(+=) incremental assignment operator
   120
(= =) comparison operator
   if statement 125
(=) assignment operator
   compared to comparison operator (==)
     63
(==) comparison operator
   compared to assignment operator (=)
     63

/* and */ comment 35
// comment 35
\" double quote escape sequence 27
\' single quote escape sequence 27
\(regular expression 323
\) regular expression 323
* regular expression 323
\. regular expression 323
\/ slash regular expression 323
\? regular expression 323
\[regular expression 323
\\\ backslash (\\) escape sequence 27
\\\ for slash regular expression 323
\] regular expression 323
\{ regular expression 323
\| regular expression 323
\} regular expression 323
\+ regular expression 323
\b backspace escape sequence 27
\b backspace regular expression 323
\f form feed escape sequence 27
\f form feed regular expression 323
\h hexadecimal escape sequence 27
\n new line escape sequence 27
\n new line regular expression 323
\r carriage return escape sequence 27
\r carriage return regular expression 323
\t tab escape sequence 27
\t tab regular expression 323

399